ONE-MAN RESEARCH: REMINISCENCES OF A CATHOLIC SOCIOLOGIST

One-Man Research: Reminiscences of a Catholic Sociologist

JOSEPH H. FICHTER

A WILEY-INTERSCIENCE PUBLICATION

JOHN WILEY & SONS
New York · London · Sydney · Toronto

Library of Congress Cataloging in Publication Data

Fichter, Joseph Henry, 1908–

  One-man research: reminiscences of a Catholic sociologist.

  "A Wiley-Interscience publication."
  1. Sociological research—United States—Case studies. 2. Sociology, Christian (Catholic) I. Title.

HM24.F49   301'.07'2   73-10261
ISBN 0-471-25793-1

Printed in the United States of America

10 9 8 7 6 5 4 3 2 1

PREFACE

If you want to "tell all" in the first person singular you have to use a style of writing that is almost alien to the way you compose paragraphs for scholarly monographs. To tell your own story of research experiences you have to be personal and subjective, the very qualities you are told by the experts to erase from the objective, value-free presentation of the findings of a research project. Not that anybody ever tells all there is to be told—that feat would demand the death of the personal censor, the "hypothetical psychic agency that represses unacceptable notions before they reach consciousness."

This book was a hard one to write, and it took longer than any of the several sociological research monographs I have had published. It was a troublesome undertaking, partly because I was constantly censoring myself so that the story would be truthful, and partly because I took the trouble to engage other "revisors"—people who were actually involved with me in these five social science projects. I prefer to call them "revisors," persons who "look over again" to

correct and improve the story, rather than censors, persons
who delete materials considered harmful to the special interests of some individual or group.

One of these revisors was a woman who had been active in
the Commission on Human Rights when we were struggling
with the organized racists of Louisiana; and she said "why
don't you leave the past alone, and look at the progress we've
made!" There were times when I felt like taking her advice,
times when I wondered whether a person can be completely
fair in talking about himself, especially when he is trying to
be defensive in his own cause and inoffensive to others. When
experiences are controversial—as some of these were—
one is tempted to make his own side look better than it was.
If that is the way this book comes out, I want to say that I
did not consciously succumb to the temptation. If it makes
me look better than my adversaries painted me—well, that
is what it is supposed to do.

Several of my revisors were social scientists—and the
Preface is the place to acknowledge their assistance—
especially Morton King and Paul Smith at Southern Methodist University and Samuel Blizzard and Dean Hoge at Princeton, each of whom read parts of the manuscript. Because they
were not personally involved in the happenings described in
this book they could be—and were—carefully objective
critics. I asked them to make a moral judgment on whether
my remarks about individuals and situations were in any way
vindictive.

The account of these research experiences was put together
not only from my memory, but especially from documents I
have in my files: newspaper clippings, letters, minutes of
meetings, written descriptions of events, and memoranda of
various kinds. As I finished the first draft of each chapter I
sent it for revision to people who were involved in the specific project. Here I want to thank John Elsner and Daniel
Quinn who were on the research team for Southern Parish;

Maria Hornung, Henry Montecino and Joan Forshag Ogilvie, who were in the middle of the fight for school desegregation; Brian Jordan, Thomas Lief and John Nelson, who know as much as I do about the study of police arrests; Carl Armbruster, Frank Matthews and Mary Schniedwind, who were acquainted with all phases of the clergy survey; and finally, the men most responsible for the study of high school students: Bernard Dooley, Edwin McDermott and Paul Siegfried.

Getting the reminiscences of these cooperative revisors delayed the completion of the manuscript by many months, but it also added clarification as well as the assurance that the account is as accurate as anyone can expect. None of them is responsible for the manner in which I took their comments and rewrote them, and I do not regret the months of delay that they added to the job of authoring.

What is left, then, in a book after a sociologist has censored himself, asked his research associates for comments and corrections, submitted his work to fellow social scientists, accepted the suggestions of the publisher's referees, and removed everything that legal experts deem libelous? It can be said—perhaps without undue modesty—that all that remains is the "unvarnished truth."

JOSEPH H. FICHTER

Loyola University
New Orleans, Louisiana
June, 1973

CONTENTS

ONE-MAN RESEARCH: REMINISCENCES OF A CATHOLIC SOCIOLOGIST

ONE

CRAFT AND CHRONICLE

When I was a graduate student at Harvard just after World War II, everybody in the new department of Social Relations was excited about William Whyte's *Street Corner Society*. Perhaps local imagination helped to augment Whyte's prestige. He had been sponsored by Harvard's Society of Fellows and spent most of his 3 years living and researching across the Charles River in the Italian section of Boston. His sociological research "style" seemed even more attractive than that of the Lynds in the *Middletown* studies, and of Warner in the first volumes of his *Yankee City* series. We discussed all of these as "models" of research projects in social science.

In those years, like sociological doctoral candidates elsewhere, we were studying research methods in the usual manner: listening to professors, reading research reports, and laying grand plans for our own future research. Yet there was something missing: the detailed description of the actual research process. It was not until 1955, in the second edition of his book, that Whyte explained in detail how he did his work in Cornerville. He told the personal, subjective story of his experiences as a researcher. He thought this story would be useful for young social scientists because "generally the published report gives little attention to the actual process whereby the research was carried out" (1).

A few other social scientists—Alvin Gouldner, Edward Shils, C. Wright Mills—took the trouble to describe their research experiences, but even as late as 1964, Phillip Hammond could say that "there were almost no chronicles of social research" (2). He took an enormous stride toward filling this need by assembling and editing eleven personal stories of research by some of the most eminent sociologists in America and publishing it as *Sociologists At Work*. Later Hammond followed this pattern by including a detailed account of his own research experience in a study of the Protestant campus ministry (3).

Is there anything that can be added to these sources of methodological information by a researcher like me who usually runs a one-man show and operates financially on a shoestring? For an answer let me turn to one of the wise comments of Everett Hughes, who has been my friend and sociological mentor for more than a quarter of a century. At the 1970 meetings of the American Sociological Association in Washington, he remarked that many graduate students and young instructors are discouraged from doing research because they cannot get gigantic grants for large-scale projects. He said: "A man with an idea, some ingenuity and hard work, can do much by himself." Looking back to a time when everything was less expensive he revealed that he had done the research for *French Canada in Transition* (4) on less than 5,000 dollars.

WHY REMINISCE? Everyone has a story to tell about himself, and when a sociologist is almost a compulsive writer

—as I tend to be—he feels that the story is worth telling. The fact that the story is personal makes it unique, but no set of reminiscences is so exclusively personal that others cannot find parallels in their own experiences. Probably every sociological research project is singular, not only because of the researcher but also because no social situation to be investigated is exactly like any other. Nevertheless, there have to be analogies and similarities, otherwise there could be no academic discipline that goes by the name of research methodology.

One of my reflections is that almost every time I tackled what I thought was a worthwhile research problem I seemed to get "in trouble." This may be due to any of several reasons: my abrasive personality (which I would hardly admit), the manner in which I conducted research (which I think was professional), the kinds of research reports I wrote (which I consider honest, ethical, and objective) or the topics I chose to study. At a farewell party at Harvard when I was ending my 5-year appointment as Stillman Professor (5), Dean Krister Stendahl remarked that I had "a cool approach to hot subjects." I liked that appraisal. The research topics were "hot" (especially race and religion) because they were too "sacred" to be prodded by an inquisitive, "profane" sociologist.

It is not my primary intention in these memoirs to prove that the people who caused me trouble were wrong and I was right—even though that conclusion should come through. I do not offer this book as a vindication of myself, and I trust that I am not read as "vindictive" because I name and describe persons who previously had been anonymous. When I received the faculty appointment to Harvard in 1965, Andrew Greeley in his syndicated column called this a "belated recognition" for pioneer research in the sociology of Catholicism. On the other hand, the White Citizens' Council of New Orleans, always antagonistic to "Harvard radicalism," publicly announced that "Harvard got what it deserved. Father

Fichter should be at home there."

No one who has watched the American scene since the end of World War II needs to be told that this has been an era of tremendous change. Within the Catholic church Pope John dramatically opened the doors to change by convoking the Second Vatican Council. The shift has been dramatic also for the sociologist who wants to research the "hot subject" of American Catholicism: it has changed from the early censorship that suppressed the findings of my own parish research to the current willingness of Catholic bishops to accept, even to pay for, sociological surveys of Catholicism. At the beginning of this period sociologists had little prestige among intellectuals and none among ecclesiastical officials (6). Now sociologists are intellectually more respectable and ecclesiastically more useful.

What happens to the image of the cool, detached, and objective social science researcher when he decides to "tell all?" Perhaps the image was a false one from the beginning. I have never pretended that I was value-free, and not intensely concerned about racial justice, about the moral implications of education, about the problems of personnel policies within the institutional church. I held strong convictions of what "ought to be" in all these situations, and in every research project I measured the actual behavior of people against the set of behavioral norms the people themselves allegedly professed. A growing number of young sociologists now insist that we must be "engaged," that we must select research projects that are "relevant" and report them in a persuasive way for the betterment of society (7).

Because I am committed to a better society does not mean that I could eschew honest and objective reporting of research results. Back in 1952 Bill Kolb and I worked this over as an ethical problem, with some pertinent observations from Eldon Powell, then a graduate student at Tulane. After much discussion and three or four complete revisions, we published the paper, "Ethical Limitations on Sociological Reporting" in the *American Sociological Review*. Our concluding remark was that the sociologist must treat the subjects of his research "with justice, understanding, compassion, and in the last analysis, love" (8).

OBSTRUCTIONISTS. I like to think that I am practicing these virtues when I write here about the people who stood in the way of me and my research projects, who tried to prevent the studies or who publicly attacked the study reports. The publicity they gave me may have been charitably intended, but the way it came out in the news media often appeared to be vicious, derogatory, and contemptuous. It is now their turn to be subjected to my appraisal, and whatever publicity comes to them from these memoirs should be virtuous if not laudatory, honest if not flattering, acceptable if not comforting.

There is a sense in which these obstructionists were a product of their times. The early fifties are now remembered as the era of McCarthyism when the spirit of free and critical enquiry—the very soul of social science—was endangered. You were disloyal to God and country if you expressed criticism or even raised questions about any American institution, sacred or secular. Overlapping the McCarthy era and carrying over into the sixties there was, especially in Louisiana where I was then doing sociological studies, the oppressive authoritarianism of the racists. I do not charge my obstructionists—at least not all of them—with McCarthyism or racism. I am quite ready to say they were sincere, which is probably the smallest compliment I can pay them.

If there is a lesson to be learned from these research reminiscences it is the fact that social science projects can be carried on successfully in the face of stubborn opposition. Probably no one will ever have to experience the simultaneous suppression of three volumes of research findings—nor would I if I had it to do over again. Yet the *Southern Parish* debacle toughened me to expect, and taught me how to resist, the opposition of racists in the school desegregation project; of police, politicians, and racists in the study of arrests; and of ecclesiastical prelates in the clergy survey. Four of the chapters of this book would not have been written, nor the research done, nor the results published, had I waited for the permission or approval of the people who ultimately benefitted the most from them (9).

Not everybody in authority was an enemy of social science research. There were a few exceptions among church hierarchs who thought that a sociological survey could be of some utility, and they permitted it under two conditions: it must not cost money, and it must not be published. One bishop of a rural diocese asked if I would study the program of the Confraternity of Christian Doctrine in his small parishes that were without an elementary Catholic school (10). When I gave him a tentative research plan and a rough estimate of the cost he wrote back to say he had no money. He guessed that I might have some graduate student who was looking for a dissertation topic and would be grateful for the opportunity to do his research. The bishop had no intention of hiring professionals for the job.

Another form of unpublished and unfinanced church research was in the numerous master's theses that gradually gathered dust on the library shelves of Catholic universities like Fordham, St. Louis, Marquette, and Notre Dame. These were done by members of religious orders who made questionnaire surveys on the "vocation background" of the people who entered their congregation. The findings provided general information, were seldom analyzed at any sophisticated level, did not cost money, and were not published (11). Building on these individual studies and far surpassing them in

magnitude was the questionnaire of 649 items distributed to
160,000 religious sisters in April, 1967, which certainly had to
have financial support but the results of which are apparently
"not for publication" (12).

There is now evidence within the Catholic church of a
positive and happy switch of official attitudes toward social
science research. Twenty-five years ago the hierarchs looked
on sociologists with suspicion and on their works with either
scorn or fear. There was nothing that social scientists could
do for the church that could not be done better by bishops
and their chancery officials, by canon lawyers, and even by
moral theologians. If there were such an academic discipline
as "Catholic sociology" it might be tolerable as long as it did
not include empirical research and above all refrained from
publishing reports of research (13). Censorship was the club
held over the head of the Catholic who taught sociology as a
profane social science and looked on organized religion as a
cultural product.

The great awakening to the need for sociological research
occurred among the American bishops several years after the
close of the Second Vatican Council. They finally accepted
the obvious fact that seminaries were emptying and priests
were departing. They voted 50,000 dollars for a study of
seminarians which was conducted by two professors at the
Catholic University of America (14). The real breakthrough
came, however, when the bishops contracted to pay the National Opinion Research Center the sum of 440,000 dollars to
do a survey of the American priesthood. Even here they
wanted some safeguards against unfavorable publicity and
hired a public relations expert whose job it was to prevent
"sensationalism" in the publication of the research findings.

INEXPENSIVE PROJECTS. I am awed and perhaps a
little envious of sociologists who get enormous financial

grants for their research projects. One of my more friendly critics, who personally makes a good living from social science research, remarked that I do research at "bargain-basement rates," and he was telling the truth—whether or not he meant it as a compliment. Of the five projects I describe in this book, the most expensive cost 10,300 dollars, and that was the educational campaign, supported by a grant from the Fund for the Republic, to prepare for the desegregation of New Orleans Catholic schools. Another, which cost less than that, was the study of police handling of arrested persons in New Orleans, supported by grants from the National Science Foundation (1,180 dollars) and the Marshall Field Foundation (6,000 dollars). This must have appeared much more expensive to the critic who called it the "50,000 dollar Fichter Report" (15).

One of the reasons my social science projects are not very costly is because for the most part I do them "on the side" while I am regularly employed on a university campus. This is possible for a bachelor priest who can work nights and weekends without the domestic distractions and demands that his married colleagues face. My research pursuits, however, have not been exclusively overtime work. The universities where I have been employed encourage faculty members to do research; they make adjustments in teaching schedules to allow time and energy for research; they also absorb some of the "hidden costs" that do not appear on the project budget.

This indirect financial assistance from the university administration was available over the years at Loyola University of the South where three of the students who were granted work scholarships were regularly assigned to the department of sociology. There I set up a social science workshop where sociology majors got a small taste of research methods, and I introduced the first IBM equipment to be used on that campus, whereby students learned at least to use a key punch and simple sorter-counter (16). Years later, while I was Stillman Professor at the Harvard Divinity School, I had a part-time research assistant and a full-time secretary who were of invaluable help on my study projects.

When I say that I did not have to do social science research "for a living" I must admit some exceptions—none of which is described in this book (17). Research was my main task for a full year, starting September 1964, when I worked for Peter Rossi at the National Opinion Research Center (NORC) on the survey of Negro college graduates. Even this spilled over to the following year when I was at Harvard and finished the research report "on the side." On a previous occasion I spent a year (1961) at the invitation of Roger Vekemans to teach research methods at the Universidad Catolica in Chile. With the help of students and junior faculty members I conducted a research project there that was published as *Cambio Social en Chile*. Still earlier (1953–1955) at the invitation of Josef Hoefner, I taught research methodology at the University of Muenster in Germany, and with the help of a student team produced a report on *Soziologie der Pfarrgruppen*.

In the competition for foundation grants the person who does research "on the cheap" may become known as a "rate-buster." I plead innocent to this charge on two counts: first, I was not very successful in getting foundation grants, and second, no one seemed to be competing to do the kind of research I inaugurated. The only instance in which there was a "competitive" cost estimate was in the replicated survey of Jesuit high school students in 1968. Although John Walsh, director of the Catholic Educational Research Center, submitted a reasonable estimate of 17,000 dollars, his center did not get the contract because his proposed research design and procedure would not allow findings comparable to those of the 1965 survey. In fact, I was not in competition for that second survey, and I had hoped that Walsh could do the work.

Access to research funds was a continuing problem for all Jesuit colleges and universities, and a solution was sought in the early fifties by setting up a Washington office for this purpose. The two successive directors of this office occasionally visited the Jesuit campuses but not any of the departments of social science. Whether it was their own concept of research or that of the leaders of the Jesuit Educational Association (JEA), they focused exclusively on the so-called physical sciences, trying to get foundation and government money for studies in biology, chemistry, and physics. At any rate, neither I, nor as far as I know any other Jesuit sociologist, was able to get a research grant through this central office (18).

SOMETHING FOR NOTHING. As I think back over my research experience since 1947, I begin to believe that there may be some truth in the folk saying: "When you get something for nothing you don't appreciate it." The two surveys I made of the American diocesan clergy in 1960 and 1966 cost the Catholic hierarchy nothing, and elicited no gratitude from them. The 1959 survey of American Jesuit seminarians, which the Jesuit General neither sponsored nor financed, was repudiated by him. The largest lack of appreciation came from Monsignor Pyzikiewicz, who paid nothing for the intensive, year-long study I made of his parish in New Orleans (19). Similarly, I did the study of police behavior in the same city without charge to Mayor Schiro or Chief Giarrusso. The findings were repudiated and I was attacked as though I were an agent of subversion to the people involved.

There are exceptions to this generalization. Repudiation of the research findings and lack of appreciation are not always the case when people get something for nothing. One of the most "satisfied clients" I had was Father Arnold Wibbert, Pastor of St. Matthew's Parish in South Bend, whose parochial school we studied in 1956–1957 (20). The financial support for that project came out of the research funds at the University of Notre Dame, and the study was done at no cost to either the parish or the diocese. Father Wibbert was not only cooperative during the whole research program but appreciative of the report that resulted from it—even though he had received an anonymous letter from someone in the New Orleans parish of Mater Dolorosa telling him that I was a dangerous man.

I suppose I have to make a mixed judgment in this regard about the 1956 educational campaign for school desegregation, which was contributed cost-free to the Catholics of New Orleans. In this instance the liberal minority among both clergy and laity was appreciative of the project, whereas the conservative majority wished that it had never been done. Archbishop Rummel and his top administrators (except the Vicar-General, Monsignor Lucien Caillouet, and the editor-in-chief of the archdiocesan weekly, Father Carl Schutten) were favorably cooperative with the whole project. Although they wearily bowed to the racist opposition and postponed for 6 years the desegregation of the Catholic schools, they were grateful that the campaign had been conducted.

Among the five sociological projects described in this book, only one was instituted, sponsored, and paid for by its beneficiaries. This was the "two-layer" survey of high school students I did in 1965 and 1968 for the Secondary School Commission of the JEA, the first at the request of Father Bernard Dooley and the other at the request of his successor, Father Paul Siegfried. It was also the one that proceeded most smoothly, with no obstructionists at hand during the collection of data and no uproar of outraged sensibilities when the research report was distributed. This was a case in which people "got what they paid for."

Perhaps money had nothing to do with it. Times and attitudes had changed. The need for sociological research was becoming more apparent. I like to think that the happy experience of the high school surveys can be attributed to the intelligent social awareness of my fellow Jesuits at this stage of development of the secondary educational system. Furthermore, the contemporary group of Jesuit Provincials seems to have a fairly sophisticated approach to the procedures of sociological research.

ONE-MAN JOBS. Most colleges and universities in the United States do not maintain the kind of social science research facilities that are operative at places like Berkeley, Chicago, Columbia, and Michigan. This means that relatively few sociologists get the opportunity of participating in large-scale, well-funded research in an organization in which they can constantly consult specialists. I had this valuable opportunity for 1 year at the University of Chicago, where many experts had a hand in the survey of Negro college graduates on which I did the report. At NORC I was able to tap the expertise of people who specialized in questionnaire construction, sampling, data collection, statistics, testing of hypotheses, analysis, and interpretation.

When a man sets up his own research project, he does all these tasks by himself. This is what I mean when I say that each of the five social science projects described in this book was a "one-man show." I had the advantage of research training as a graduate student at Harvard, supplemented by summer courses with Rupert Vance at the University of North Carolina and with W. Lloyd Warner at the University of Chicago. But it remains true that the craft is learned and the skill is acquired by actually doing research. Without becoming an expert at any of the subspecialties of methodology I had to hold myself accountable for every stage of the process.

In the late 1950s I thought a great deal about cooperative research and teamwork centered around the sociology of religion. In my opinion the Catholic Church in the United States was desperately in need of sociological research, and the Catholic hierarchy should have been willing to find financial support for a large-scale research organization. I discussed this with Monsignor John Egan, who was then assembling a small research staff in his Office of Urban Affairs in Chicago (21). Later I discussed it also with Thomas McDonough, Peter Rossi, Morton Grodzins, James Davis, and Andrew Greeley, all of whom were associated with the University of Chicago. Nothing came of this proposal.

In 1965 the American bishops encouraged the establishment of the Center for Applied Research in the Apostolate (CARA) in Washington, with a trained anthropologist, Father Louis Luzbetak, as its first director. I was a member of the Research Committee of CARA which met sporadically but with no clear understanding of its duties. The bishops took no financial responsibility for CARA, which had to raise its own money and which became in essence a kind of "middleman" or clearing house for church research. When CARA got research funds from the Knights of Columbus, the Serra Club, or any other source, it "farmed out" the research project to social scientists.

At about the same time the Jesuit Institute of Social Order, which had existed since the late 1930s at St. Louis University, was undergoing a reorganization. For more than a year I was at least peripherally involved in the planning of this group which finally relocated itself in the neighborhood of Harvard University with a new name, the Cambridge Center for Social Studies. I was an associate of the center and a member of the board of directors when it opened in September 1965. My hope was that we could emulate successful research institutes like Berkeley and Columbia, where large-scale cooperative studies could be conducted by a team of social science specialists. This hope was not realized, and I resigned from the Center in January 1967 (22).

The men at the Cambridge Center were also doing "one-man jobs" of research, but with the usual professional contacts with other social scientists. In this sense no researcher works completely alone. With the exception of a few eccentrics, there is, fortunately, a kind of "fellowship of concern" among the great American sociologists. Like genuine scientists in other academic fields, they are willing to share knowledge and techniques with their colleagues, seek counsel and give it, and provide encouragement for younger scholars. The bigger the man, the more likely is he to be cooperative. In my earlier years as a researcher I received counsel from so many great sociologists that it would be embarrassing for me to try to list them here.

The one-man research project is like the book that has a single author who takes all responsibility for the contents. Yet the single author often gives a list of acknowledgements of his debts to other people. Three of the projects described in this book could not have been carried out successfully without teamwork: the studies of parish life, police behavior, and school desegregation. The two others were surveys, done by mailed questionnaires which required assistance mainly in technical data processing and computer work. The surveys of diocesan clergy and of high school students would have been interminable without sophisticated data processing.

UTILITY OF RESEARCH.   It seems to me that, next to the pursuit of virtue, the noblest activity of human beings is the search for truth. Most of us at some time or another philosophize about the ultimate meaning of existence, but the scientific researcher is professionally busy about intermediate meanings. Knowledge is ordinarily more useful than ignorance, unless to dispel ignorance requires more reform than persons and groups are willing to undertake (23). If knowledge is useful, then the research source of knowledge is the beginning of social utility.

Most American social scientists think that research is a good thing for the society; it opens up the potential for intelligent and guided change, so that eventually something useful will result from their research. People who pay for sociological research (except some large, disinterested foundations that will underwrite basic research) usually want some practical findings that can be turned into practical improvements. I am not talking here about product research that leads to inconsequential variations in consumer goods, nor about market research that finds ways of attracting the largest number of customers for goods.

Big business and industry have long since learned that it "pays" to study human relations and to discover that labor peace ensues, absenteeism declines, and productivity rises when workers are intelligently managed. The utilization of manpower has become the focus of extensive research projects, not only in private-profit organizations, but also in political, military, and educational systems. Social planning, which is becoming increasingly necessary in all large social collectivities, is unthinkable without preliminary research.

This pragmatic view has been a guiding principle for me in inaugurating every social science project I conducted. Certainly I wanted first-hand knowledge that would improve the content of my sociology lectures, but more importantly I wanted research knowledge that would be useful to the people I studied. At first it was my mistake to assume that everybody, especially church people, would recognize the obvious advantage of collecting and analyzing information about human groups. I have often remarked that the greatest problem of the Catholic church in America was the absence of trained leaders, and the best evidence of their lack of training was their refusal to take research seriously (24).

This ecclesiastical ignorance and opposition were so bothersome to me that I wrote a special appendix, "The Utility of Social Science for Religion," for my 1954 book, *Social Relations in the Urban Parish* (25). I gave a dozen reasons why empirical research is useful for the operation of city churches and dioceses, and I suggested that this pragmatic argument could be extended to include the whole ecclesiastical system. One of these was the plea for substantive content in the whole area of "pastoral theology," and it grew partially out of my own seminary experience of a totally inadequate academic course in this subject (26).

There are research studies that lie fallow. How useful can a project be if its findings are not adequately interpreted or its report judiciously publicized? One example of a "wasteful" study was the "census" of American Jesuits in preparation for the 1967 conference on the "Total Development of the Jesuit Priest." The first volume of the *Proceedings* contained 212 statistical tables emerging from the questionnaire survey conducted by Eugene Gerard and John Arnold, but there was no interpretation or analysis of the data. I urged that these important findings be utilized, or at least that their utility be investigated. These data have not yet been probed, except for three small secondary studies I made from them and published in the *Jesuit Educational Quarterly* (27).

Curious as I am about the practical utility of my sociological studies, I have had relatively little feedback from them, except sometimes to hear that they did "more harm than good" by arousing suspicion, fear, and antagonism. In some cases, however, sending out the research report was like throwing it off a cliff on a dark night. It just seemed to disappear. This was certainly not the case with studies that dealt with race relations in New Orleans. If ever there were people who needed empirical knowledge about race relations they were the members of the New Orleans police department,

and the parents, teachers, and priests who were faced there
with the approach of Catholic school desegregation.

APPLICATION OF RESEARCH. One of the persistent
problems I encountered in all these sociological studies was to
clarify the difference between the person who does the research and the person who implements the findings. Even at
the beginning, when I was still planning the parish research
program and discussing it with Archbishop Rummel, he
asked me, "Why don't you write a book telling us what to
do?" Even after reading the typescript of the second volume
of the abortive *Southern Parish* series, he was still pleading
for a "blueprint" that could be followed in the operation of
Catholic parishes (28). This was the attitude, too, of the bishops I addressed at a closed conference at Fordham University
in June 1967. They wanted answers from the researcher
without paying attention to the research data out of which
they themselves would have to fashion the answers.

I still believe that planning and development are specialized
fields of human relations, quite distinct from the role of sociological researcher. There were a few such specialists in the
Louisiana colleges and universities when Catholic school officials were talking about desegregation, and later when public
school officials faced the same decision. As far as I know,
none of these specialists was consulted during the period
(1952–1960) that Morton Inger calls "the wasted years"
(29). The blundering manner in which two white public
schools in low-income areas were reluctantly desegregated in
the fall of 1960 is clear evidence that the expertise of professional planners, even if they were consulted, was not put to
use (30).

It is true that in the report on *Police Handling of Arrestees*
I appended a list of recommendations for the improvement of

this aspect of police behavior. These practical recommendations were based on the research findings, but they were formulated mainly by specialists, Aaron Kohn and his associates,
who had been working for more than a decade in New Orleans to better the relations between the police and the
community. In the final analysis, of course, the reform of police behavior had to come "from the inside" as Chief Giarrusso contended, but it would probably never have occurred
without the prodding of research findings provided by "outsiders."

The much heralded "renewal" of the role and status of
Catholic priests in the United States is another case in point.
The people "in charge," the superiors of dioceses and religious orders, were chiefly responsible for putting into effect
the recommendations of the Second Vatican Council and for
formulating the local implementation of research findings on
the clergy. Some of the planning implications were clear
from research done even before the Council: the need for
shared responsibility, for better communication between bishops and priests, for improved seminary training and continuing education. I felt that it was not my task as a researcher to
outline these improvements for ecclesiastical management,
nor was I ever in an administrative position from which I
could direct a program of reform. The fact that my 1966 survey of diocesan priests found many of the same problems that
had shown up in the 1960 survey suggests that ecclesiastical
managers did little to reform the situation in those 6 years.

The only project in which I attempted to discover whether
my research findings had led to improvement was the 1968
survey of the Jesuit high schools in the United States. This
was a replication, with the same questionnaire, of the 1965
survey of those schools. I knew that close attention had been
paid to the findings of the earlier survey, especially at a
workshop of delegates from these schools held the following
summer at Loyola University of Los Angeles. The research

report was meticulously scrutinized by the assembled educators, who drew up a list of recommendations for the reform of these schools (31). The extent to which any particular Jesuit high school followed these recommendations is known only to the people locally involved in the school.

I have always wanted my research to be ultimately applicable and useful, and although I separate the function of research from that of planning and development, I have often been curious about the practical "results." I wonder, for example, what Catholic chaplains did with my research report on military trainees at Lackland Air Force Base, whether the survey of Catholic parents in the Peoria diocese resulted in a better vocation program, whether the minor seminary in the St. Paul diocese, the parish in Ellensberg, Washington, the Newman Foundation in Oklahoma, the Boston Confraternity of Christian Doctrine, the Alumni Office of Loyola University of the South, ever made any practical use of the research I conducted for them. Were the findings filed away and forgotten?

MEASURING SOCIAL RELATIONS. Although most sociologists would not win prizes for their literary style, they attract the largest number of readers when their reports are narrative or descriptive. The opposite of this is the stereotype of sterile statistics, of "counting noses," of putting people in pigeonholes. I have tried to avoid both extremes: mere description or mere statistics. There is, of course, empirical value in the description of a racially integrated audience, a church wedding, a police "show-up," a school playground. There is value also in columns of comparative statistics showing similarities and differences between two or more categories of people.

Except for trained scientists and scholars, most readers of sociological reports need help in ferreting out the meaning of research findings. This means that the factual data that have been laboriously collected must be interpreted, or measured against some set of pertinent behavioral norms, but these must not be subjective norms based on the personal values of the social scientist (32). For my own satisfaction and, I think, for the ultimate utility of the research I have done, I have consistently and in each instance spelled out the normative expectations involved in the particular social system under investigation. The gap then that exists between the accepted norms and the actual behavior constitutes the measure of success or failure.

Although put in quantitative terms, this is a qualitative interpretation. It was not enough to discover "what goes on" in a Jesuit high school classroom; I had to ask first "what is supposed to go on?" This second question could be answered in the so-called philosophy of Jesuit secondary education as explained at a generalized level by its theorists and at a particularized level in the brochures and bulletins issued by the schools themselves. If the brochure says that religion *is* (but means that it *ought* to be) the most important subject taught in the school whereas the students themselves rate religion lower than say, English, history, and mathematics, we have a gap between what ought to be and what is.

The measurement of "religiosity" has been a sticky problem for behavioral scientists and has probably not yet been satisfactorily resolved, especially by researchers who omit the sociological dimension of religious affiliation with others. In the *Southern Parish* study I employed as criteria the widely taught norms of Catholicism to establish a rough typology of parishioners: nuclear, modal, marginal, and dormant. Variations of this typology have been tested subsequently by sociologists who introduced the extra psychological dimension of "inner experience," which is either basically immeasurable or sociologically irrelevant (33). The formula is still applicable, but it must be altered to accommodate the changing criteria

of Catholicism that have been introduced since the Second
Vatican Council.

In some instances I had to deal with a conflict between
normative systems, a situation exemplified in the 1950s and
1960s by the difference between southern white norms and
democratic American norms of expected behavior between
the races. If one accepted the southern white pattern of separate racial schools, which was declared unconstitutional in
1954 but continued in New Orleans until 1960, there would
have been no "gap" to measure by sociological research. The
central "problem" of race relations lay in the resistance of
southern racists to the acceptance of behavioral standards
contained in the United States Constitution and spelled out
by the Supreme Court.

THINGS HAVE CHANGED.   I started this chapter by
saying that a chronicle of some of my research experiences
might be helpful to others, especially younger social scientists
who do not have access to large research grants or to organized institutes that have such access. Perhaps the younger sociologist just starting on his professional career today has a
distrust of the establishment in the form of large, well-orga-
nized research bureaus and would prefer to be a "loner."
Whether from choice or necessity, it seems to me there will
always be room for the self-starter, for the person who is
willing to do one-man research jobs on a frugal budget.

Joining a well-established research bureau, whether in university, government, or industry, means fitting oneself into a
fixed project and doing the research segment to which one
had been assigned. This has its advantages in terms of on-
the-job training, but it is probably distasteful to some of the
free spirits of the new sociological generation—those who
want to be thought of as imaginative or creative or even radical. It may also hamper the efforts of those who—like

myself—are committed to a better society and believe that social science research can make a contribution to that goal.

Sociology is more exciting than it ever was; sociologists are more prestigeful than ever; the need for sociological enquiry is ever increasing; but the pedestrian, day-by-day hard work of research remains pretty much the same. You still have to interview people, observe their behavior, perhaps participate in it, collect data by mail and from documents, analyze trends and comparisons, and try to make sense out of research findings. What is different now—compared with a quarter of a century ago—is the wide availability of the computer, and this labor-saving device is best appreciated by those who once manipulated their data by counter sorters, or even manually.

It is a truism to say that the whole American sociocultural system has changed since the period immediately following World War II. Although social scientists always worry about potential threats to freedom, about reactionary movements among the people and authoritarian gestures by government, they must recognize a general loosening of restrictions throughout the American culture. It is almost true to say that only the personal taste and tact of the researcher place limitations on what he will study and how he will present the results. Censorship of access to data and of publication still exists, but in more subtle and rational forms than previously.

There are probably more "crises" in the United States now than ever before—at least there seems to be a greater social awareness of the "problems" in which our society is involved. Some people, like civil and ecclesiastical authorities, who are not comfortable with the all-pervading curiosity of the social science researcher, think that sociologists focus only on problems and publish only exposés of human misconduct. I have been associated with both Lewis Coser, who is sometimes called a "conflict sociologist," and Talcott Parsons, who seems to be best known for his interest in the "equilibrium" of social systems. In my own approach to research I lean to the latter when I try to discover "what works" to keep a collectivity going successfully, but my research reports (especially in race and religion) have been criticized as though they simply "exposed conflicts."

Are there now different and larger social problems that call for scientific research? Some of them are old phenomena seen anew, such as poverty, city ghettoes, and racial discrimination. Some of them are relatively new phenomena (nothing is really new), such as the counterculture that involves education, feminism, military service, and the general area of radical protest. This means that there is more than enough to engage the talents of the sociological researcher. Perhaps the most significant change is the image shift of the sociologist: from the aloof positivist who stood above it all and affirmed the value-free posture, to the dedicated activist who stands in the middle of it all and affirms the central values of the culture (34).

Because this chronicle is personal and autobiographical (in a limited sense) I should not omit the fact that I, too, have changed over the years. Aside from the knowledge and skill that accrue to any diligent scientist who works long enough and consistently enough at his craft, there has come to me a genuine appreciation of the virtue of prudence. It took me several years to realize how imprudent I had been in submitting to the suppression of three volumes of the *Southern Parish* study. The prudent person is one who has the courage to act in a situation where action is necessary and salutary. This means to reveal the truth—the findings of sociological research—and then to implement those findings in programs of social betterment. Over the years I have observed not only acts of imprudence but a kind of habitual imprudence in civil and ecclesiastical authorities who lacked the courage to accept, publish, and implement the findings of sociological research.

NOTES

1. William Foote Whyte, *Street Corner Society* (Chicago, University of Chicago Press, 1955), p. 279. Appendix to second ed.: "On the Evolution of *Street Corner Society*," pp. 279–358.

2. Phillip E. Hammond, *Sociologists at Work* (New York, Basic Books, 1964), p. 2. See p. 14, footnote 4, for references to Gouldner, Mills, and Shils.

3. This is an Appendix to *Campus Clergyman* (New York, Basic Books, 1966). Among other examples see the prize-winning book by Elliot Liebow, *Tally's Corner: A Study of Negro Streetcorner Men* (Boston, Little, Brown, 1967), especially "A Field Experience in Retrospect," pp. 232–256.

4. Everett Hughes, *French Canada in Transition* (Chicago, University of Chicago Press, 1943).

5. The Charles Chauncey Stillman Chair of Roman Catholic Studies was first held by the late historian, Christopher Dawson. It is a nontenured faculty appointment which I held from 1965 to 1970.

6. For a lively article on this subject see Bennett M. Berger, "Sociology and the Intellectuals: An Analysis of a Stereotype," *The Anticoch Review*, Vol. 17, No. 3 (Autumn 1957), pp. 275–290.

7. For the beginnings of this "movement," see Maurice Stein and Arthur Vidich, *Sociology on Trial* (Englewood Cliffs, N.J., Prentice-Hall, 1963). See also Howard S. Becker, "Whose Side Are We On?" *Social Problems*, Vol. 17 (Winter 1967), pp. 239–247, and Alvin Gouldner, "The Sociologist as Partisan: Sociology and the Welfare State," *American Sociologist*, Vol. 3 (May 1968), pp. 103–116.

8. Joseph H. Fichter and William L. Kolb, "Ethical Limitations on Sociological Reporting," *American Sociological Review*, Vol. 18, No. 5 (October 1953), pp. 544–550.

9. In a sympathetic letter to me on the occasion of the *Southern Parish* suppression, Robert Lynd revealed that the people who financed the *Middletown* study refused to have it published, but when Lynd insisted they predicted that no publisher would touch it.

10. The Confraternity of Christian Doctrine is mainly concerned with the religious education of Catholic children in public schools. While at Harvard I conducted a questionnaire survey of

lay men and women teaching in this program at the high school level in the Boston archdiocese. The research grant for this project did not come from Catholic sources.

11. They were accessible, however, through library loans, and I consulted some of them for the summer courses in "Sociology of Vocations" I gave at Notre Dame and Fordham, and in preparatory research for my book, *Religion as an Occupation* (Notre Dame, University of Notre Dame Press, 1961).

12. Separate reports were distributed to all the religious congregations participating in the survey with cautions against releasing the data for publication. The survey director, Sr. Marie Augusta Neal, analyzed some of the findings in the H. Paul Douglass Lectures for 1970. See *Review of Religious Research* (Fall 1970), pp. 2–16 and (Spring 1971), pp. 153–164.

13. In the early 1950s most members of the American Catholic Sociological Society no longer thought there was anything peculiarly "Catholic" about their sociology, but they had the habit of obedience. In 1951 I asked for, and expected, organized support of this group in protest to the suppression of *Southern Parish*. It was not forthcoming.

14. Raymond Potvin and Antanas Suziedelis, *Seminarians of the Sixties* (Washington, CARA, 1969). The NORC survey of priests was under the general direction of Andrew Greeley, whose occasional "confrontations" with the bishops were widely publicized in the press, especially in the *National Catholic Reporter*. For Greeley's own "final" remarks see his *Priests in the United States: Reflections on a Survey* (Garden City, Doubleday, 1972). For my own comments on this book see *America* (May 20, 1972), pp. 531–534.

15. Hubert J. Badeaux, *Commentary on the Fichter Report* (New Orleans, privately printed, 1964), p. 105.

16. The computer center at Loyola University of the South was established in 1964 by John Keller who from then on, with the competent assistance of Norma Batt, processed the data from my research projects.

17. Three books are the products of this relatively full-time research: *Soziologie der Pfarrgruppen* (Muenster, Aschendorf, 1958); *Cambio Social en Chile* (Santiago, Editorial Universidad Catolica, 1962); and *Graduates of Predominantly Negro Colleges* (Washington, D.C., Government Printing Office, 1967).

18. When I urged both Bernard Dooley and Paul Siegfried to get

assistance from this Jesuit Office of Research for the two high school surveys, they said they had been "advised" by officials of the Jesuit Educational Association not to do so.

19. When the pastor showed reluctance to return the typescript of the second volume, and did so only at the insistence of Archbishop Rummel, I offered to sell him the typescripts of all four volumes at 2,500 dollars each.

20. He is the pseudonymous pastor described in *Parochial School: A Sociological Study* (Notre Dame, University of Notre Dame Press, 1958).

21. This office, established by Cardinal Meyer, became in some ways a model for Catholic concerns about inner-city problems in other urban dioceses. It was suppressed by Cardinal Cody in 1966. See my article, "Chicago's Archdiocesan Office of Urban Affairs," *America*, Vol. *113* (October 23, 1965), pp. 462–465.

22. Some research grants were obtained by the members of the Cambridge Center for Social Studies, but most financial support was provided cooperatively by the ten American Jesuit Provinces. The center was closed in the summer of 1971, and the social scientists there received faculty appointments elsewhere.

23. It is probably not unfair to label this "opportunistic ignorance." Myrdal discussed the "convenience of ignorance" as a form of "opportunistic escape" in the area of race relations. See Gunnar Myrdal, *An American Dilemma* (New York, Harper, 1944), pp. 40–42.

24. One of the "cordial recommendations" of the Vatican II was that religious and social surveys be made through offices of pastoral sociology, and that the bishop ought to "employ suitable methods, especially social research," to learn the needs of his diocese. *Bishops' Pastoral Office in the Church*, articles 16, 17.

25. *Op. cit.*, Appendix, pp. 235–248. This was an expansion of my article, "The Southern Parish Controversy," *The Priest* (January 1952), pp. 21–26.

26. Efforts are being made to remove this lack. See Eugene Weitzel, Ed., *Pastoral Ministry in a Time of Change* (Milwaukee, Bruce, 1966). Even more promising is the statement of Cardinal Krol that "the NCCB has appointed a new committee to promote the pastoral implementation of the study," p. vi in *The Catholic Priest in the United States: Sociological Investigations* (Washington, United States Catholic Conference, 1972).

27. These were in successive numbers of the *Jesuit Educational Quarterly*, Vol. *31*, Nos. 2, 3, 4, "Hardworking Jesuits" (October 1968), pp. 91–100; "Preparation of the Jesuit Professional" (January 1969), pp. 148–158; "Pastors and Professors" (March 1969), pp. 189–198. This *Quarterly* ceased publication in March 1970.

28. As early as July 6, 1948, the Archbishop said, "I hope that your study will give us some practical outlines that will enable us to make suggestions for a more fruitful application of our spiritual, moral and social resources in the operation of parish life."

29. Morton Inger, *Politics and Reality in an American City: The New Orleans School Crisis of 1960* (New York, Center for Urban Education, 1969), p. 17. See also *The New Orleans School Crisis* (Washington, D.C., Government Printing Office, 1961).

30. See the article by James Lawrence, "The Scandal of New Orleans," *Commonweal*, Vol. 73 (February 3, 1961), pp. 475–476.

31. This was published under the title *The Christian School—A New View* (Washington, Jesuit Educational Association, 1966) and distributed to all Jesuit high schools in the United States. A later pamphlet, *The Jesuit High School of the Future* (September 1972) although composed by the Commission on Research and Development, completely ignored the findings of the surveys of 1965 and 1968.

32. The values and intentions of the sociologist are at the basis of the way he interprets not only his findings but the whole sociological enterprise. See Peter Berger, "Sociology and Freedom," *The American Sociologist*, Vol. *6*, No. 1 (February 1971), pp. 1–5.

33. See my "Sociological Measurement of Religiosity," *Review of Religious Research*, Vol. *10*, No. 3 (Spring 1969), pp. 169–177.

34. In his presidential address to the American Sociological Association at Washington, August 31, 1970, Reinhard Bendix made a plea for the sociologist's "combination of passionate concern and scholarly detachment which is the hallmark of reasoned inquiry in our field." See his "Sociology and the Distrust of Reason," *American Sociological Review*, Vol. *35*, No. 5 (October 1970), pp. 831–843.

TWO

THE DYNAMICS
OF SUPPRESSION

At this point in the history of the quickly changing Catholic church, the official ecclesiastical *Index of Prohibited Books* has become outmoded. For a long time this index had served as a warning to Catholics that danger to their faith and morals lurked in the published works of immoral and heretical authors. Usually the prohibition was not a suppression of the book after publication except in places where church authorities could control bookstores and sellers. Obviously it was not a prevention of publication since a book had to be printed and in circulation before it was placed on the index.

There was, however, a common procedure for preventing an author from publishing his work. Back in the days when censorship was taken much more seriously than it is now, a dangerous work by a Catholic author could be kept off the market by the disapproval of the official *censor librorum* (1). The unique aspect of my own experience with ecclesiastical book suppression is that I had received the official approval of the appointed censors, but still my work was suppressed. Not only that; I know of no one other than me who has had three books suppressed *at the same time*. This happened in 1951 at a time when such things could happen, long before the Second Vatican Council. Now 20 years later, such an occurrence is virtually unthinkable (2).

"The Southern Parish Case" was the title of an article by Paul Courtney in *Commonweal* for November 30, 1951. The opening sentence was as follows: "This is a report on an incident in New Orleans in which a few overly sensitive clerics lost their heads and Catholic America lost three valuable volumes of original sociological research." Courtney, a diocesan priest, had not consulted me before writing this article. He implied that Archbishop Rummel was the key to the book suppression since he did not "reopen and force the issue." He was closer to the truth when he added that my religious superiors "apparently" failed to support me and my work (3).

The first volume of a projected four-volume series, reporting the results of a year-long (1948) sociological study of a New Orleans Catholic parish, was titled *The Dynamics of a City Church*. The manuscript was completed in August 1949, accepted for publication by the University of Chicago Press in September 1950, and released on the fall list of 1951. This first volume had been personally approved by Archbishop Rummel, received the *imprimi potest* of Father Harry Crane, provincial of the southern Jesuits, the *nihil obstat* of Monsignor J. Gerald Kealy, Chicago's official archdiocesan censor of books, and the *imprimatur* of Cardinal Samuel Stritch (4).

The second volume, *Social System of a Parish*, dealing with the various organizations, or "societies," of the parish, was completed in August 1950 and submitted to the same multiple scrutiny by the same ecclesiastical authorities, except that a new provincial, Father William Crandell, had taken office that same month. It was passed by the Jesuit censors of the southern province and by the archdiocesan censor of Chicago, and approved by Archbishop Rummel. In November of that year, the readers for the University of Chicago Press submitted their commentaries and recommended that this second volume of the *Southern Parish* series be published.

Another year passed and the manuscript for the third volume, *Parish School and Home Life,* was nearing completion. On Wednesday, August 28, 1951, my work was interrupted by a telephone call from Archbishop Rummel. Unlike most other prelates of this high rank, he was easily accessible in person and by telephone and often made direct calls without benefit of secretaries. He said, "You seem to be in real trouble. Monsignor Joseph is very angry about the book you wrote on his parish. I know that I gave it the green light— and told him so—but he demands that you stop all publication and withdraw the book from the market."

This message stunned me, and I was not sure how to respond to the archbishop. Only a few days earlier I had sent an autographed prepublication copy of *Dynamics of a City Church* to Monsignor Joseph Pyzikiewicz, the pastor of Mater Dolorosa Parish (5). I had inscribed it with a note of appreciation for his kindness and cooperation during the year in which we studied his parish. Although by this time he was no longer happy with me and my team of researchers, I erroneously thought that the book itself would please him and give him a sense of pride in the parish.

THEORETICAL ORIGINS. The conceptualization of the research project that caused all this excitement goes back to the days when I was a graduate student at Harvard University just after World War II (6). I was intrigued with Durkheim's concept of anomie and listened to Sorokin's lectures on the "dire" manner in which modern norms and values were shifting in the direction of an increasingly sensate culture. I was impressed with Kluckhohn's remark that the

Roman Catholic church, with its integrated system of values and its high quality of organizational competence, could potentially restore a sense of balance to Western civilization.

Furthermore, at Harvard, while searching through literature on empirical sociological studies, I discovered that American Catholicism was virtually an untouched field of sociological research (7). I became convinced that my personal interests and religious convictions could combine well with theoretical knowledge and scientific training to point me in this direction (8). A research project must start with a preliminary design and a set of testable hypotheses. Why not study the total American Catholic church as a sociocultural system to test the hypothesis that the church would demonstrate an internal solidarity flowing mainly from its integrated core of values?

Of such stuff are the grandiose dreams of graduate students made, and the stuff diminishes—and sometimes evaporates —when it comes time to do the research. There were two themes then under discussion by the Harvard social scientists that seemed to negate this large-scale approach to the church. People such as Stouffer and Parsons were talking about informal patterns of behavior in ostensibly highly formalized organizations. Military behavior had been studied during World War II by social scientists who found that action was often most effective when it bypassed rigid regulations. From the functional point of view it was to me an exciting suggestion that repetitive procedures in the Catholic church become informally organized and could be studied alongside the formal flow charts and systematic procedures of the church.

If this notion were to be applied to the study of American Catholicism it would require participant observation of the manner in which Catholics actually behave. What do the members of the church do and say? What does it mean to be a Catholic in the day-to-day experiences of life? In what ways, and to what extent, does the informal practice of Catholicism differ from the formal expectations of the official church? It seemed to me that a worthwhile research project had to look systematically at the *real* church of living human beings rather than at the descriptions provided in textbooks on Catholicism.

A second theme then popular among Harvard social scientists centered around the study of small social groups. Homans was developing his theories along these lines and encouraging his students to do research in manageable limited collectivities. Exploratory studies of this kind had been done with Navy personnel, particularly among crews of air force bombers during the war. All the graduate students in sociology read William Whyte's *Street Corner Society* and paid close attention to the study of the bank wiring room done by Roethlisberger and Dixon. This was the kind of ground-level research introduced by LePlay in Europe and largely ignored by the so-called "system builders" among sociological theorists.

It was obvious to me that the Catholic church in America—complex, organized, and institutionalized—contained within itself almost innumerable human groups. It would be a gigantic research task to study all of these simultaneously and to investigate not only their informal, functional, internal *modus vivendi* but also their structural and meaningful interdependence. A more practical approach would be to select some social unit within the system: a chancery office, a seminary, the Knights of Columbus, a diocesan school system. Parsons at one time suggested that I study the informal social structure of the American Jesuits, or perhaps one of the ten American provinces of the Society of Jesus.

I had no intention of embarking on an empirical research project of this nature before finishing my doctoral program of study at Harvard. As a matter of fact, although the implication was later made that I had done the *Southern Parish* study for my doctoral dissertation, I selected a completely different subject in which to fulfill this requirement. Under the direction of Carle Zimmermann, with Parsons and Sorokin as thesis readers, I made a study of family legislation of the Roman Emperor Augustus. This dissertation was completed and approved in the summer of 1947, after which I returned to Loyola University of the South, ready for teaching and further research.

Research projects, or their preconceptualizations, never turn out quite the way they were planned. Combining the notions of informal function and small structure in the study of American Catholicism, I looked also for the kind of collectivity that would represent the total system. Most of the Catholic groups I had considered represented some component of specification and differentiation within the ecclesiastical system. Even before returning to New Orleans I thought about the Catholic diocese, of which there were then 132 in America, as a kind of replica of the whole Catholic church, *ecclesiola in ecclesia.*

In a relatively small diocese the episcopal pastor, his ministers, and people, might be conceptualized as a miniature replica of the universal church (9). The problem I faced was that the New Orleans archdiocese was not a "small" group of Catholics. According to the official statistics in the *Catholic Directory*, there were at that time 461 priests, 1658 sisters, and 140 brothers, ministering to 421,262 Catholic lay people in the archdiocese of New Orleans. This large social unit of the church could indeed be studied sociologically, but not with the research project I had designed.

Another strong influence on my research orientation was W. Lloyd Warner, under whom I had taken a course at the University of Chicago in the summer of 1946. Sorokin used to criticize Warner's preoccupation with social status and stratification, saying that he made "mince pie" out of the New England community he studied. Yet, what attracted me to Warner's social anthropology was the fact that he attempted to include the total community in his research design. He was very encouraging when I suggested to him that I might employ his community concept in studying a Roman Catholic parish. This idea stayed with me during my final year of graduate work at Harvard.

CHOICE OF A PARISH.   The Catholic church is everywhere made up of local dioceses, and each diocese is everywhere made up of local parishes. From the territorial and juridical points of view, the basic social unit, or smallest component, of organized Roman Catholicism is the parish. From the point of view of church members, the parish is meant to be the "community of the faithful," of all the baptized Catholics living within certain fixed boundaries, and attending a church presided over by an appointed pastor. In the New Orleans archdiocese in 1947 there were 140 of these parochial units, some large and long established, others newly formed with only a makeshift place of worship.

Like any other diligent research designer I prepared a mimeographed memorandum in the hope of attracting research funds and, in this case, for the edification of academic and ecclesiastical administrators. This was to be my first "big" study, and I wanted people to know what I was trying to do, especially the "right" people who could in some ways be of help to the project. In it I explained the (a) reasons for the study, (b) selection of the parochial research site, (c) the method of research, (d) frames of reference, and (e) the need for a financial grant.

In this preliminary memorandum I included my *basic postulate:* "The influence of the church for the integration and solidarity of the larger community depends very much upon the internal integration of the church itself," and my *tentative hypothesis:*

From a purely sociological (not theological and supernatural) point of view, the internal structure and functioning of the parish is a significant index of the whole church as a solidaristic, sociocultural system of logico-meaningful behavior. In order to test this hypothesis, we do not intend to study a "problem parish" where there appears to be a relative lack of solidarity. Briefly then, we wish to select a "successful parish" in an effort to discover *what makes it successful* (10).

I do not know whether the choice of another parish—and another pastor—would have averted the ultimate disaster of suppression. At any rate, I worked out ahead of time the negative criteria for selecting a research site as follows:

All downtown parishes were eliminated because of the instability and transitory character of the congregation. National and Negro parishes and those operated by religious orders or in conjunction with educational institutions were considered a-typical. Of the remaining parishes, some were excluded because they were too recently established, others because the pastor was either on the inactive list or had not been in office long enough.

In my memorandum I said that there were also positive criteria for the tentative judgment of a successful parish:

In general we looked for a parish in which the majority of its members are overtly behaving as Christians according to their orthodox inner beliefs and values. Insofar as Catholic conduct can be measured in a scientific way the following characteristics were used as norms: vocations coming from the parish, children in parochial school, type and activity of parish organizations, number of children per family, attendance at Mass and the sacraments, attendance at weekday devotions, proportion of mixed marriages (also divorces and separations), presence or lack of juvenile delinquency, number of converts.

When I talked with Archbishop Rummel about my wish to select and study a successful parish, he asked, "Why not Holy Name?" This is the parish in which Loyola and Tulane Universities and two Catholic women's colleges. St. Mary's Dominican and Ursuline Brescia, were located. It was a flourishing parish, giving excellent service to the people, and widely known because of its weekly radio broadcast of the Sunday mass. I told the archbishop that I had talked with Father William Harty, the Jesuit pastor of Holy Name, who was willing to have his church studied, but that I turned down his invitation for two reasons. First, the normal complement of parish clergy was augmented by the presence of almost forty Jesuit priests on the Loyola University faculty who often assisted in parochial duties. Second, the congregation was swollen by large numbers of students who had only temporary residence there and could not be termed "typical" parishioners.

Besides Archbishop Rummel and Father Harty, some of the others who advised me in my search for the "best" researchable parish were the diocesan chancellor, Monsignor Charles Plauche, the superintendent of Catholic schools, Monsignor Henri Bezou, the pastor of St. Rita's Church, Monsignor William Castel, the archbishop's secretary, Father Joseph Vath, and a seminary professor, Father Vincent O'Connell. They understood what I was trying to do, and after numerous conversations and a process of elimination, they helped me narrow the list of potential research sites to three parishes: Incarnate Word, Mater Dolorosa, and Our Lady of Lourdes.

After visiting these three parishes and talking with their pastors I decided in November 1947 that Mater Dolorosa Parish was the one we should study. In retrospect it seems to me remarkable that I got almost unanimous agreement among these consultants when I told them of my final choice (11). Perhaps a scientific "pilot study" would have led me elsewhere, and would certainly have prolonged the choice. What I had was a matter of hearsay and reputation, and it led me to believe honestly that this parish had a good active pastor and a good "mixture" of people who joined in good parish societies and sent their children to a good parochial school. In spite of the controversy that later surrounded the findings of the research report, I am still ready to say that this was probably the best parish I could have chosen for the study.

Everything was "good" about Mater Dolorosa Parish in the opinion of these clerical consultants, who had both wide knowledge and long experience in the New Orleans archdiocese. When I transmitted these high opinions to the pastor, Monsignor Joseph, he said that "it feels good" to hear them, and that he had tried during the 15 years of his pastorate to build up this kind of reputation for his parish. Perhaps my approach to him on that autumn afternoon in 1947 contained an element of flattery, but it was not one of deception. From that moment the pastor was friendly and cooperative —as I tried to be—and this kind of relationship between us continued most of the time for almost 2 years.

I ought to point out that neither then nor later did I think that Mater Dolorosa was an "average" parish from which conclusions could be extended to the whole American parochial system. I was apparently not successful in making this point in the typescripts of the first and second volumes I submitted for publication to the University of Chicago Press, some of whose readers commented that I was "going beyond the data." Although I believed that my research findings were generally useful, I knew that the conclusions from the study of one parish were not universally applicable.

GETTING UNDER WAY.   Before granting permission and promising cooperation, the pastor queried, "What do you want to know?" Neither he nor I was sure what I meant when I answered, "Everything." Without attempting to explain my vaguely formed hypotheses about informal organization, social solidarity of small groups, the parish as miniature mirror of the whole church, value consensus as a basis of both mutual love and cooperation, I simply said that I wanted to get a true, detailed, objective picture of how a successful urban Catholic parish operates.

On several occasions, Father Joseph, a title by which everyone knew him and which he preferred to that of monsignor, said that he knew "everything there is to be known" about his parish. He had been ordained in 1921, and his very first assignment—for 4 years, till 1925—had been as assistant priest at Mater Dolorosa Parish. He claimed personal knowledge of all the (white) Catholics there, all the fine parishioners as well as some whom he called "bad eggs." He liked to contrast himself with his immediate predecessor, Monsignor J. Francis Prim, who died in 1933 leaving the new pastor with a tremendous (184,000-dollar) burden of debt. He was proud of his competence as a fund raiser, and his record proved that competence.

The pastor was a ready conversationalist, freely expressing the generally "conservative" level of opinion about labor unions, welfare recipients, Eleanor Roosevelt, Negroes, Protestants, and Jews. Lest this description sound condemnatory, or give a negatively critical impression, let me quickly add that the social attitudes exhibited by Father Joseph were quite typical of most New Orleans pastors over 50 years of age. The way he thought was also pretty much the way his older, middle-class, white parishioners thought. In an article in *Social Order* (December 1949) I reflected on the data from our study and wrote that the social role of the priest "is formed more on the patterns of the secular community than on the social teaching of the Church" (12).

I was less interested in his social philosophy—except as

it was reflected in his sermons and in dealings with
parishioners—than I was in the vast amount of information
he provided in our many conversations. I sat with him in his
rectory office an average of three times a week, and after
each occasion I made notes of all I could remember. After a
while he invited me to celebrate the nine o'clock children's
mass on Sundays—which I did on forty-one Sundays during the year of the study. This meant that I had breakfast
with him or one of his curates on most Sunday mornings (13). The pastor gave me a 5-dollar stipend for "helping
out" on these Sundays, and occasionally a bottle of I. W. Harper's bourbon.

Even before we started the daily schedule of research in
January 1948, I introduced Father Joseph to my ten
assistants—all of them students at Loyola University. Four
of them were women, and four of the men were veterans of
World War II. At this time I was still worrying about financ-
ing the project. The academic dean of the university, Father
William Crandell, who later became provincial of the southern
Jesuits, saw no reason for paying the students for doing what
he thought was "simply part of their class work." In my
early memorandum on the study I had said that "there is always the remote possibility that the parish or the diocese may
be approached for a partial subsidy," a possibility that was
never actualized. I soon had assurance, however, that my request would be granted for a 5,000-dollar subsidy from the
Carnegie Foundation for the Advancement of Teaching.

At any rate, the student researchers came to know the parish priests—the curates, Fathers O'Neill and Whitney, as
well as the pastor (14)—during the ensuing months, but
knew the teachers in the parochial school and the leaders and
members of the various lay groups in the parish even better.
They were everywhere, watching everything, talking with
everyone. Father Joseph was pleased with them—even pro-

viding a special outing for them on one occasion—but he seemed to feel that they were not discovering anything that he did not already know.

I instructed my research assistants to become personally acquainted as soon as possible with all the parishioners they could meet under any circumstances—on the streets, in their homes, in church, at parish society meetings and programs. What we wanted was all the information available about the parish from people who were in any way involved in the parish. I divided the parochial territory into sections according to census tracts and street addresses in the city directory, and then assigned a section to each researcher. I explained the concept of participant observation to my assistants and divided among them the seventeen lay groups: eleven for adults (three male, six female, and two mixed) and six for youths (four male, two female).

Each research assistant spent an average of 10 hours a week among the parishioners of Mater Dolorosa and soon became very popular with the most active lay leaders. People like to talk about that which interests them most, and these people willingly expressed both praise and criticism of the way in which their parish was operating. The students were instructed to be "helpful" in all the parish groups, but not to take initiative in any way, and never to voice any opinions, either of praise or blame. As a result they were soon made part of every group and became confidants of the lay leaders and active parishioners. One criterion of their effectiveness and popularity was the fact that there was never a complaint made either to me or to the parish priests about their conduct.

EXCHANGE OF INFORMATION. One of the methodological research questions to which there seems no satisfactory answer is: how much of your findings do you tell your "client" while the research is still in progress? (15) Rightly or wrongly, my answer in the Mater Dolorosa study was: as little as possible, for two reasons. First, I did not want an input of research data that might effect change in the parish during the middle of the year. I felt that any changes introduced must come from other sources. Second, I did not want the pastor to become disturbed by piecemeal findings that become intelligible only when integrated into the total analysis.

One example of a fact unknown to the pastor emerging from the preliminary house-to-house canvas we made of the parish territory was when we discovered that more than one-third of the white people who claimed to be Catholics were really "dormant" parishioners in the sense that they never went near the church. With data from the parish records we extimated that there was a large "leakage" from the potential parish population because more than one-third of the infants baptized were not brought up as Catholics by their parents (16). From a careful count of attendance at mass on every Sunday we estimated that almost half the parishioners (over 7 years of age) were not regularly going to mass.

At the end of June 1948, I prepared a "progress report" for the Loyola University Faculty Committee of the Carnegie Foundation for the Advancement of Teaching. I did not show this to the pastor, but I did discuss it with Bishop William Mulloy of Covington, Kentucky, to whom the first volume was dedicated, and with Archbishop Rummel. The latter said that "your findings practically confirm what I have long since deducted from other sources, namely, the fact that not more than 50 to 60 percent of our so-called church membership can be classified as practicing Catholics. This is indeed a rather sad commentary upon our combined efforts to bring religion home to all our people as a vital influence in their lives."

From frequent discussions with Father Joseph I surmised that he would not agree with our findings along these lines nor with the archbishop's estimates—at least, if they were applied to Mater Dolorosa Parish. Occasionally he was curious about how the research team could keep so busy, and he asked them what they were doing and what they were finding out. He did not seriously question our methods of investigation, although he did not always like it when the researcher took notes of what he said at public meetings. My research assistants did indeed discover many facts that did not fit into the rosy picture of the parish drawn by Father Joseph, but I instructed them that such facts were confidential to the research team alone.

Withholding information was not one-sided, practiced only by the research team. The parish census is a case in point, in which the pastor concealed his main reason for wanting the census. As part of the research program, we planned to go back to the households of Catholic parishioners with a census schedule modeled on the one used earlier by Coogan and Kelly in Florida (17). There had been no census taken in Mater Dolorosa for many years. The pastor was delighted with this idea, paid to have the census forms printed, and encouraged lay people as volunteers to help take the census.

With the generous help of adult parishioners we distributed the census forms to Catholic households during the first week of Lent in 1948, asked the people to fill them out, and collected them in sealed envelopes the following week (18). The pastor allowed us to assure the parishioners that the census had nothing to do with collecting money from them. What I did not know till later was that Father Joseph intended to use the census as a basis of a fund-raising drive for the autumn of that year for the purpose of building a new sisters' convent atop the parochial school. Ignoring the pastoral value of the census, what he wanted, and obtained, was an exact listing of parishioners: their names, addresses, and telephone numbers.

There was another and more important kind of pastoral information collected in the census which was never followed up by either the pastor or his curates. This was personal data revealing those parishioners who had been married "outside the church," had not made their Easter duties, or seldom attended Sunday mass. Zealous parish priests show concern for such lapsed or semilapsed Catholics. Father Joseph liked to say that he knew them all without the help of a census, but if this were the case he should not have been so disturbed when he read the results of the study. In answer to a complaint that the priests did not visit the sick he said: "People move in and out of this parish and never make themselves known at the rectory. We can't read minds" (19).

Father Joseph told me more than he seemed to realize, or later to remember: how well he got along with his "close friend" former Mayor Robert Maestri, head of the city machine, and how he did not like the current mayor, Chep Morrison, head of the Reform Party and parishioner of Mater Dolorosa; what he thought about "Mississippi niggers" who move into New Orleans; how he took care of beggars by asking to see whether their hands had signs of "honest toil"; about the three ex-priests who were now his married parishioners. Much of this I had no intention of including in the published reports, but the detailed descriptions I did provide in the typescripts of the first and second volumes led the pastor to charge that I had hidden microphones in strategic places. There is also a humorous aspect to this charge in a later conversation with the archbishop, when Father Joseph thought that "to transcribe" meant "to tape."

In retrospect, in a letter of July 29, 1951, the pastor expressed very decided views about our relationship and about the contents of the second volume of the study. He felt that my account was libelous and revengeful, that I was telling malicious half-truths and making wicked innuendos. He believed it was, in short, a personal and deliberate attack on him, his assistant priests, and his parishioners. To him this was all the more ungracious of me because he and his people had treated me in such a kindly and brotherly fashion.

COLLAPSE OF HYPOTHESIS. Meanwhile we went about the daily job of collecting data on "everything" in the parish and also held a meeting of the research team on every Saturday morning to discuss our findings. We were trying to make sense of this mass of data in the light of the hypothetical conceptualization I had formulated before we began the study. What was the evidence for, or against, the parochial solidarity of Mater Dolorosa emerging from a common core of values? This concept gave us more trouble than anything else during the whole research project. We looked for an internal social integration of the parishioners that would be manifested in daily human relations and that would be peculiarly Catholic and parochial. We failed to find it.

Perhaps my "ideal norm" of Catholic solidarity among the parishioners was completely unrealistic, but as the months of research passed I would have settled for a lower level of social love and cooperation that was clearly based on the common sharing of Catholic religious beliefs and practices. Unfortunately, the data from Mater Dolorosa demonstrated the untenability of this central hypothesis (20). I had to admit, as I said in a paper delivered in December 1949 at the Chicago meetings of the American Catholic Sociological Society, that "urban Catholic parishioners are for the most part united more on secular ideologies than on common religious beliefs."

It could be said—with some reservation—that there was a closer social bond in sharing the same occupation than there was in sharing the same religion. Professional people —lawyers, dentists, teachers, and the like—in Mater Dolorosa Parish had more frequent, congenial, and mutually respectful relations with fellow professionals regardless of religious affiliation than they had with fellow parishioners, regardless of occupational status. In general, we found the same phenomenon of social solidarity on the basis of similar economic status, and also of similar educational achievement. Common membership in the parish did not cross the social lines that separated the poor from the wealthy, the college graduate from the elementary school graduate.

The two largest "national" categories in the parish were those of German and French descents, but we had little evidence that common national background was an important basis for social relations and solidarity. This had not always been the case. At the time of the Franco-Prussian War, the Catholics of Carrollton maintained two separate parish plants—with church, rectory, school, and sisters' convent —on opposite sides of the street near the levee (21). At times of greatest tension between the German Catholics and the French Catholics, armed parishioners stood guard at night on both sides as protection against each other. When Monsignor Prim became pastor in 1898 he was charged by Archbishop Shaw to consolidate the parishes, which he did by building a new Mater Dolorosa in 1908 on Carrollton Avenue and selling the French parish, St. Joan of Arc, to the Negro Catholics of the area.

These were events of the distant past. When we took the census in 1948 we found that the greatest incidence of marriage "mixture" was between people with French and German names. The conflict had long since subsided, and the memory thereof was lost. Like the German Lutherans who had a flourishing church just two blocks from Mater Dolorosa, the German Catholics had largely abandoned their ancestral ties and were absorbed into the local culture (22). There was a minority of families of distant French background who had moved into the parish from the rural, so-called "Cajun country" of Louisiana, and ethnic social solidarity continued relatively strong among them.

The historical problem of national-language rivalries was not mentioned in any way when Mater Dolorosa celebrated its 100th anniversary in 1948, the year of our study. The sermon preached on that occasion in September by Father Joseph Vath, who had grown up in the parish, selected the positive and triumphant aspects of the parish history (23). He completely omitted reference to the racial problems of the parish, or to the fact that when the new church was built 40 years earlier the old church building was sold to the Negro parishioners so that they could have a "parish of their own." Race relations among Catholics was a continuing moral and organizational problem, but one that church leaders were expected to "soft-pedal."

If social solidarity found its basis in the sharing of occupational, educational, and economic status among Catholics, it was even more securely anchored to race. We searched long and unsuccessfully for cordial race realtions, which may stem from the fact that the individuals involved were Catholics living in the same parish. There were always some whites who attended mass at St. Joan of Arc church, and more Negroes who did so at Mater Dolorosa church, but in each case they tended to sit in separate pews (24). Sharing the eucharist, the "sacrament of love," and sharing the liturgy, the "expression of community," had no measurable effect that I and my coworkers could discover in the relations of local Catholics across racial lines. On the parish level there was simple, and outright failure to demonstrate the internal religious and parochial solidarity we hypothesized.

This matter of racial relations among local Catholics was so irritating to Father Joseph that he could not hold an objective, intelligent conversation about it. Like many other immigrant priests in the South, he tended to absorb local white cultural attitudes and practices. Although he and I maintained fairly cordial relations throughout the year of the study— and although I avoided the subject of race as much as possi-

ble in talking with him—he sometimes expressed displeasure over remarks I made in my sermons. Once he said, "I
don't want you emptying out my church with your race sermons." On another occasion I displeased him by failing to
read from the pulpit the announcement of a forthcoming
minstrel show (with whites in black make up) for which the
ladies were selling tickets at the church door. On the Sunday
when the archbishop canceled the Holy Name Rally because
the city stadium officials insisted on racially segregated seating, I preached another "racial sermon" that made the pastor
unhappy (25).

Interestingly enough, several of his parishioners who were
students at Loyola University and Dominican College were
active members of the student interracial group I instituted in
the late spring of 1948. A year later, in April 1949, when I
helped establish the Commission on Human Rights of the
Catholic Committee of the South, two of its most active leaders were parishioners of Mater Dolorosa. While I was direct-
ing the southern parish project my effort at organized opposition to racial segregation within the Catholic church was
slowly gaining momentum, and it was at the end of 1951 that
Courtney called me "a man who is intensely admired or se-
verely criticized by laity and clergy, because of his efforts after
racial justice in conservative New Orleans."

It is true, of course, that the Negro Catholics had "their
own" parish, St. Joan of Arc, in which there existed all the
typical parochial groups including an elementary school. For
all practical purposes of sociological investigation we accepted Mater Dolorosa as a segregated white parish and con-
fined our search for Catholic solidarity to its white parishioners. This we found in small primary groups of parishioners
who cooperated well in performing functions for the parish.
They were for the most part the inner core of each of the
seventeen parish societies, but even here there was a range of
difference from the most to the least solidaristic. There were

occasions of fairly close cooperation among these groups, when "all worked together," as in the centennial celebration, taking the census, and the fund drive for the sisters' convent.

By and large, however, the hypothesis of a genuine community of Catholics, united in belief, worship, and love, did not test out. I have often since used the analogy of the "service station" where the people come as individuals for their religious needs. In a sense, the pastor has the "franchise" to provide this service because he has the official obligation imposed by the bishop to take care of their spiritual welfare (26).

WHAT WENT WRONG? Despite this failure of my central hypothesis on the integrative force of the Catholic value system, there were many positive findings that helped to explain why Mater Dolorosa was judged by many to be one of the most successful parishes in New Orleans. After the study was completed I believed, as I still believe, what I wrote in the foreword to the first volume, "that St. Mary's should be ranked high among the successfully operating parishes of the diocese" (27). This is a relative statement, and what the first volume of *Southern Parish* demonstrated was that Mater Dolorosa was *relatively* successful in its religious practices when these were measured against the high ideals of Roman Catholicism. At the end of the book I said that "when the standard of parochial accomplishment is set as high as it has been in this book, it is certain that no parish anywhere reaches this ideal" (p. 270).

At the end of most chapters I made judgments based on the collected evidence. I said that on Sunday mass attendance the parishioners "may be called better than average Catholics" (p. 153). On the reception of the sacrament of confirmation, the parish is "somewhat above normal" (p. 95). The record on the sacrament of matrimony "appears to be very good" (p.

110). On developing vocations to church service, the parish is "fairly good" (p. 111). On providing the last sacraments, we found that "the priests are more prompt to respond to the needs of the dying than the parishioners are to ask for the last sacraments" (p. 135).

What was it about this objective sociological report on a parish's religious patterns that irritated Father Joseph to the point that he told the archbishop he was going to have a heart attack if it were not suppressed? Father Wilson, pastor of St. Joan of Arc Parish, later told me that Father Joseph resented most bitterly the description given of him as a "short, stockily built man in his fifties who was born in Hungary and who came to the United States at the age of thirteen and still speaks with a slight foreign accent" (28). (For purposes of anonymity, I "altered" the facts that he was born in Poland in 1895, and came to this country in 1911, not knowing a word of English.) Father Wilson said, "He doesn't believe he has an accent and thinks he's a good preacher."

One area in which I could not give Mater Dolorosa high marks was that of preaching, and even on this my appraisal was restrained. "The general quality of the sermons indicated that the priests were competent and pedestrian preachers but they lacked great eloquence and artistic merit" (p. 210). I did point out that the pastor's sermons were longer than those of the other priests. From the notes of my research assistants who attended every mass and heard every sermon, I reported that parishioners often avoid the eight o'clock mass on Sundays because the pastor is "so slow and talks so long." Furthermore, the people sometimes "sighed audibly in relief" when he finished talking, which he did "with a slight accent, with very little inflection, but with intense sincerity" (p. 207).

Reference to his foreign accent and lengthy sermons was only one source of personal grievance to Father Joseph. He told Father Wilson that I "made him look bad" by reporting that he seldom visited the sick or bore the "drudgery" of the confessional on Saturday afternoons and by describing certain incidents, like the time he publicly scolded a child at the communion rail or when he delayed sending a marriage certificate to the city registrar until the stipend for the wedding ceremony had been paid. He did not deny that these incidents were true. He said that I was "out to get him" by reporting them.

None of these personal grievances was publicly aired when Father Joseph tried to have the first volume, *Dynamics of a City Church*, suppressed in 1951, when he hand-picked three of his clerical friends as the "Archbishop's Committee" to review the book. Their long critical review appeared in the diocesan newspaper, then called *Catholic Action of the South*, on October 4, 1951, saying that the book contained "inappropriate reporting"; it had "not much pastoral usefulness"; it failed to conceal the identity of Mater Dolorosa Parish. Interestingly enough, this book review avoided naming either the pastor or the parish.

Three excerpts from this review seem worth mentioning here: (a) "Neither the Church nor the rectory should be turned into a common public place for the sake of statistical observation. Nor should a church parish be turned into a kind of 'guinea pig' for the sake of almost unlimited dissection, probing, and any sort of reporting, whether trivial or not." Some months later, in March 1952, Father Leonard Feeney, director of St. Benedict's Center, which was outside the walls of Harvard University, took note of my book and said that I was "merely a loyal Harvard man using Catholics as guinea pigs for a sociological survey" (29).

Behind the obscurantist, antiscientific aspects of this criticism there is probably a general horror of profanation. Physical experimentation with laboratory animals is, of course, a far cry from the scientific observation of animal behavior, both human and nonhuman. One may have great reverence, as I do, for sacred persons, rituals, and institutions, but at the same time accepting the demonstrable fact that the behavior of people in religious groups is still human behavior. Sociological methodology need not be feared as an intrusion into the sanctuary, except perhaps by those inhabitants of the sanctuary who are very unsure of their religious beliefs, commitments, and practices.

(b) "Measurement of Catholicity by 'ideals' can be very subjective. Whilst the Church unquestionably works for perfection, still the works of the Church are not to be mathematically judged by the number of those who are perfect." One wonders what other norm, or ideal, the busy pastor uses when he keeps a census of his parish and faithfully reports to the chancery office the (mathematical) number of baptisms, communions, marriages, and funerals. He knows what his parishioners are supposed to do as Catholics; in fact it is his pastoral function to guide and encourage them to the fulfillment of these behavioral ideals. Are these expectations of the Catholic religion simply "subjective" when they are constantly expounded in papal teachings, episcopal letters, theological tracts, catechisms, and even Sunday sermons from parish pulpits?

(c) "As it stands, it must be asserted that *Southern Parish* in many respects does an injustice to, and misrepresents the Catholic parochial life of the South." This criticism goes far beyond anything I did, or tried to do, in the research project and its report. An objective reading of the book reveals two facts: first, that the book does not pretend to represent anything more than the study of one parish, Mater Dolorosa, and second, that it does not misrepresent or do any injustice to the parishioners and priests of this one southern parish.

Besides this attack by the committee of the pastor's friends, there were two other severe criticisms published against the book. One of these was by the highly respected social philosopher and metaphysician, Paul Furfey, of Catholic University. He courteously sent me a prepublication copy of the criticisms he had made and invited me to have dinner with him in Washington to discuss the research project and his opinions of it. At that dinner we reviewed all the major points of criticism, after which he expressed himself fully satisfied with my explanation.

In spite of this amicable agreement, and much to my surprise, Furfey allowed his critical review to appear in *The Catholic Educational Review* for December 1951. He had seemed satisfied when I said that the methodology of the study would be explained in an appendix to the fourth volume of the proposed series, and he questioned the arithmetical accuracy of some of the tables. His erroneous statistical interpretation of my data also appeared in *Commonweal* for November 16, 1951, and I can only suppose that he was perturbed by my easy correction of his manner of handling statistics (30).

The other attack appeared as an editorial, "A Controversial Work," in *The Priest* for November 1951, although the editor later admitted (January 1952) that this so-called "editorial" was done by "our reviewer" (31). This review largely rewrote the statement of the "Archbishop's Committee" which had appeared in October in the archdiocesan weekly newspaper, and it too was written by Father Thomas Balduc, one of the pastor's three friends on that committee. I had written a refutation of the committee's attack and submitted it to Archbishop Rummel whom I did not want to embarrass by publishing it. As though to balance, or offset, the harsh statements of the pastor's committee, the weekly Catholic paper published the syndicated review column by Father John Kennedy, who wrote that my book "is immensely stimulating and constructively disturbing, worthwhile as a dissolver of complacency and a spur to zeal" (32).

At this late date I think it is futile to quote the great majority of social scientists and religionists who reviewed the book with favor. Perhaps I should have been less considerate of the archbishop's status and more aggressive in my own defense. After the turmoil ceased I meditated on the central questions that had been raised in the sociology of religion as a result of discussions on my book. I analyzed these together with the points I made in rebuttal to *The Priest* "editorial," and published an article under the title, "Major Issues of Parish Sociology," in May 1953 (33).

STEPS TO SUPPRESSION.   In spite of the pastor's vehement objections, the first volume of the *Southern Parish* series, published September 21, 1951, was neither suppressed nor "taken off the market." The three remaining volumes were prevented from publication. The person ultimately responsible for the suppression of these books was not Father Joseph, who voiced his disapproval, nor Archbishop Rummel, who voiced his approval, but the Jesuit provincial, Father William Crandell, who, unlike his predecessor, Father Harry Crane, decreed that I had to obtain the consent of the pastor before publication.

The segments of this story of suppression can be neatly assembled from letters and other documents dealing with the event. In August 1949 I completed the manuscript for the first volume, which I originally called *The Religious Life of a City Parish*, and dutifully submitted it to Father Crane for Jesuit censorship. After receiving the critical comments and helpful suggestions of the two censors, I revised the manuscript, which then received the official *imprimi potest* of the provincial. I then sent a copy to Archbishop Rummel, whose eyesight was poor but who told me he "had it read" to him "from cover to cover."

The archbishop did not find in it "any startling information" that would be intensely interesting to clergy or laity. "The story is told quite simply and realistically, but the information should be known by anyone fairly familiar with the ordinary operation of a parish church." This was a reaction quite different from that of Everett Hughes, with whom I talked about the whole research project in December 1949 at the Chicago meeting of the American Catholic Sociological Society, where I delivered a paper on "Parochial Solidarity." He urged that I send the manuscript to the University of Chicago Press, and I said I would do so after I had finished the manuscript of the second volume on *The Social System of a Parish*.

William Couch was then director of the University of Chicago Press. I sent him the manuscript for the first volume in May 1950 and for the second volume in the following September. During these 4 months he had the first manuscript read by experts such as Sally Cassidy, Kurt Wulff, Everett Hughes, and David Selznick, all of whom made suggestions that I incorporated into the final revision. The readers employed by the University of Chicago Press are not considered "censors," but in practical effect they perform the same useful role for the author as do the religious or ecclesiastical censors—the readers are an invaluable guide for the publisher's decision to accept the manuscript and for the author's readiness to revise and improve it.

At any rate, the "controversial" first volume of *Southern Parish* was accepted in September, together with an invitation to come to Chicago in October to discuss plans for the whole series of four books with Bill Couch and his assistant, Fred Wieck. They already had in hand a preliminary copy of the manuscript for the second volume, and (although I did not know it at the time) engaged as readers Ralph Gallagher, Franz Mueller, Gerald Kelly, Clement Mihanovich, and John Ford. At that meeting we laid grand plans for the whole series, tentatively setting publishing dates for the succeeding volumes for September 1951, April 1952, September 1952, and April 1953.

The irony in this situation is that 1 month later, on November 21, 1950, Bill Couch was fired because he had published a book that Robert Hutchins, chancellor of the University of Chicago, wanted to suppress. Editor Fred Wieck then resigned in protest. A few weeks later, the *Chicago Tribune* reported that Couch "lost his job as director of the University of Chicago Press because he had published a book which Chancellor Robert M. Hutchins, at the request of the University of California, had sought to suppress." Vice President James Cunningham, a spokesman for the University of Chicago, said that the reasons for the dismissal were private: Couch's "inability to get along with subordinates or superiors" (34).

What now seems even more ironic was that Morton Grodzins, author of the disputed book, *Americans Betrayed*, later replaced Couch as director of the Press and worked vigorously to prevent the suppression of the three remaining volumes of *Southern Parish*. As a graduate student in political science at the University of California, Grodzins wrote a doctoral thesis that was critical of the way both California and the federal government handled the "relocation" of Japanese-Americans during World War II. There was an alleged agreement between him and the University of California that he could have access to the essential materials for the thesis on condition that he would not publish the doctoral thesis. Couch was unable to verify this agreement, and he proceeded with the publication of Grodzins' book.

Meanwhile in New Orleans a shift had taken place of my own religious superiors when Father Crane completed his 6-year term of office. In August I submitted the manuscript of the second volume to the new provincial, Father William Crandell, who was not satisfied with the arrangement whereby the ecclesiastical *nihil obstat* and *imprimatur* would be issued by the Chicago archdiocese. Nor was he satisfied with informal reading and approval of the manuscript by

Archbishop Rummel in New Orleans. This prolonged the process of censorship by several months, but the manuscript was finally approved for publication after multiple and extraordinary scrutiny.

Ordinarily a book manuscript is read by two Jesuit censors, but in this case the provincial appointed a third censor. Archbishop Rummel's official censor, Father Patrick Gillespie, provided the *nihil obstat* for New Orleans, and Cardinal Stritch's official censor, Father J. Gerald Kealy, provided the *nihil obstat* for Chicago. Together with the five readers engaged by the University of Chicago Press, this drawn-out process resulted in the most thorough critical prepublication appraisal I have ever had of any book manuscript. The process dragged on until the provincial introduced a *new* condition on June 7, 1951, when he said that I had to have the approval of Monsignor Joseph, the pastor of Mater Dolorosa.

This newly and arbitrarily imposed condition—that the report of my research project could not be published as long as Father Joseph had any objection to it—was quite different from the understanding I had with the pastor from the beginning of the study. Since I am as scrupulous as any social scientist about the validity and reliability—and indeed veracity—of my research reports, I had expected from the beginning that the pastor would read the manuscript and help me to avoid errors of both fact and interpretation. The sad story is that he cut me out of his friendship in the late summer of 1949, and after that I saw him only once—at the dedication of the sisters' new convent—and even then had no conversation with him.

As a matter of fact, the pastor was both hostile and inaccessible to me—a situation I explained fully to the provincial, who had hoped prayerfully that I could "patch things up." He informed me on June 18, 1951, that "if you prefer that I submit the manuscript to Monsignor Joseph, I will gladly do so." I should say here that I never put the blame on the pastor for the suppression of my three volumes. The provincial preferred to believe the pastor's version of our original understanding—that he would have final decision over what could be published—rather than my version, which called for the pastor's collaboration in correcting and improving the manuscript.

From this point on, as the chancellor, Monsignor Plauche, said, the pastor "held all the cards." He refused to meet with me; he had no intention of helping me revise the manuscript of the second volume; he was insistent that nothing be published about his parish; and he had the word of the provincial to support him. On Saturday, July 21, the archbishop called and asked me what to do with the manuscript of the second volume, which had been read to him and which he had approved. I asked him to have it delivered to the pastor, to whom I wrote on the same day, explaining that I would appreciate his cooperation in turning out the best manuscript possible.

After about a week's delay Father Joseph "put me on notice" in a letter dated Sunday, July 29, but postmarked 2 days later and sent by registered mail. After a paragraph charging me with libel, malice, wickedness, and revengefulness, he put me "on notice" that I was not to publish the content of *Social System of a Parish* either in book form or in journal articles. In spite of all this he must have found the monograph interesting and useful, because he said that he intended to make a thorough study of it, discuss it with sociologists and lawyers, and reveal the contents to selected parishioners. He wanted especially to get the reaction of the officers and members of the various parochial societies described in the book.

In my reply to this letter I suggested that his criticisms were much too general to be of use in improving the book. I asked also that he specify the particular points, by page and line, where he thought the work ought to be corrected, and I promised to follow scrupulously any reasonable suggestions.

Since he had already had the manuscript in his possession for 11 days, I proposed that he take 2 weeks further to supply the items necessary for an adequate revision. "If you do not care to make these specific suggestions before August 15th, and return the manuscript by that time, I shall proceed to publication with the other copy I have."

I held the firm—if naive—conviction that the pastor would be satisfied, even proud of his parish, when he saw the results in book form. As a member of the Jesuit Order I had the logical expectation that my provincial would soon remove the stringent condition he had placed on the manuscript. Both the pastor and the provincial seemed to become even more unbending when the first volume, *Dynamics of a City Church*, was published.

NEGOTIATING THE SUPPRESSION.   If the pastor's reaction was vigorous after reading the typescript of the second volume in July, it became explosive in August when he had in hand a prepublication copy of the first volume which I had delivered to him. It was at this time that Archbishop Rummel telephoned to tell me that I seemed to be "in real trouble." As I now reflect on my own reaction to the archbishop's disturbing phone call, I realize that I pursued the wrong strategy. The pastor had gone to his ecclesiastical superior, the ordinary of the diocese. I decided to go to mine, the Jesuit provincial. I thought it reasonable to assume that a kind of "high level" negotiation between the archbishop and the provincial would settle the matter in my favor, since the former gave full approval of the research project and its report and the latter would give full support to one of his fellow Jesuits.

This reasoning was incorrect and this assumption was invalid. The provincial was then making his annual visitation of southern Jesuit communities and could not return to New

Orleans (except when important financial matters arose). He delegated Father Thomas Shields, the president of Loyola University of the South, as his representative in this crisis. I expected that the president of the university at which I was professor and head of the department of sociology would carry on negotiations on my behalf with the archbishop, and especially with the pastor of Mater Dolorosa Parish. Only later did I learn that these "negotiations" consisted of placating the pastor and agreeing that the latter could choose a three-man board of judges to publicize the "errors" in the book.

The president of Loyola University, like the provincial of the southern Jesuits, seemed to feel that it was necessary to have "peace at any price" between the diocesan clergy in the parishes and the religious order priests at the university. Father Joseph pushed his complaints to the point of demanding that the University of Chicago Press withdraw the book from circulation and that the Jesuits assume the cost of this procedure. When the publisher set this cost at 14,750 dollars, the pastor's demand was promptly considered unreasonable. This was a price too high to pay, even to placate an irate pastor whose friendship neither helped nor hindered Loyola University of the South and the Jesuit priests on its faculty.

The Jesuit decision not to "buy up" the first edition of *Dynamics of a City Church*, and thus effectively suppress its publication, was made on September 5, 1951. At a conference with the archbishop and the president on the following Saturday, the pastor insisted that "I reserve my right to say the book must be suppressed." At this meeting Father Shields presented a prepared statement, the reasoning of which was based "on the accepted moral principle that when one is necessarily confronted with a choice between two evils he must choose the lesser evil."

What were the "two evils" between which a choice would have to be made? On the one side there was the offense against the pastor of Mater Dolorosa, who saw no solution except suppression of the book. On the other side there was a series of "evils" that would result from the suppression: it would (a) bring odium on the Catholic church for suppressing facts and interfering with freedom of the press; (b) bring embarrassment and offense to Cardinal Stritch who had given the book his official *imprimatur;* (c) create a demand for the book on the suspicion that it contains horrible or salacious scandals; (d) not solve the problem because the University of Chicago Press had the legal right to publish a second printing even if all copies of the first printing were bought up.

Obviously, the "lesser of two evils" in this case was the alleged offense against the pastor, especially since the cost of suppressing the first printing of the book was 14,750 dollars. This would have ended the matter in spite of the pastor's protestations had not Father Shields suggested that a "compromise" be offered to soothe the ruffled feelings of Father Joseph. The idea was that the book should be handed over to a committee of three priests who would study it carefully and submit their opinion of it to the archbishop (35).

Who was to serve on this three-man commission? The archbishop had great confidence in his official censor, Father Patrick Gillespie, and in Monsignor Prendergast, and he suggested that the third man be a Jesuit. Gillespie and Prendergast were out of town at the moment and would not return for several weeks. Incredibly, what happened then is told in a letter from Father Shields to Archbishop Rummel, saying that although his excellency had proposed that a Jesuit be named to the commission, he declined this offer and allowed Monsignor Joseph to name all three persons who were to make a critical study of my book.

These "negotiations" were being carried on without my knowledge. For some still unfathomable reason the president of my university had opened the door wide for the pastor to walk in and select three clerical friends to do a "hatchet job" on me. Two of his choices were fellow pastors, Monsignor Joseph Boudreaux and Monsignor Francis Baechle, who had undergraduate degrees in theology and no knowledge of social science research. The third was Father Thomas Balduc, professor at the seminary and a perennial opponent of my activities in the field of race relations.

Two days after this committee was formed, Father Shields studied the contract I had signed with the University of Chicago Press. He then informed the provincial that the work of the committee examining the book would be useless since no one could stop publication by the University of Chicago Press under terms of the contract. He also relayed this information to the archbishop, who on the next day (September 11) told all three members of the panel about the publishing contract and added that "it really looks as though there is no way of preventing the circulation of Volume I." Nevertheless, after the three-man panel met on September 13, Monsignor Baechle concluded his report to the archbishop as follows: "It is eminently desirable that what remains of Volume I should be taken out of circulation, even if the Jesuit Fathers must buy up the issue."

The three-man panel of the pastor's friends made its report to the archbishop on this same date, offering an "alternative" action in case the book could not be suppressed (36). This was to be a statement to the press, intended to point out "glaring inaccuracies, fictions that are indistinguishable from facts, many gross canonical errors, imprudent divulging of serious confidential matters, many half-truths, numerous inappropriate reportings that have a close relationship to the sacred character of the clergy and parochial life, and an abundance of irrelevant trivialities."

Father Joseph, who denied any "collusion" with the three clerics of the panel, actually had a copy of the report before it reached the archbishop, and he spread the word among his friends in the parish that he had "put me in my place." His story was, as telephoned to me by a parishioner, that the "official" committee had condemned the book, decreed that it must be suppressed, stated that the publishing contract must be voided, and commanded that the Jesuit Order buy up all copies of the book. This information I passed on to the president who, with the pastor, was invited to meet with the archbishop the following night (September 14) to receive and discuss the panel's report. Before anything else could be said at that meeting Father Shields revealed that the contents of the report were already known to parishioners of Mater Dolorosa church. This disturbed both the archbishop and the pastor. The latter fumbled a reply that "they must have gotten it from someone else" and demanded to know the name of the parishioner who had "spread that story."

At any rate, the "alternative" to suppression was agreed upon that night, with the understanding that the whole case would be closed once the panel released its critical review to the press. Father Shields readily agreed that this review, released in the name of the panel, would be written by Father Balduc. Earlier he had failed to insist that someone less inimical to me be included on the panel, and now he failed even to suggest that a balanced book review be written with the help of someone less prejudiced to me than Father Balduc. Even Archbishop Rummel had some misgivings about this since he had praised the book in manuscript. After the review was printed in the diocesan weekly (October 4, 1951) he expressed displeasure that the panel had presumed to call itself the "Archbishop's Committee."

The agreement of the night of September 14 was meant to close the matter, but on the next day the pastor had second thoughts about it. With the help of a lawyer he filed a "brief" with the archbishop in which he called himself the "plaintiff" in this issue and me the "defendant." He decided that the agreement of the previous night was a "preliminary decision" that satisfactorily covered the matter of complaint, but that a further decision was to be made by the three-man committee. This decision was to elicit from me a formal agreement that I would never make public, whether in spoken or written form, and especially not in my university lectures, any of the research information I had gathered in the study of his parish. His demand was that I sign such an agreement in the presence of the archbishop, the Jesuit Provincial and a notary (and presumably with God as my further witness) promising to refrain "from now on and for all time" from writing or lecturing about the findings of my research project.

PERMANENT SUPPRESSION. The pastor's demand that I sign such a legal document was rejected for the insult that it was. The negative and distorted book review that appeared in the diocesan weekly did not greatly disturb me, except that many people thought Father Balduc's criticisms were those of an "official Archbishop's Commission." In subsequent weeks more than a hundred copies of the book were sold in New Orleans, largely at the Catholic book store. Monsignor Baechle phoned the proprietor there and told her she was "violating church regulations by selling a condemned book," and added, "Take that god-damned book off your shelves or I'll come down and do it myself."

Father Balduc's zeal sought further outlet in opposition to the contents of the book. He prepared a long critical article for the *American Ecclesiastical Review* and submitted it for the archbishop's approval, which was not forthcoming. He supplied the review that was published as an "editorial" in *The Priest* for November 1951. Except for the criticisms of Balduc and Furfey, the book got a "good press" in both ecclesiastical and sociological journals. A great scholar, Joachim Wach, called it a "major count in the field of sociology of religion in the United States" and said that church people who have to deal with such problems "will be grateful to the courageous and conscientious pioneer work of the author" (37).

I was willing to let Volume I stand on its own merits, but was very unwilling to sit back and watch the suppression of the second, third, and fourth volumes take place. In early October, despite my request of August 1, Father Joseph still retained the manuscript of the second volume and had not yet provided me with the list of errors to be corrected. He was sure it would never be published because the provincial said it had to have his approval. I telephoned the provincial and asked, "If I can get the archbishop to order the pastor to withdraw his objections, would you still insist on the pastor's approval?" Father Crandell replied, "I doubt that the archbishop will ever do that, but if he does, you can go ahead."

I thought it was worth a try. After all, the second volume had already been passed for publication by multiple censors. Now I was ready to have it censored once again, but this time by a panel of my own choosing: Auxiliary Bishop Abel Caillouet, Diocesan Chancellor Monsignor Charles Plauche, and Catholic school superintendent Monsignor Henri Bezou. At my request, the archbishop invited these men to a conference on October 5, together with the president of Loyola and the bishop's brother, Monsignor Lucian Caillouet—the latter to "represent the pastor's interests."

After I had explained my proposal for a board of review for the second volume, and also reported the provincial's willingness to go along with the archbishop's order to publish, the latter said that he could not "override" Father Joseph. At this point, the pastor's personal plea of ill-health was revealed. He had had a heart attack in 1944, and had recently promised the archbishop that he would have another if my three remaining volumes were published. This touched the archbishop, who believed that worry over the first volume had made the pastor a sick man, and that if he would order publication of the other volumes he would be responsible for "gravely injuring a good priest of the diocese not only spiritually and mentally, but even physically."

Father Joseph's health may have been ill-affected by the "worries" my research project brought on him—although he lived to celebrate his retirement from the pastorate at age 74 (November 1969). Nevertheless, I wanted the opinions of "my" three-man panel, and asked for a meeting with the same people on October 17. At the previous conference I had asked Monsignor Caillouet whether there was any possibility that, after having read the second volume, he might approve it. He said, "No, I'll still oppose it," which he did. I was pleased, however, that Bishop Caillouet and Monsignors Plauche and Bezou viewed the manuscript favorably and urged its publication. At this meeting Monsignor Bezou also strongly approved the publication of the third volume on the parochial school, the manuscript copy of which I had given him.

Having completed and revised the manuscript of the third volume, I sent it to the provincial for the usual censorship of the Jesuit Order. Without giving it to the Jesuit censors he immediately returned it with the curt remark that he "will never grant the *imprimi potest* without the pastor's approval." Father Crandell was annoyed from another direction—that of the University of Chicago Press. Hayden Carruth, associate editor there, had written to tell him, "I think any suppression of *Southern Parish* would be a great shame, and indeed a virtual misdemeanor." He was displeased, too, when the new director, Morton Grodzins, wrote to him about the moral and contractual obligations between author and publisher. Father Crandell told me later that he resented any layman, especially a Protestant, giving him "moral advice."

As the word spread throughout the country that the three remaining volumes of the *Southern Parish* series had been suppressed, I began to get carbon copies of letters written by both social scientists and religionists in support of their publication. *Ad hoc* committees of the Catholic (38) and Southern Sociological Societies and an informal group in the American Sociological Association made a study of the case and decided that this was an "internal Church matter" rather than a violation of academic freedom (39). Most of the communications were addressed to Archbishop Rummel in the mistaken notion that he was responsible for the suppression. In discussing these petitions, the archbishop said to me, "After all, it was *your* superior, not I, who suppressed the books by insisting on the pastor's approval."

Morton Grodzins was convinced that "things could be talked out." He came to New Orleans in March 1952, and was graciously received by the archbishop and the chancellor, who pointed out that they had no objections whatever to the publication; they had in fact already officially approved the second volume. He assured Archbishop Rummel that he and I were willing to revise the three manuscripts and proposed to pay the pastor the regular readers' stipend if he would list all the corrections needed in the books. He suggested further that the archbishop write a laudatory preface for each of the volumes pointing out the excellent service rendered to the church by the anonymous paster of pseudonymous "St. Mary's" parish.

The archbishop willingly agreed to this and promised to try again to persuade the pastor to change his mind. On March 27 he wrote to Grodzins, reporting that he had invited Monsignor Pyzikiewicz to come to his study and talk over the matter with him and his chancellor, Monsignor Plauche. During a "very lengthy conference" he presented again all the reasons why the pastor should accept the proposed condition under which the remaining volumes of the research study could be published. He said that Monsignor Joseph remained "adamant" in opposition despite all the persuasive arguments that he and the chancellor brought to bear on him.

The cooperative response Grodzins received from the archbishop and his chancellor was quite different from that of my Jesuit superiors, the provincial and the president. He was unable to get an appointment with the Jesuit provincial, who said, "There is nothing to discuss," but spent some time with his representative, the president of Loyola University. Grodzins was frustrated by this "pleasant bureaucrat, who has no scholarly or scientific interests, and who seems unwilling to take a stand on anything troublesome."

A greater frustration came for Grodzins at an elaborate dinner to which the pastor invited him and the critical committee of Baechle, Balduc, and Baudreaux. This dinner was in "superb good taste," as Grodzins said, "a demonstration that I was not dealing with some backward southern priests who didn't know their way around." The effort was to charm this representative from a great northern university, and at the same time to convince him that he had misread the character of his author. The Chicago guest later told me, "I've never heard clergymen use the kind of foul language they used in talking about you."

The pastor remained adamant. The archbishop told me, "I tried to persuade him to cooperate, but I couldn't budge him." The provincial also remained adamant, and I could not "budge him." My recourse was with the Jesuit authorities in Rome. On January 10, 1952, I wrote to Father Vincent McCormick, the American assistant to the Jesuit general, but received no reply. On January 17, Morton Grodzins also wrote him a long, closely reasoned letter, setting forth the pertinent reasons why the three volumes should be published. He also received no reply. I waited till October 10, 1952, before writing to Father James Naughton, the Secretary of the Jesuit Order, a friend of many years, asking him to bring this case to the attention of the Jesuit General, Father Janssens. He recommended *corragio* and *pazienza* because it takes Roman officials a long time to make decisions.

The virtue of *pazienza* kept me going until the following year (April 20, 1953) when I wrote directly to the Jesuit General, enclosing a copy of my earlier letter to Father McCormick and requesting that the ban be removed on the publication of the three remaining volumes. There was no reply to this letter, and I determined to go personally to Rome, an opportunity made possible by the fact that I received an appointment as Fulbright Visiting Professor to the University of Muenster in West Germany (40).

Jim Naughton had prearranged my appointment in Rome with Father Janssens, with whom I spent almost an hour on Sunday, December 27, 1953. The general was sympathetic and deeply concerned about sociological studies of the Catholic church, and from a digest of the correspondence he showed a remarkable acquaintance with the *Southern Parish* case. From my point of view, the two most significant things he said were first, that the manuscript did not really require the approval of the pastor, and second, that he would request that the censor's reports on Volume II be sent to Rome, and if these were in order, he would authorize the publication of the book.

Religious superiors, like top administrators of other large organizations, do not always get their decisions carried out by subordinates. One of the questions he asked me was, "How can I get your provincial to answer letters?" He asked me to give a memorandum of our talk and his decision to Father McCormick, who would take care of the affair. As far as I could discover, the latter did not carry out his task, and I continued to wait patiently for a solution.

Meanwhile at Muenster I had a research team of thirteen university students—four of them women, five of them divinity students—with whom I did a study of the lay societies of a local German parish (41). To complete this work I stayed in Muenster through January 1955, having received an extension of my Fulbright grant. This book was published under the title, *Soziologie der Pfarrgruppen*, with a Foreword by Josef Hoeffner, then Director of the Institute for Social Science, later Bishop of Muenster, and currently Cardinal of Cologne.

In effect then, I had a study similar to that of the second volume of the series in print, but it dealt with Catholic lay groups of another urban parish in another country. The years were passing, but I had not given up hope that in 1956, when Father Crandell's term of office ended, the whole matter would be reopened under more reasonable conditions. The new provincial was Father Laurence O'Neill, to whom I immediately wrote requesting a reconsideration of the *Southern Parish* manuscripts. I should have realized that church administrators, like those in other bureaucracies, are reluctant to put a predecessor in a "bad light." The answer, of September 27, 1956, said that he considered it "untimely" to take up a matter that might involve the reversal of a decision by his predecessor who had only recently left the position of provincial.

For the academic year, 1956–1957, I accepted an invitation as visiting professor of sociology at the University of Notre Dame (42). Here I again assembled a research team, this time of graduate students of sociology, and conducted a research study of a local parochial elementary school. During the course of the study, the pastor of the parish received an anonymous "warning" about me from someone at Mater Dolorosa Parish in New Orleans. He showed it to me laughingly and told me not to worry because every once in a while he gets "crank letters."

The report of this study was published by the University of Notre Dame Press under the title *Parochial School: A Sociological Study* and later widely circulated in a paperback edition. In a sense, then, I had the third volume of the series in print, although it was a study of an elementary parish school in a midwestern city rather than in a southern parish. After this experience I returned to my teaching position at Loyola

University of the South, still awaiting word from the Jesuit general at Rome.

I wished that there could be further recourse, but I doubted that any ecclesiastical authority could be more effective than that of the Jesuit general. Nevertheless, when Jim Naughton came back to the United States for a visit, I telephoned him to say that if I could not get some response from the Jesuit Curia at Rome I would lodge a formal complaint to the Vatican Congregation of Religious. This he did not want because he felt that Jesuits should settle their problems without appeal to "outsiders." I told him I wanted an answer from the general.

The answer finally came in the Jesuit general's letter of February 15, 1959, in which he said he did not wish to force (*exigere*) the provincial to grant the *imprimi potest* and asked that I accept the decision of superiors in a "spirit of humility and obedience" and to turn my effort and energies to other social problems (*quae certe non deficiunt*). It was still within the discretionary power of the Jesuit provincial, Father Laurence O'Neill, to allow publication of the three volumes by removing the arbitrary condition that the pastor's approval was necessary. This he was unwilling to do despite my repeated requests. It was then, in a spirit of weariness and frustration, rather than of "humility and obedience," that I abandoned hope for the publication of the complete *Southern Parish* series.

When Roger Vekemans invited me to come to Chile in 1961 to teach sociological research methods at the Catholic University of Santiago, I thought for a while of researching family life in a Catholic parish down there. This would have provided materials to "replace" the fourth volume of *Southern Parish*, as had been done only partially in Muenster for the second volume and in South Bend for the third volume—partially in the sense that only the focus of the studies remained the same. I did not actualize this idea, but one of the research projects I directed was a study of the Christian Family Movement in Santiago, the report of which was gratuitously delivered to the movement's leaders, but still remains unpublished.

NOTES

1. Canon lawyers used to point out that excommunication was the penalty for violation of some of the provisions of canons 1395–1405 on prohibited books.

2. Hans Küng, *Infallible? An Inquiry* (Garden City, Doubleday, 1970) would certainly have been listed as a prohibited book in 1950, for attacking the doctrine of papal infallibility.

3. Paul Courtney was the pseudonym for a Louisiana priest who later left the priesthood. This fact about him still protects his anonymity since so many of his clerical colleagues have also resigned the priesthood.

4. The first volume is better known as *Southern Parish*, the general title for the four proposed volumes.

5. Before he brought wide publicity upon himself, his identity was hidden as "Father Urban," Pastor of "St. Mary's" in "Riverside."

6. I discussed these earlier reflections with Donald McDonald, *Catholics in Conversation* (Philadelphia, Lippincott, 1960), "Perspectives," pp. 32–50.

7. Even the *American Catholic Sociological Review*, which began publication in March 1940, reported little research on Catholics. An article by Francis J. Friedel, "Catholic Sociological Research," Vol. 3, No. 3, (October 1942), pp. 129–136, suggested the Catholic parish as a subject of research.

8. But I was also influenced by a book that at that time seemed to question the "purity" of scientific objectivity in social science and was not widely popular among graduate students. It was Robert Lynd, *Knowledge for What?* (Princeton, Princeton University Press, 1939).

9. It is only relatively true that a diocese is a small-bore model of the total church. The concept simply does not fit at all when applied even to the largest urban parish. See, however, "The Nature of a Diocese," pp. 34–44, in Karl Rahner, *Bishops: Their Status and Function* (Baltimore, Helicon, 1963).

10. Both the postulate and the hypothesis are still wide open questions. I still do not know whether the chain (church) is only as strong as its weakest link (parish), nor am I as confident as I once was that the value system of Catholicism is the basis for reordering Western culture. See my optimistic article, "Religion: Integrator of the Culture?" *Thought* (Autumn 1958), pp. 361–382.

11. The only consultant who was hesitant about the choice of Mater Dolorosa as a successful parish was Father Joseph Vath, who had grown up in the parish and who knew it more intimately than any of the others. He is now the bishop of the new diocese of Birmingham, Alabama.

12. "The Social Role of the Parish Priest," *Social Order* (December 1949) was reprinted in the *Catholic Mind* (August 1950) and brought to the attention of the pastor who complained about it to the Jesuit provincial. The article did not identify the parish, but the editors gratuitously "placed" the parish in New Orleans.

13. I was the "Father Bruno" of *Dynamics of a City Church*, about whom relatively little is said in the book.

14. Father Landry, a curate when I first came to Mater Dolorosa, was transferred to another parish during the first month of the research study.

15. See the remarks by John W. Riley, "The Sociologist in the Nonacademic Setting," pp. 789–805, in Paul Lazarsfeld, William Sewell, Harold Wilensky, Eds., *The Uses of Sociology* (New York, Basic Books, 1967).

16. For statistics on baptisms, communions, and confirmations, see *Dynamics of a City Church*, pp. 38, 62, 95.

17. See George A. Kelly, *Catholics and the Practice of the Faith* (Washington, D.C., Catholic University Press, 1945). See also his chapter, "The Parish Census," in C. J. Nuesse and Thomas Harte, Eds., *The Sociology of the Parish* (Milwaukee, Bruce, 1951).

18. Announcement of the census was made on two Sundays, and the pastor at his mass said, "If there's something you don't like on the census, you can just leave it out." The rest of us urged the people to answer all questions.

19. *Dynamics of a City Church*, p. 126.

20. Some European Catholic sociologists clung to the concept of the parish community and were unhappy with my findings. I re-

sponded in "La Paroisse Urbaine comme Groupe Social," *Paroisses Urbaines, Paroisses Rurales* (Casterman, 1958), pp. 84–94, and "The Parish and Social Integration," *Social Compass*, No. 1 (1960), pp. 39–47. See also the comments of Joseph Schuyler, *Northern Parish* (Chicago, Loyola University Press, 1960), pp. 54 f.

21. Carrollton was then a separately incorporated town, "out in the country" with its own main street, post office and ferry crossing.

22. Father Joseph was the fourth pastor of Mater Dolorosa, all of whom were foreign-born. In 1970, when the parish was 122 years old, it got its first American-born pastor.

23. For the account of the parish centennial, see *Dynamics of a City Church*, pp. 241–244.

24. Gunnar Myrdal, *An American Dilemma* (New York, Harper, 1944), pp. 870 f., had already pointed out that "In the South, especially in southern Louisiana where the French and Creole traditions are dominant, the Roman Catholic Church is the only one where Negroes are allowed to attend white churches."

25. Father Joseph always expressed deep loyalty to the Archbishop, but said he did not "understand" his attitudes on race relations. Morton Inger, *Politics and Reality in an American City* (New York, Center for Urban Education, 1969), p. 22, remarks that "As early as 1949, Rummel had cancelled a Holy Hour service because the religious procession would be segregated."

26. See this point in my "Conceptualizations of the Urban Parish," *Social Forces* (October 1952), pp. 43–46.

27. *Dynamics of a City Church*, p. vii. The opinion of an "outsider," however, was that the book "removes the halo which members of other urban churches are sometimes prone to ascribe to the Roman Catholic parish as a social institution." William J. Villaume, *The City Church* (January 1952), p. 15.

28. *Dynamics*, p. 17.

29. This was in a small monthly paper, *The Point*, published by the Center before Father Feeney was excommunicated. He and I lived in the same Jesuit community in Boston in the academic year, 1946–1947. He had an aversion to the "Harvard Jesuits," all graduate students at the university. See Catherine Clarke, *The Loyolas and the Cabots* (Boston, Ravengate, 1950), pp. 63–66.

30. This was in two letters to the editor of *Commonweal* on December 14, 1951, and February 1, 1952.

31. The reviewer, Thomas Balduc, had to be anonymous here because the Archbishop had told him and his fellow "committeemen" not to pursue the attack on my book. I did not know that he was the "editorial reviewer" when I did my rebuttal, "The Southern Parish Controversy," *The Priest*, Vol. *8*, No. 1, January 1952, pp. 21–26.

32. *Catholic Action of the South*, December 13, 1951.

33. *American Ecclesiastical Review*, May 1953, pp. 369–383. In it I made no mention of either Balduc or Furfey. I expanded this piece and published it as Chapter 15 in *Social Relations in the Urban Parish* (Chicago, University of Chicago Press, 1954).

34. The remarks of William Couch and James Cunningham were reported as news stories in the *Chicago Tribune*. The controversial book was by Morton Grodzins, *Americans Betrayed: Politics and the Japanese Evacuation* (Garden City, Doubleday-Page, 1969), first published by the University of Chicago Press, 1951.

35. At this point, as far as I could learn, there was no talk of publicizing this proposed memorandum. Father Shields already knew that the Jesuits would not "buy up" the first printing of the book. It was the infuriated pastor who insisted that Father Balduc's attack on the book be published in *Catholic Action of the South* (October 4, 1951).

36. This was the "boomerang" of the Loyola president's "moral principle" of choosing the lesser of two evils. The pastor could also play this game.

37. Book review in *The Journal of Religion*, Vol. *32*, No. 2, April 1952, pp. 139–141.

38. At the 1955 convention of the American Catholic Sociological Society I received the annual book award for *Social Relations in the Urban Parish*.

39. In 1952, I talked with Bishop Edwin O'Hara, then honorary president of the American Catholic Sociological Society, asking him to make a statement in support of publishing the three remaining volumes of *Southern Parish*, but he refused to do so.

40. Where I remained from the end of August 1953 till the end of January 1955. Aside from my duties of research and teaching at the university, I made several lecture tours of Germany under the auspices of the United States Information Agency, delivering

twenty-six lectures, most of them on race relations in the United States.

41. I lectured on two chapters of the research report, one in Frankfurt, the other in Madrid. They were published as "Die Sozialstruktur der Gruppen in Einer Pfarrei," *Kölner Zeitschrift für Soziologie und Sozialpsychologie*, Heft 1, 1955, pp. 43–54; and "Las Reuniones de las Associaciones Parroquiales," *Revista de Estudios Politicos*, Madrid, March–June 1956, pp. 141–156. The whole research report was translated by Franz Schmidt, *Soziologie der Pfarrgruppen* (Muenster, Aschendorf, 1958).

42. I gave a course on the "Sociology of Vocations" in the three summer sessions of 1956, 1958, and 1960 at the University of Notre Dame and in the 1959 summer session at Fordham University. Out of these lectures grew my book, *Religion as an Occupation* (Notre Dame, University of Notre Dame Press, 1961).

THREE

THE DESEGREGATION PROJECT

The practical uses of sociology are many and varied, and the knowledge derived from sociological research is applicable in all social groups in which human beings pursue their common goals. My experience and training in social science did not focus exclusively on sociology of religion nor on the study of parish life in the Catholic church. New Orleans had other problems, and even as a graduate student after World War II I foresaw the possibilities of using social science for the improvement of race relations in Louisiana. Armed with my doctorate I returned there for the fall semester of 1947.

With the advice of Gordon Allport and Samuel Stouffer of the Harvard faculty, I had worked out a tentative program that would eventually integrate Negro students into Loyola University of the South (1). I saw this as the first step to the eventual and complete desegregation of Catholic schools in Louisiana and then of all Catholic facilities of whatever kind. From the beginning I favored the procedure "from the top down," rather than starting from the kindergarten and moving up to the graduate school—which was the preference of Archbishop Rummel and some of his advisors (2).

In late 1946, at a luncheon in Cambridge with Father William Crandell, then academic dean of Loyola University, I outlined my plan for gradual desegregation of the university. It seemed to me the essence of simplicity and prudence. In the fall semester of 1947, I would invite black students from Xavier University to meet occasionally with me and Loyola students to discuss the problem. If this went well, I would conduct a seminar in the spring of 1948 for students from both universities, the academic credits for which would be granted from the campus at which the student was registered. This experience, I believed, would prepare for the formal admission of Negro students at Loyola University for the fall term, 1948.

This careful and reasonable plan depended for its success on the goodwill and cooperation of the administration and faculty of Loyola University, which were not forthcoming. I had underestimated the racial prejudice of some of the faculty, and had overestimated the prudential courage of the administrators. Although there were undoubtedly racist white students on the campus there was no overt opposition from them—at least not until the spring of 1955, when the propaganda of the recently organized White Citizens' Council began to infect all southern institutions.

Although Loyola was the first private white campus in Louisiana to accept Negro students, the process whereby they were accepted did not go according to my plan (3). Expediency forced a change in my strategy. A small group of students met occasionally throughout the winter, alternating the meeting place at Loyola and Xavier, and also brought in some interested students from Dominican and Ursuline Colleges. In April 1948 they formally established themselves as an Interracial Committee under the umbrella of the National Federation of Catholic College Students. I acted as their chaplain.

In the larger community of New Orleans there existed a Committee on Race Relations, the primary concern of which was "to further understanding among people of different races living in New Orleans." Eighty-four citizens of both races formed this committee under the chairmanship of Rabbi Emil Leipziger. An institute for teachers of both public and private schools was successfully conducted in 1946 under the direction of Professor Clarence Glick of Tulane University. This interracial institute was repeated in the fall of 1947, at which time I acted as assistant director of the program. Classes were held at the YWCA building, and public school teachers who participated received 18 hours of in-service training credit (4).

My experience with this institute and with the Catholic college students convinced me that there was need for a group of adult Catholic lay people to work for racial desegregation of all Catholic facilities of the archdiocese. Here again we had an already existing "umbrella" organization, the Catholic Committee of the South (CCS) formed in 1939 by the Catholic bishops of the south, with Archbishop Rummel as chairman of the board. In January, 1949, I proposed to Father Vincent O'Connell, executive secretary of the CCS, and to Professor Vernon Miller, Dean of the Loyola University Law School, that we revive and expand the interracial unit of the CCS. Dean Miller issued personal invitations to fifty people, of whom twenty-two appeared on Monday night, February 21, at Loyola University.

PROLOGUE TO DESEGREGATION. The story of race relations among Louisiana Catholics goes back many decades before the formation of the CCS and of the Catholic intercollegiate, interracial committee, back to the priests and brothers of the Divine Word, the Josephite, and the Holy Ghost Orders, who attended the spiritual needs of Negroes; to the Sisters of the Blessed Sacrament, who taught in Negro schools and established Xavier of New Orleans, the first black Catholic university in the world; to the Sisters of the Holy Family and the Knights of Peter Claver; to concerned Catholic lay people of both races, who deplored the incongruity of "separate but equal" facilities among Catholics (5).

Much more can be said about these historical activities of cooperative effort between the races, but I want to concentrate here on the activities leading up to the spectacular drive in 1956 to desegregate the Catholic school system. In the early fifties the basic assumption of the organized lay Catholics, both students and their elders, was twofold. First, they felt that despite strong racist attitudes among many Catholics the time had come for a successful removal of racial barriers within the church in Louisiana. They saw, perhaps vaguely, the direction in which the American society was moving toward civil rights. Second, they felt that the moral leadership in the civil rights movement should come from the churches, especially their own church in Southern Louisiana (6). They saw the NAACP winning legally; they were convinced that their church could win morally.

These were also, of course, my own assumptions and convictions, and I worked closely with the two Catholic lay organizations in their promotion. I was chaplain and consultant to the two groups till their dissolution in 1957, with the exception of the 18 months I spent in Germany, when Father Henry Montecino, professor of philosophy at Loyola, replaced me, and the academic year, 1956–1957, when I was at the University of Notre Dame, during which time Father Alvin Pilie, professor of theology at Loyola, acted as chaplain. These were years of excitement and of close collaboration between the college students and their elders. Other organized voices were gradually silenced by the virulent local racists; by 1956, these lay Catholics represented the only interracial group still working publicly for improved race relations (7).

The student organization, after incorporating students

from Sacred Heart College of Grand Coteau and Spring Hill College at Mobile, renamed itself SERINCO (Southeastern Regional Interracial Commission). They met monthly on one campus or another for serious discussion about the race problem and issued a monthly newssheet, *The Christian Conscience*, dealing with the larger question of Catholic desegregation but also specifically concerned with desegregation on the Catholic college campus (8). There was a lighter and congenial side of the program: interracial parties at private homes and picnics on the grounds of the Catholic orphanage, Hope Haven, across the river in Marrero. Public facilities like Audubon Park and City Park were not then available for interracial picnics.

The interracial unit of the CCS renamed itself the Commission on Human Rights (CHR) and began distributing its own newssheet, *The Christian Impact*. On the last Sunday of each month the members attended mass together and afterwards had breakfast and a meeting. The original plan was to alternate the monthly mass at white and Negro parishes, but this had to be revised because St. Raphael's and St. Louis Cathedral were the only white parishes where we were acceptable. We were, however, most welcome at the convent chapels of the Madames of the Sacred Heart, the Ursuline Sisters, and the Missionary Servants of the Most Holy Eucharist. CHR was dedicated to the complete desegregation of all local Catholic activities: parishes, schools, hospitals, social service agencies, and all parochial and diocesan organizations (9).

Between 1948 and 1956 these two interracial groups joined in sponsoring an annual public program, Catholic Interracial Sunday, regularly scheduled on the second Sunday of Lent which usually coincided with National Brotherhood Week. Catholic Interracial Sunday was the occasion when all parish churches in the United States took up a collection for the Negro and Indian missions. Besides myself, there were a number of Catholic clergymen, mainly nonparochial men like

Monsignors Bezou and Plauche, Fathers Montecino and Twomey, who participated in interracial programs. The priests in Negro parishes were always cooperative, but this could be said of only a few priests serving in white parishes.

Aside from this limited clerical encouragement, the whole thrust for improved race relations within the New Orleans Catholic church was basically the work of the laity. Among the lay leaders were members of the interracial faculty of Xavier University: Philip and Maria Hornung, Victor Labat, Numa Rousseve, and Stephen and Patricia Ryan. Among the student leaders were Harry Alexander, now a Washington judge, Charles Palazzolo, professor at Villanova University, Daniel Quinn, Lt. Col. U.S. Army, Norman Francis, President of Xavier University, Donald Nicodemus, lay theologian and author, Aaron Henry, leader of the Mississippi Freedom Party at the Democratic Party convention in 1964.

The constant, but most frustrated, effort of these lay Catholics was to get action from the clergy, particularly to get Archbishop Rummel to move toward official desegregation of all Catholic facilities. On occasions when I talked with him about the second-class status of Catholic Negroes, he said: "You and the Josephite Fathers complain about these things, but I'm not getting any complaints from Negroes themselves." It is probably true that Negro protest, both inside and outside the church, did not reach its full strength till years later. Yet, the archbishop was aware of rumblings of discontent among Catholic Negroes in Louisiana (10).

A special word should be said about this prelate, whom I greatly revered and who basked in a vague international reputation as a progressive, socially concerned churchman. In spite of his brave proclamations about the immorality of racial segregation and of his frequent exhortations to brotherly love, he was ineffectual as a social activist. Until it was "safe" to do so, that is, till after the public school system was forced to desegregate, he refused to take decisive action. He failed to recognize and utilize two forces at his disposal: a faithful group of dedicated and knowledgeable lay people and a handful of social scientists in local universities willing to advise his program.

With exceedingly high motivation, Archbishop Rummel was ineffectual in race relations because of an excess of prudence and a failure of nerve. He did not lead the campaign for racial desegregation, but he did cooperate with the laity in a benign and interested way. For example, he appeared at each of the eight annual Catholic Interracial Sundays, closing each program with an inspiring homily. In April 1950, he had as his house guest, Black African Bishop most Reverend Joseph Kiwanuka, who was featured at a public program sponsored by the two lay organizations.

Cardinal Stritch and other members of the Catholic hierarchy were present at this program honoring Bishop Kiwanuka. He and the other prelates had dinner with the Jesuit Fathers that night—the first time a Negro had ever been invited to a meal in the Loyola Faculty Residence. While walking to the auditorium I asked the Cardinal to say a few words condemning racial segregation but he answered, "I can't say this in another man's diocese" (11). A different answer had been given by Monsignor Fulton Sheen, who spoke annually at the Loyola Forum to thousands of Orleaneans. I asked him also to come out forthright in condemnation of segregation (as Clare Booth Luce had done before addressing a Loyola Forum). His response was, "This is a problem that can be solved only by prayer."

THE NEED FOR ACTION. As a clergyman I had great faith in prayer, but as a sociologist I saw the necessity for combining action with prayer in any attempt to alleviate the racist immorality among my fellow Catholics. The virtue of patience and the belief in gradualism were simply maintaining the status quo. In September 1952 one of our CHR members, A. P. Tureaud, who was also the chief lawyer for the NAACP, filed a suit against the New Orleans school board. Less than 2 years later, May 17, 1954, the U.S. Supreme Court issued its famous decision on the unconstitutionality of racial segregation in public schools.

The inevitability of public school desegregation seemed to be assured by that decision. During my absence in Germany, Father Montecino and the lay leaders of CHR and SER-INCO continued their vigorous public program for racial improvement within the Catholic church of New Orleans. On my return in late January 1955 I confidently cooperated with them in trying to persuade the archbishop to announce the end of Catholic school segregation. We hoped that he might do this on the occasion of our seventh annual Catholic Interracial Sunday in February.

My personal request to Archbishop Rummel was that he set a date as of September 1955 for the removal of discriminatory practices from the Catholic school system as well as from all other Catholic facilities and organizations of the archdiocese. Unfortunately, like many other southern leaders of good will, the archbishop temporized while the racist forces gathered in opposition. By the end of 1954, the White Citizens' Council had spread from Mississippi to New Orleans, where some of its organizers and many of its members were Roman Catholics. From then on, the White Citizens' Councils, with civic leaders such as Leander Perez, Emile Wagner, and Emmet Irwin, were the strongest opponents of Catholic efforts for racial improvement.

The campaign of propaganda and education I proposed at the end of 1955 was largely born out of frustration at the slow pace of change. For years the archbishop had been preaching that racial discrimination is immoral. The typical response, especially from black Catholics, was, "Well, why not stop it—at least among Catholics?". The cautious prelate, who was under great pressure from racist Catholics, felt that the time was not "ripe." He was not ready to move, he said, because the people—white Catholics—were in need of preparation, enlightenment and instruction. There was great need of specific education on the race question, but no person or group within the church seemed ready to mount a concerted, diocese-wide program to fulfill this need. There was also no money available from local sources to subsidize a first-rate educational project of this kind.

In December 1955 I contacted Frank Loescher, who had reported on a study of race relations among Protestants and who was then working with the Fund for the Republic (12). At a luncheon with him in Philadelphia he urged that I apply immediately to the secretary-treasurer of the fund, David F. Freeman, for a grant of 10,000 dollars to launch the program. This I did in a letter to Mr. Freeman on December 31, whose response was that the board of directors would require two documents: a letter of approval from Archbishop Rummel and an assurance that Loyola University of the South would administer the monies which I received. The board of the fund moved fast and authorized the grant on January 16, 1956.

The procedures and content for such an educational project had been worked out over the years, even before the Supreme Court decision of 1954. I had discussed it not only with members of CHR and SERINCO, who would sponsor the project, but also with my colleagues in education and sociology at Loyola, Louisiana State, Tulane, and Xavier Universities. This was not a research project, but an action program. It was designed specifically and scientifically for its propaganda effect to influence Catholic parents, teachers, and clergy in New Orleans. It was meant to provide basic preparation and motivation to accept the proposed desegregation of the parochial school system in September 1956 (13).

I did not think of this as a "scattershot" program for better race relations, brotherhood, or social improvement. It was specifically aimed at certain people to reach a definite objective within a limited period of time. As I viewed the social climate at that time, the three categories of people we were trying to reach were at different levels of readiness for Catholic school desegregation. (a) The teachers, especially the religious sisters, in both the elementary and high schools, were ready to make the move to racial integration. (b) The priests, especially those in parishes where they had to contend with parents' clubs, would be ready only if an order to desegregate came from the archbishop. (c) Catholic parents of school-age children at the elementary level were more fearful of the proposed change than were those who had children of high-school age.

Our first step was to assemble a mailing list, which varied around 4,000 names and addresses, containing all the priests in the city, all principals and many teachers in the Catholic schools, and all lay persons who were members of the parents' clubs of Catholic elementary schools. Starting on January 18, 1956, and ending on August 27, we sent out fourteen separate mailings with a total of 201,200 pieces of printed or mimeographed materials. Each mailing included *The Christian Impact* of CHR, and every other mailing *The Christian Conscience* of SERINCO. Besides the findings of experts at the lecture meetings of our program, there were also reprints of articles and news stories pertinent to the question of school desegregation.

The hypothesis on which I operated was the expectation that reliable and scientific information about race relations would help clear up the jungle of myths and half-truths that pervaded the Catholic Louisiana milieu. I made the large assumption that people who professed a common and basic Catholic morality, and who were close enough to the Church to be involved in Catholic schools, were open to an acceptance of the truth. Psychologists realize that knowledge alone is not sufficient to remove prejudice. Nevertheless, I felt that the dissemination of knowledge was the preliminary step to the alleviation of racial prejudice and to the logical move for Catholic school desegregation.

THE TESTIMONY OF EXPERTS. People who did study and research in race relations—and not only in the South—were aware that a series of stereotypes was a basic and widespread reflection of ignorance about this subject. Gunnar Myrdal's *An American Dilemma* had done much to dissipate this ignorance, but this book was violently attacked by racists who refused to relinquish the stereotypes. The recently established White Citizens' Councils made Myrdal a favorite target of attack and were busily engaged in reviving the ancient southern myths and stereotypes (14).

The obvious antidote to these false beliefs was the public testimony of experts who could objectively repudiate them one by one. This was no novel idea. The whole university system is geared to the discovery and dissemination of truth. The Citizen Forum on Integration, of which I was an active member, had only recently twice tried to answer the common stereotype: "School integration is a failure. It doesn't work." Alvin Hackett spoke to this public forum in December 1955, explaining how public schools had been integrated in St. Louis. One month later, Dr. Margaret Butcher came from Washington, D.C., and talked to the same audience about the integrated public school system there.

The first lecturer I invited dealt with the same theme. On Sunday, January 22, 1956, Father James Hoflich, superintendent of Catholic elementary schools in the St. Louis archdiocese, described how Cardinal Ritter had effectively instituted desegregated Catholic schools years before the public school system took this step. Father Hoflich was invited by Archbishop Rummel to give the same talk to all the New Orleans Catholic clergy, and he spoke also on the following night at a parents' club meeting at Dominican College.

A by-product of the Hoflich meeting was the publicity of the remarks of Monsignor Plauche who introduced him. The *Times-Picayune* next morning printed the headline, "Mixed Classes Possible in 1956," on the basis of the chancellor's answer to a question from the audience. He said, "It's very possible that it may be this year. But no definite decision has been made, and it's equally possible it may be delayed." The newspaper also reported his answer to a question about racial intermarriage. "We are opposed to the marriage laws as they exist. Is anybody here going to say that a couple in love should be refused marriage because their grandparents were Negroes?"

The second racist stereotype was the assertion that the admission of Negro children would "spread social disease" throughout the Catholic school system. A nationally known health expert talked to this question on Sunday, February 5. He was Dr. S. Ross Taggart, Chief of the Venereal Disease Division of the U.S. Department of Health in Washington. His medical knowledge and experience, as well as a thorough familiarity with school health surveys, disposed of the fear of "health hazards" through racial integration of the local Catholic schools.

A third typical statement of white racists was that "Negroes themselves don't want to go to white schools." The forum on this question was held on February 26, at the eighth annual Catholic Interracial Sunday. The principal speaker was the Honorable Hulan Jack, Borough President of Manhattan, whose speech was greeted in laudatory terms by Archbishop Rummel, who presided at the program. This event set off an explosive attack by Emile Wagner and his fellow racists, and deserves separate discussion later.

Catholic Interracial Sunday was notable also for the issue of the archdiocesan weekly, *Catholic Action of the South*, published under that date. Editor Millard Everett did a long article on the legislation proposed on February 15 by a group of Louisiana legislators "that would directly invade the operation of Catholic and other privately supported schools" (15). The front-page headline proclaimed "Church Rights are Threatened. Proposed Measures would invade Catholic Schools: Excommunication Possible." This was the first warning to Catholics in the Louisiana legislature, and it was repeated on several occasions in subsequent years.

The second big story on the front page was oddly headlined "No Final Decision on Integration in Catholic Schools." The story contained the complete text of the Archbishop's pastoral letter on "The Morality of Racial Segregation" which he had sent out to the clergy on February 11, with instructions that it be read in all the parish churches on Sunday, February 19. It was a long message, and it stated clearly that "racial segregation is morally wrong and sinful" because (a) it is a denial of the unity and solidarity of the human race; (b) it is a denial of the unity and universality of the redemption; (c) it is basically a violation of the dictates of justice and the mandate of love.

Near the end of the letter he wrote, "Nothing would please us more than to be able at the present moment to render a decision that would serve as a guide for priests, teachers, and parents. However, there are still many vital circumstances which require further study and consideration if our decision is to be based upon wisdom, prudence, and the genuine spiritual welfare of all concerned."

Without directly mentioning the current educational campaign, the news story remarked that "a group of competent attorneys, physicians, priests, religious educators, and sociologists is studying objections that have been raised against integration in the schools." One of these "objections" was the oft-repeated fear that acceptance of Negro children would "lower the intellectual standards" of all children in the Catholic schools. Our fourth lecturer, who handled this subject on March 11, was Benjamin Pasamanick, professor of psychiatry at Ohio State University, whose extensive research among preschool and school-aged children made him one of the country's experts on racial differences of intelligence.

A fifth objection, voiced by many white Catholics, was that the decision of the Supreme Court on school desegregation had "nothing to do with private schools." On April 8, William Hepburn, dean of the Lamar School of Law at Emory University, talked about the constitutional aspects of private school integration. This was becoming increasingly important because of the Louisiana legislature's threatened reprisals against parochial schools that planned to desegregate.

The next speaker of the series dealt with the ancient, but recently revived notion, that "the Bible proves God was the first segregationist." I had invited Father John McKenzie, renowned scripture scholar and author, to speak on this subject on Sunday, March 25, but Archbishop Rummel suggested a postponement. "Let us have peace on Palm Sunday," he said. The lecture was given on Sunday, April 22, but only over the vigorous objection of Father Thomas Balduc, rector of the Archdiocesan Seminary, who attempted to convince the archbishop in my presence that the church forbids the open public discussion of biblical and doctrinal matters (16).

The seventh forum of the series, on May 6, met the widespread claim of racists that the admission of Negro children into the Catholic schools would immediately raise the delinquency rate among white children. A nationally known sociologist, Professor Albert Reiss of Vanderbilt University, presented the findings of his factual studies to refute this assumption.

The final speaker of the series was a Negro priest and convert to the Catholic church, Father Clarence Howard of St. Augustine Seminary (17). His task, on May 20, was to counter the frequently stated objection by white racists that the immorality of racial segregation was a "new teaching" of the church which neither they nor their parents had heard about while they were being educated in the Catholic schools.

I was personally responsible for inviting these eight experts to New Orleans, but I did so only after much correspondence and more telephone calls to all parts of the country, and after considerable discussion with the lay leaders of CHR and SERINCO. Anyone connected with the forum series in any way was branded an "integrationist," which was not the most popular label to carry in New Orleans in 1956. Whatever "credibility" an integrationist could have had at that time might have been enhanced if all of our experts had been white, southern-born Catholics (18). The fact is that only three came from the South—the law dean from Georgia, the criminologist from Tennessee, and the moralist from Mississippi. Only four of the eight were Catholics, of whom one was a Negro layman, one a Negro priest, and two were white priests.

There was, however, a large number of local experts involved in this series of lectures. With one exception, there was at each forum a panel of four to six New Orleans people on the stage. They were men and women of professional status in the community: educators, physicians, psychiatrists, sociologists, social workers, lawyers, and theologians. The panelists made comments and raised questions concerning the main speech, and while this was being done written questions were submitted from the audience. The whole proceedings, including the question period, were recorded on tape.

Although the eight principal lecturers were "outsiders" to New Orleans, all forty-two panelists were professionally well-known citizens of Louisiana. Thirty were Catholics and twelve non-Catholics; there were thirty-three whites and nine Negroes, thirty-five men and seven women. Their names were published as contributors to the digest of this lecture series, which was printed in a forty-page booklet, *Handbook on Catholic School Integration*. This was published in a limited edition of 8,000 copies, about half of which were distributed in the final mailing of this educational project on August 27, 1956. The rest were distributed mainly to Catholic school systems in other southern dioceses.

It was not a simple matter to arrange for the locale where these lectures were held. The committee in charge of such arrangements, led mainly by Patricia Ryan, felt that no single parochial school would, or should be asked to, sponsor all eight lectures. They were unable to find any pastor or principal of an elementary school in a white parish willing to allow an "integration" forum on the premises. They were forced to look elsewhere and arranged for two meetings at Xavier University, one each at St. Mary's Dominican College, Ursuline College, Loyola University, and the downtown Jesuit parish that had no elementary school, and two in high schools run by religious orders, St. Joseph's Academy and Cor Jesu High School.

MAXIMUM PUBLICITY. A regular stream of information about this educational campaign was going out through our mailing list to priests, teachers, and parents. The Sunday afternoon attendance at the forums, depending on the convenience of the meeting place, ranged from about one hundred at the smallest gathering to almost one thousand on Catholic Interracial Sunday. Relatively few priests, seminarians, and sisters attended the lectures, an absence explained by the archbishop on the fact that Sunday afternoon was the only time these church people had to visit with their friends and relatives.

Anything that had to do with the race question, especially with a group deliberately promoting racial integration, was "big news" in New Orleans (19). The three white newspapers, the *New Orleans States, New Orleans Item,* and *Times-Picayune,* gave excellent coverage to each lecture and published pictures and interviews with the speakers, as well as descriptive accounts by news reporters. The Negro paper, *Louisiana Weekly,* frequently featured the materials provided in the mailings from CHR and SERINCO and headlined the speakers. The archdiocesan weekly, *Catholic Action of the South* virtually ignored the educational program, a fact I pointed out to the archbishop in April.

Television station WDSU sent a cameraman to the lecture forums and then included a run of the pictures twice, and sometimes three times, in the Sunday night news reports. This station also arranged for a half-hour panel show with Father McKenzie and four college students. The WDSU radio station broadcast 5-minute interviews with each of four of the featured lecturers. Without offering an explanation, I must confess that the WWL radio station, owned and operated by Loyola University where I taught, did not cover the lecture series. This fact I pointed out to the president, Father Patrick Donnelly, who said that the whole program was "too controversial."

My colleagues and I were convinced that the public schools would eventually have to integrate, and our strong hope was that the Catholic schools could set up the model by being first to desegregate. Fuel had been fed to the "controversy" in the second month of our educational campaign when, on February 15, 1956, Judge J. Skelly Wright of the federal district court in New Orleans ordered the public school board to admit children "on a racially nondiscriminatory basis with all deliberate speed." Mayor Chep Morrison, who had his eye on the governorship, said nothing. Dr. Clarence Scheps, Tulane University comptroller and member of the New Orleans school board, reflected the opinion of his four fellow board members when he said in 1956 that the New Orleans schools would never be integrated.

In other words, no one else was preparing for the desegregation of the schools besides the organized Catholic integrationists. Politicians and civic leaders were confident that it would never happen, and even as late as May 1960, after all appeals had failed, the public school board admitted to Judge Wright that no desegregation plan had been formulated. Liberal and moderate groups had practically disappeared by the spring of 1956. The New Orleans Committee on Race Relations had ceased to exist, as had the short-lived Citizen Forum on Integration. The National Urban League had been cut from the United Fund; the NAACP had been shamefully pilloried, as had Jim Dombrowski and his Southern Conference Educational Fund. (20).

I was in no way surprised, therefore, that the White Citizens' Councils recognized this educational campaign for Catholic school desegregation as the largest single public threat to its own program of white supremacy. Its leaders and their mimeograph machines gave full attention to this group of lay Catholic integrationists. They aimed their attack at the highest authority in the diocese, Archbishop Rummel, as though he were the responsible promoter of the campaign. Leander Perez publicly advised Catholics to "cut off his water," that is, stop contributing to the church. A regularly repeated charge was that those Catholics who favored school desegregation were following the Communist party line, were the unknowing dupes of the Communist conspiracy to weaken America by "mongrelizing" the people.

I want to emphasize that this opposition was not an anti-Catholic crusade mounted by old-fashioned Southern bigots. One of the most vocal segregationists in New Orleans was Emile Wagner, member of the city school board and a product of Catholic education from kindergarten through law school. Perez was a Catholic, as were several of the most vocal leaders and officers of the White Citizens' Councils. By this time, however, racist Catholic pastors were no longer publicly expressing their views, and at no time did a Catholic priest act as chaplain, or offer the benediction, at meetings of the White Citizens' Councils (2 1).

The most explosive publicity of the campaign—and one that involved the Communist smear—was engineered by Emile Wagner. It surrounded the eighth annual Catholic Interracial Sunday, February 26, 1956, when the principal speaker was the Honorable Hulan Jack, borough president of Manhattan, New York. He praised Archbishop Rummel for his "courageous leadership" in the struggle for racial justice. The archbishop responded with praise of Hulan Jack, but also took the opportunity to throw back the Communist charge on the segregationists, suggesting that they should ask themselves "whether they are doing the work of those striving to introduce the principles of atheism and infidelity and Communism into the United States."

The irony of these countercharges about Communism became apparent only as an aftermath of the Catholic Interracial Sunday. When the program ended that day the archbishop invited several of us, including Bishop Caillouet, Hulan Jack, and his secretary, Stanley Rose, to a luncheon at his residence. During the luncheon I was called to the telephone to talk to a news reporter who wanted to check on a story he had just received about Hulan Jack. It was to the effect that Jack had been widely involved in various "Communist fronts." I handed the phone to Stanley Rose, who said, "if this isn't a case of mistaken identity, it's an outright lie."

It was not a case of mistaken identity since Hulan Jack, former assemblyman and now borough president, was too easy to identify. The story unravels as follows. During the week before Jack's appearance in New Orleans, Emile Wagner asked Leander Perez to check the Washington "files" for information on Jack. Perez sent the request to Senator James Eastland and through him to the Senate Internal Investigation Committee, which passed it on to the House Un-American

Activities Committee (HUAC). Back from Eastland through Perez to Wagner, on Friday morning February 24, came the record of Jack's "participation in Communist-dominated activities," listing his membership in the Negro Labor Victory Committee, the fact that he had sponsored a testimonial dinner for Ferdinand Smith, and had favored presidential clemency for Earl Browder. The inference drawn from the HUAC file was that anyone who did such things was a dangerous and "un-American" person, if not exactly a Communist.

When Emile Wagner obtained this information on Friday morning he wanted to be "fair" to Loyola University where Jack was to appear and from which he himself had obtained his law degree. He felt that Father Donnelly, the president of Loyola, should be warned ahead of time and perhaps force a cancellation of the program. He sent a fellow segregationist to talk with the university president, under strict orders not to reveal that he came from Wagner (22). Not wanting to "add to my worries," as he later said, the President asked Father Louis Twomey's advice. During the conversation, and in the presence of Wagner's messenger, Father Donnelly phoned New York to question Father John LaFarge, a close friend of Jack.

Father LaFarge had nothing but praise for the borough president of Manhattan. Wagner's messenger was assured that Jack was an outstanding American, a loyal Roman Catholic, a devoted family man, and a democratic opponent of Communism. This made no impression on Emile Wagner, who saw the civil rights movement as an obvious part of the Communist conspiracy to destroy the southern way of life. He surfaced as the instigator of this "investigation" on Sunday after the Hulan Jack program, when he distributed copies of the HUAC "file" to news reporters. At that time he also remarked, "I am not going to say that Mr. Jack is a Communist or anything like that—I don't know." Nevertheless, he was highly incensed that he had failed to persuade his alma mater to deny a platform to a black integrationist from New York.

The charges against Jack immediately became national news, and among liberals made him a quasi-hero. He had had the courage to "invade" a southern stronghold of racism at a time when the Montgomery bus boycott, under the leadership of the Rev. Martin Luther King, Jr., was in full swing. He was beseiged by newsmen on his return to LaGuardia Airport and at a press conference he called at the municipal building in New York. Jack told reporters he might press libel charges against Emile Wagner and made reference to the incident in subsequent speeches. He was endorsed in laudatory terms by presidential candidate Adlai Stevenson and by Governor Herbert Lehman of New York. He was defended by Mayor Robert Wagner of New York as the "highest type American I know" (23).

At the time of the Hulan Jack program, Emile Wagner said that he did not represent any group, thus dissociating himself from the White Citizens' Council. He explained that he and A. Konrad Lagarde took it upon themselves as individuals to "try to check on all people coming to speak here on integration because we fear some outside force is at work." His failure to destroy, or even slow down, our propaganda campaign to promote Catholic school desegregation seemed to convince him that he needed organization. Two weeks later, on March 12, 1956, he filed articles of incorporation with a notary public for the Association of Catholic Laymen. There were thirty charter members who listed as one of their purposes "to seek out, make known, and denounce Communist infiltration, if any there be in the integration movement."

Wagner and his associates "infiltrated" the meetings of parents' clubs of a number of Catholic elementary and high schools and spoke heatedly against the school desegregation we were promoting. As an additional element in our educational campaign we conducted an essay contest for parents who had children in New Orleans Catholic schools. The title of the essay was "Why an Integrated School is Better than a Segregated School." Thirty-seven parents submitted essays, of which nine were judged worthy to share in 550 dollars of prize money. These essays were published in a pamphlet, of which 10,500 copies were distributed, entitled *Southern Catholic Parents Speak Up for Integrated Schools.*

To publicize this contest we took quarter-page ads in the diocesan weekly for 5 weeks and ran smaller ads in two of the daily papers for 1 week at a time. We had also intended to conduct a similar essay contest for teachers in the Catholic schools, but our funds were not adequate for this. Without thought of entering a "contest," fifty-three teachers submitted short statements on school desegregation. The contributions of two Negro teachers and six white teachers, half of them lay persons and half religious sisters, were published in another pamphlet, *Southern Catholic Teachers Favor Integrated Schools,* of which more than 6,000 copies were distributed.

THE OPPOSITION GROWS. One of the persistent questions I discussed with the leaders of CHR and SERINCO was whether this high-powered educational campaign of propaganda was achieving desired results. There were white Catholics of good will in the community who felt that we should go more slowly, that perhaps we were "doing more harm than good," were "stirring up trouble" and solidifying the racist opposition. The vigor of the campaign and its wide publicity were directly linked to the establishment of the segregationist Association of Catholic Laymen. During the late spring the parents' clubs in three white parochial schools went on record as voting against the desegregation of their schools.

Some of the parents on our mailing list asked to have their names removed. "In the future keep such trash as this out of our home. It tends to demoralize and decay the Christian atmosphere by introducing such a radical movement." One parent misquoted Our Lady of Fatima concerning "sins of the flesh which you encourage by socializing colored boys and girls in school functions." Another wrote that "if racial segregation is a sin then our religious and teachers have been condoning sinful practices for generations." Still another decreed that "the Jew shall have the gift to make money; the white man shall have the gift to govern; the Negro shall be a servant" (24).

These are a small sample of the "printable" objections I received in the mail, all of them from parents who signed their names, strongly opposed to the move to desegregate the Catholic schools and who wanted the whole propaganda campaign stopped. The contents of anonymous letters were for the most part not repeatable in respectable print. They foreshadowed the racist hate letters I received in 1964 in the controversy over my research report on police arrests in New Orleans (25). One non-Catholic reminded me that "your church has mixed races since it began in 325 A.D. under Constantine. How you must hate Caucasian Israelites (Protestant whites). See Rev. 13:18 and Rev. 12:9."

Although our educational campaign was not aimed at either the general public or at the New Orleans public school system, the leaders of the White Citizens' Councils saw it as a threat to both. They were concerned about what the Catholics were doing, or might do. They evidenced their displeasure by a rally at Pelican Stadium on Thursday, May 17, 1956, where Archbishop Rummel's name was loudly booed and hissed, and after which a fiery cross was erected on the seminary grounds near his residence (26). On the following Sunday the officers of CHR met to draw up a "model" resolution, referring to this incident and pledging our "complete support of the program of his Excellency in the removal of all barriers to the integration of Catholics." This was released to the press on the following day and also sent to all Catholic lay organizations of the diocese requesting its adoption.

The CHR also prepared a longer press release, which got full coverage in newspapers, radio, and television and which said in part that "we object vigorously to the importation of rabble-rousers like Senator Eastland of Mississippi and Governor Griffin of Georgia into our peaceful New Orleans community." This press release also stated that "we brand those people who appeared last week on the racist program at Pelican Stadium as anti-American, anti-Southern, anti-Catholic, and irreligious people."

On May 27, Dr. Emmett L. Irwin, chairman of the White Citizens' Council of New Orleans, issued a statement denying all these charges and demanding that they be either substantiated or retracted. I was glad to comply with this invitation by issuing a long statement that was published in its entirety by the New Orleans newspapers on Monday, June 11. In it I dealt with the anti-Americanism of the White Citizens' Councils, listing ten examples of their "subversion," in word and practice, of the American ideology and commenting that "out of the mouths of segregationists themselves comes the obvious conclusion that the white supremacy groups are anti-American in both spirit and practice."

This was too much for the chairman of the White Citizens' Council who then turned for help to J. Edgar Hoover and the Federal Bureau of Investigation. He concluded his letter of June 15 to the FBI with the paragraph: "It is further urged and requested that the Federal Bureau of Investigation make a searching investigation of the activities of the Rev. Joseph H. Fichter S. J., and his secret organization, the Commission on Human Rights of the Catholic Committee of the South of which he is reported to be the founder. Such an investigation may reveal most interesting information, showing why these organizations withhold the names of members from the public" (27).

On the same day Dr. Irwin took careful public note that I had received a grant of 10,000 dollars to combat segregation from the Fund for the Republic, "long suspected of Communist leanings." It was public knowledge that the fund was then being threatened with an "expose" by the House Un-American Activities Committee. In early June, announcement had been made by Chairman Francis Walter that HUAC would begin public hearings on the Fund for the Republic toward the end of the month. On June 11, Robert Hutchins, president of the fund, issued a statement in defense of the fact that "in the field of race relations the fund has given 732,000 dollars to religious organizations representing nearly every denomination."

There was, of course, no "case" against the Fund for the Republic, but this fact did not deter the organized segregationists from frequently slandering the fund and its beneficiaries. By the middle of July it appeared that HUAC Chairman Walter would not hold formal hearings on the fund but would attempt to discredit it by conducting investigations on a series of topics that provided an opportunity for hostile witnesses to attack the fund indirectly. The New Orleans racists kept this in mind for subsequent attacks on me as well as on other people who worked for improved race relations.

Meanwhile there were forces at work in the Louisiana legislature aimed at hampering, if not eradicating, people and groups who favored desegregation (28). One of its tactics was to require that all organizations in Louisiana send a list of their membership to the secretary of state in Baton Rouge. If this order had been complied with, the segregationists would know the names of all Louisianans who favored desegregation and could expose them to the harrassment meant to curtail their activities. Most organizations complied with this order, and the listings that piled up at the state capitol were ignored because they did not include those of groups like the NAACP, National Urban League, and the Southern Conference Educational Fund. Nor did we submit the membership lists of CHR and SERINCO.

This refusal to make public the names of our members is the reason why Irwin complained to the FBI that I was the head of a "secret organization" (29). On the advice of our lawyer-members, John McCann, Janet Riley, A. P. Tureaud, and Frank Weller, I insisted that church organizations were exempt from this kind of official order and that this unreasonable demand constituted political interference with the operation of a religious group. Interestingly enough, if the White Citizens' Council had been willing to spend the necessary time and effort they could have researched the New Orleans newspapers since 1949, and in the news reports of our activities over the years could have found the names of practically all active members of our "secret organization."

EFFECTIVE OPPOSITION.   There were other ways of getting at bothersome integrationists and of hampering their activities. One of them directly affected some of the most active and competent members of CHR who were public school teachers, both Negro and white. It was a two-pronged attack by the Louisiana legislature which voted on and approved Act 15, requiring that any high school graduate who wanted to attend a state college or university have a certificate of eligibility, or statement of good moral character, signed by a local school official.

Negro students had been attending Louisiana State University under federal court order since 1950. The author of Act 15 claimed that he was not countering this court order and that the act indeed had no racial implications at all since it applied to all high school graduates in the same way. White students would also need this document to be eligible for study at a state college or university. The deception in this statement is seen in the fact that the legislature at the same time amended Act 250 on the teacher tenure law to permit the firing of school teachers and of school officials who act toward the integration of the races in the public school systems of the state of Louisiana.

These two legislative actions of 1956, strongly and publicly endorsed by the White Citizens' Councils, contained a double threat to public school educators who favored desegregation. The teacher, principal, or other administrator of a Negro public high school, who certified to a graduate's eligibility to attend Louisiana Sate University automatically performed an "act toward integration." Furthermore, the members of CHR who were public school teachers, both Negro and white, placed themselves in jeopardy of losing their jobs because they belonged to an organized group that clearly promoted racial integration.

At a special meeting in June, CHR members agonized over both the moral and legal aspects of continued membership for those employed in the public school system. For a public school teacher to stay in the group could mean exposure by the racists even though the list of members was never submitted to the secretary of state of Louisiana. CHR was not quite as "secret" as the segregationists alleged. On the other hand, could resignation be considered a kind of moral defection from the high Christian principles for which the group stood? One teacher said she was willing to sacrifice her career if she could get a clear-cut statement from the archbishop that the morality of the race question demanded action as well as preaching. The attorneys in the group, however, strongly advised the public school employees to resign from CHR.

Both groups, CHR and SERINCO, continued the educational campaign throughout the summer, but at a slower pace. Monthly meetings were held and the 4,000 people on the mailing list continued to receive our integrationist propaganda: in June the pamphlet containing the parents' essays, in July the essays written by Catholic teachers, and at the end of August just prior to the opening of the school year, the *Handbook on Catholic School Integration*, which summarized the scientific and objective knowledge provided by our expert lecturers.

The financial grant from the Fund for the Republic had been exhausted and actually "overspent" by more than 300 dollars. I had been invited as visiting professor of sociology for the coming academic year by the University of Notre Dame, but before leaving New Orleans I wanted to obtain a financial subsidy that would allow the continuation of the educational program. To this end, I again contacted David Freeman of the Fund for the Republic, who suggested that the application for a further grant be made at the end of August and that we had a good chance of receiving continuing support.

Father Henry Montecino of Loyola University, who had energetically and successfully replaced me as chaplain during my previous absence in Germany, agreed to act in the same capacity again with CHR, but did not have the time to devote to SERINCO. He took up the negotiations with David Freeman, in the course of which he informed Father Donnelly, president of Loyola University, that the Fund for the Republic was likely to make another grant for the campaign against racial segregation. The president informed him that the university board of directors had voted not to accept any further grants of this kind which simply required the university to act as disbursement office for Catholic lay groups (30).

Father Montecino then took up the matter with the chancellor of the diocese, Monsignor Plauche, who had been most cooperative throughout the educational campaign. The point at question was whether the archdiocese itself, as a tax-exempt corporation, would act as recipient of the proposed financial grant from the fund for the Republic. At this point,

Archbishop Rummel seemed to be weary of all the racial controversy and especially of the continuous attacks made upon him by racists. "He thought we had done enough and that it might be better not to conduct another campaign for the desegregation of the Catholic schools" (31).

Nevertheless, the archbishop was unwilling to disappoint his most loyal supporters. He would not "stand in the way" of the continued effort if CHR could obtain the grant through the Catholic Committee of the South, which then had its headquarters at Rocky Mount, North Carolina, under the general secretary, Father Maurice Sheehan. Some years earlier he had received a grant of 17,000 dollars from the Fund for the Republic. Despite telegrams, registered letters, and attempted telephone calls, no response could be obtained from Father Sheehan (32). It appears that the bishops of the south had gradually withdrawn their interest and support so that the Catholic Committee of the South was then on the verge of dissolution.

The 1956 educational project for racial desegregation was also a kind of climax for SERINCO. Before I left New Orleans Father Donnelly told me that the board of directors had seriously considered banning the National Federation of Catholic College Students from the Loyola campus. This was not done, however, because the Jesuit Educational Association had urged that Jesuit colleges belong to the NFCCS. On the Loyola campus the only active unit of the federation was the student interracial commission. I recommended that Father Alvin Pilie, of the theology department, be appointed as my replacement.

During the fall semester, while I was at Notre Dame, I did not receive the regular monthly issue of *The Christian Conscience*, but I attributed this to carelessness on the part of the student editors. As the time approached for the official brotherhood week of 1957 I began to make inquiries about the students' plans for the ninth annual Catholic Interracial Sunday.

I wrote to Father Donnelly at Loyola, to Philip DesMarais, vice-president of Dominican College, to Sister Josephina, President of Xavier University, to Bishop Caillouet, and even to Archbishop Rummel, asking all of them to encourage the students in promotion of this annual program.

It was only then that I learned how Father Donnelly succeeded, where his predecessor Father Thomas Shields had failed, in suppressing both SERINCO and its monthly newssheet, *The Christian Conscience.* In a letter of February 21, 1957, he told me, "interracial activities are now back under the control of the Sodalities where I sincerely believe they ought to be (33). They are under the Social Action Committee of the Sodalities of Loyola University. . . . Their organ of publication is the *Christian Accent*, a copy of which is enclosed." There was to be no Catholic Interracial Sunday; SERINCO was dead; the segregationists had won another victory.

EXCOMMUNICATION.   Except for the minority of outspoken integrationist priests—most of whom were in nonparochial positions—the Catholic clergy of New Orleans were at best lukewarm to the whole program of desegregation within the church. Emile Wagner told the archbishop that many of his priests were honestly opposed to the integration of the races but were now fearful of reprisal from higher authority if they publicly spoke their convictions. Wagner wanted open dialogue, frank discussion, and freedom of speech for both clergy and laity on both sides of the question. This was the man who tried his best to prevent freedom of speech for Hulan Jack at the Catholic Interracial Sunday and who, as member of the public school board voted against the use of the Rabouin School by the Citizen Forum on Integration, and who favored the banning of the Urban League, NAACP, and SCEF.

Many New Orleanians who were not Catholics but who strongly approved school desegregation could not understand why the archbishop of an "authoritarian" church was so dilatory about coming to a decision on such an important moral problem and why he did not simply excommunicate recalcitrant Catholics. They were dismayed when Archbishop Rummel apparently capitulated in announcing again the postponement of Catholic school desegregation (34). In their eyes, the segregationists had scored another victory when the prelate declared that the schools would not be integrated "before September, 1957."

Excommunication from the Catholic church is a severe penalty which in this day is relatively seldom imposed by church authorities. Twice during 1956 Archbishop Rummel let it be known that the threat of excommunication hung over certain Catholic racists. One had to do with the segregation laws proposed in the Louisiana legislature that would interfere with the operation of Catholic schools. The diocesan weekly editorialized that "if the laws were put into effect automatic excommunication would be incurred by those who worked for and voted for their passage, and by those who appealed to lay authorities for their application." This was a warning to the Catholic members of the state legislature.

The second threat of excommunication accompanied the archbishop's order that Wagner's Association of Catholic Laymen be disbanded. The archbishop sent every member of the board of directors a letter stating they were liable to the penalty of excommunication if the association continued. The group bowed humbly in obedience but also sought recourse to higher authority by preparing a brief on their moral position to be delivered to the pope through the apostolic delegate in Washington. Wagner remarked that "as good Catholics, we bow to His Excellency's authority, but we question the propriety of the decision."

I tended to sympathize with Wagner and his associates, not

only because I took the liberal position—which they did not—that freedom of speech and organized protest should be permitted in the Catholic church as elsewhere in the American society, but also because Archbishop Rummel had previously failed to impose excommunication in more serious and provable cases. I did not believe that excommunication was out of keeping with modern liberal and democratic ideology. There are certain basic expectations and rules of conduct for members in any formal organization, the violation of which entails the expulsion of the member, or his resignation.

On three occasions prior to our 1956 educational campaign, such violations occurred. The most publicized of these happened in October 1955 at Jesuit Bend, a town south of New Orleans, when four white men prevented a Negro priest, Father Carlos Lewis, from celebrating Sunday mass in the parish church (35). Another occurred in a parish across the river from New Orleans when a white "usher" (with a gun in his holster) took over the seating arrangements for the congregation at mass and ordered Catholic Negroes to move to the back pews of the church. Still another was the physical assault of a Catholic Negro student from Xavier University after Sunday mass at a white suburban parish.

The persons guilty of these offenses were easily identified and their names were given to the archbishop. These cases constituted flagrant interference with the public worship of the church and were the kinds of behavior that should not go unpunished. After each of them, Father Louis Twomey and I visited the archbishop and urged that he excommunicate the guilty persons. In his charitable leniency he refused to do so, but he asked these people to reflect and pray and to come to a moral conversion of conscience. In the case of Jesuit Bend he interdicted the parish church in which the great majority of parishioners who had nothing to do with the unfortunate incident, were deprived of religious services.

The effect of this leniency seemed to embolden the segregationists, some of whom publicly declared that they had the archbiship "on the run." They could defy him with increasing vigor, and they did. Senator James Eastland noted this in April 1956, when he told an American Legion convention in Tupelo, Mississippi, that "the South owes the people of southern Louisiana a great debt of gratitude for resisting integration moves by the Roman Catholic church." He praised that area for "holding the line against tremendous odds" and "against the threat of a Roman Catholic archbishop to integrate schools there."

Only God knows what might have been had the archbishop acted promptly against Catholics who disrupted public worship services, but it was my conviction that excommunication, imposed at the right time for the right reasons, would have been an effective check on racist Catholics. The penalty of excommunication was indeed imposed, but only when it seemed too late, and for the wrong reasons. In the spring of 1962, after the public schools had been desegregated, Archbishop Rummel finally decided to bring parochial schools into compliance. Three racist Catholics who continued to voice their objections were officially declared excommunicated from the Catholic church in April 1962. The incongruity of this condemnation lay in the fact that these three, Una Gaillot, Leander Perez, and Jackson Ricau, were punished for their words and thoughts, and not for the kind of action (interference in church services) that had gone unpunished 6 years earlier when performed by others.

WAS IT WORTHWHILE?   The archbishop's decision not to start desegregating the Catholic schools, at least on the high school level, was a disappointment to me and the zealous lay Catholics who worked on the educational campaign of 1956. I personally felt that the process of desegregating all

Catholic facilities and organizations should have begun immediately after World War II, or at the latest in the September following the Supreme Court decision of May 17, 1954. After that, the segregationist forces, both in the larger community and within the Catholic church of New Orleans, gathered strength and numbers while the integrationists gradually withdrew into the background.

In my final report to the Fund for the Republic I attempted to evaluate the educational campaign to which they had given financial support. It was true that the parochial schools, with a few scattered exceptions, were still racially segregated, but it was also true that Catholic priests, teachers, and parents had a great deal more knowledge about race relations than they had previously had. I pointed out certain by-products of the educational campaign.

(a) The program helped us to learn more about the nature and strength of the opponents of school integration. We were able to distinguish between the friends and the foes of integration, between the fearful and the courageous, both within the Catholic Church and the New Orleans population. Although the campaign was meant to be an "internal" Catholic promotion of school desegregation, it spilled over as an object of controversy to the whole citizenry. Strong opposition came from some Catholics; strong support came from some non-Catholics.

(b) The program of education and propaganda demonstrated a lack of cooperation, both lateral and vertical, among the Catholic lay organizations of the archdiocese. The larger groups, like the Holy Name Societies, the Sodalities, the Knights of Columbus, lent no support to our efforts, nor did their officers state publicly that they endorsed the archbishop's moral position on the race problem. With the exception of the Legion of Mary, the Knights of Peter Claver, and the Catholic Students Mission Crusade, the organized Catholic laity in effect dissociated themselves from CHR and SERINCO.

(c) This refusal of the laity to cooperate with either the project or the archbishop could be laid largely at the door of the priests who acted as chaplains or directors of these groups. They had no plans, and apparently no intentions, for the eventual racial integration of Catholic lay groups. This lack of planning, of knowledge and techniques, of social engineering, was apparent also at the highest administrative levels of the archdiocese. There is no doubt that the archbishop, as he said, consulted his advisors on the race problem, who dealt admirably with the canonical and moral aspects of segregation but seemed to know little about the practical procedures of desegregation. At the end of the 1956 campaign there was still the widespread notion that you can "let things ride; things will work out by themselves; time will solve it; you are only causing trouble."

(d) This concentrated campaign of information and propaganda, and the enormous publicity which attended it, challenged the influence of the White Citizens' Councils of southern Louisiana. All other moderates and liberals who favored racial desegregation had been driven under cover. The work of CHR and SERINCO was no small achievement at a time when most of the political officials, both at Baton Rouge and New Orleans, were under the domination of the White Citizens' Councils and were preparing a massive program of resistance to public school integration.

I was back in New Orleans, teaching at Loyola University of the South, in the fall of 1960 when the so-called "New Orleans school crisis" occurred. I watched the repetition of the same central blunder. The civic officials of 1960, like the church officials of 1956, had no carefully planned, empirically viable program for school desegregation. In reference to the public school board, Inger says that "from 1956 to 1960, when they could have been preparing the public for desegregation, the board members were telling the public desegregation was not coming" (36). Church officials kept telling Catholics that the desegregation of parochial schools was coming, but after 1956 did practically nothing to prepare them for it. If there was a "Catholic plan," it was simply to imitate in September 1962 what the public schools had done successfully in September 1961.

Robert Crain pinpoints the public school crisis with a subtitle: "The Failure of an Elite," the civic leaders who failed to defy the White Citizens' Councils or to put pressure on Mayor Morrison and the school board members (37). Most of this civic elite were Catholics whom we had unsuccessfully invited to membership in the Commission on Human Rights as early as 1950. One of them agreed, and then declined, to be the principal speaker at the Catholic Interracial Sunday in 1953. Several of them were close advisors of Archbishop Rummel. They privately disapproved of the White Citizens' Council, but were "not yet" ready to favor school integration, and one was a member of Emile Wagner's Association of Catholic Laymen.

Is there any causal link between the public school crisis of 1960 and the Catholic desegregation campaign of 1956—and especially the previous 8 years of public interracial activities of CHR and SERINCO? This organized Catholic lay action was in preparation for the desegregation of Catholic schools by September, 1956, but it obviously failed since the Catholic schools remained segregated. It could be argued that this failure was a triumph for the racists, who may have felt that since they kept the Catholic schools from integrating in 1956, they could also keep the public schools from integrating in 1960 (38).

The White Citizens' Councils and their racist friends were indeed stronger in 1960 than they had been in 1956, but they also had a stronger opponent: Federal Judge J. Skelly Wright, who held steadfast throughout the whole period to the directives of the U.S. Supreme Court. The legal conscience of the court and its officials succeeded whereas the moral conscience of the Catholic church and its officials failed (39). Archbishop Rummel was old and tired when he finally resigned his office in October 1962, 1 month after he saw the opening of white Catholic schools to Negro pupils. He died in November 1964 at the age of 86.

His successor, Archbishop John Cody, was as formal and inaccessible as Archbishop Rummel had been informal and accessible. I could not reach him in the spring of 1963 when I proposed an interview survey of Negro Catholic parents whose children were then attending the integrated parochial elementary schools. Through one of the chancery functionaries he expressed disapproval of this research project, but our interviews with these parents revealed a high degree of satisfaction with the "new" situation, particularly with the Catholic sisters teaching in the schools. I did not pursue the research further because I was already then involved in the study of police handling of arrestees.

NOTES

1. I attended Allport's graduate seminar on the nature of Prejudice from which he later published a book with the same title (Reading, Mass., Addison-Wesley, 1954, and paperback in Anchor Books, 1958). And I also discussed with Stouffer his research findings on discrimination in the United States army. See Samuel Stouffer *et al.*, *The American Soldier: Combat and Its Aftermath* (Princeton, Princeton University Press, 1949).

2. The "model" for this procedure was St. Louis University where Negroes were admitted first to the graduate school, then to the college. The Catholic high schools in St. Louis were then integrated before the parochial schools.

3. In the spring semester of 1948 I conducted a class on inter-group relations in the evening division, in which most of the lectures were given by Negro professors. Negro students attended Loyola University for the first time in October 1950, when Father Louis Twomey established the Institute for Industrial Relations. These students earned "certificates" and not regular college credits toward an academic degree. The first Negro students, "officially" registered to obtain academic credits, were two religious Sisters of the Holy Family, who began taking Saturday courses at Loyola in September 1951.

4. The following year, 1948, I urged that this teacher institute be held on the campus of Loyola University which would grant the inservice credits, but this recommendation was rejected by the university administration.

5. For historical information see John T. Gillard, *Colored Catholics in the United States* (Baltimore, Josephite Press, 1941) and John LaFarge, *The Race Question and the Negro* (New York, Longman, Green, 1943).

6. Others had a similar expectation of New Orleans, which at least later "was considered the chink in the wall of the South's resistance to change. New Orleans was Catholic, tolerant, cultured, and residentially integrated." Morton Inger, *Politics and Reality in an American City* (New York, Center for Urban Education, 1969), p. 70.

7. This fact is largely neglected in the various accounts of New Orleans school desegregation. See *The New Orleans School Crisis*, eighty-three-page report of the Louisiana Advisory Committee to the U.S. Commission on Civil Rights (Washington, D.C., Government Printing Office, 1961); Warren Breed, "The Emergence of Pluralistic Public Opinion in a Community Crisis," pp. 127–146, in Alvin Gouldner and S. M. Miller, Eds., *Applied Sociology* (New York, Free Press, 1965); William A. Osborne, *The Segregated Covenant* (New York, Herder and Herder, 1967), pp. 74–76, and Robert L. Crain, *The Politics of School Desegregation*, Part III, "Desegregation in New Orleans," pp. 223–325 (Chicago, Aldine, 1968). Morton Inger, *op. cit.*, was based on the materials in Crain's book, on which he had given research assistance.

8. See the articles, "Southern Collegians Resist Racism," *The Catholic World* (December 1950), "Catholic College Students Active in Race Relations," *The Claverite* (April 1952), and "We Don't

Take Negroes Here," *The Catholic World* (January 1956). One of the older (now deceased) professors at Loyola University wrote to the editor of *The Catholic World* demanding the names of the students who submitted these articles.

9. For an earlier article see T. James McNamara, "The Catholic Committee of the South and the Negro," *Interracial Review* (July 1947) pp. 102–104.

10. "According to one unverified account," the archbishop's failure to speak up in the 3 years, 1957–1959, "was in part due to his advisers' having persuaded him that his pronouncements had gone beyond the demands of the Negroes." Crain, *op. cit.*, p. 249.

11. He did say that night that "we have a job to make democracy work, and we can do it only by being a brother to everyone who is a brother in Christ."

12. Frank S. Loescher, *The Protestant Church and the Negro* (New York, Association Press, 1948).

13. The archbishop had said that the Catholic schools would be desegregated "not before September 1956." This was a negative statement, but when that date approached he definitely promised to start school desegregation in September 1957 on a grade-per-year basis.

14. On December 29, 1954, Leander Perez addressed the Young Men's Business Club in New Orleans, ridiculing the Supreme Court for accepting the word of Myrdal whom he called "New York's political NAACP's hired social science consultant."

15. Everett won the James J. Hoey Award for Interracial Justice. His integrationist views were not shared by his editor-in-chief, Father Carl Schutten.

16. Father Balduc is featured in the previous chapter as the severest critic of my report on the *Southern Parish* research project. See pp. 52, 63. His objection to the McKenzie lecture was based on a statement of the Pontifical Biblical Commission, December 15, 1955, saying that meetings of scriptural experts should not be open to outsiders poorly prepared to evaluate what was being said. See *Enchiridion Biblicum* (4th ed., 1961), pp. 622–633.

17. Father Howard had spoken to my class in social problems in April 1948, the first Negro priest ever to have lectured at Loyola University of the South. In the class was policeman and part-time student, Hubert Badeaux, who later wrote a racist

"Commentary" on my research report of *Police Handling of Arrestees*. See p. 148.

18. This is, of course, mere speculation. In 1959 I was one of three co-chairmen of Save Our Schools (SOS) which, says Crain, "was full of Jews, integrationist Catholics, and non-Southerners. Hence they were unable to attract the moderates of the city even though SOS strategy wisely emphasized open schools rather than integrated schools." *Op. cit.*, p. 251.

19. In light of this tremendous publicity and of available printed accounts, it is disconcerting that Breed, *op. cit.*, p. 131, could write off this integrationist campaign with one sentence: "An organization backed by the Catholic hierarchy published pamphlets and presented a series of excellent speakers, but attendance was negligible and nothing further was tried." It is true that Professor Breed did not participate in the program, but others from the Tulane faculty did, among them Helen Cassidy, Munro Edmunson, William Kolb, Harold Lief, and Robert Lystad.

20. The Young Men's Business Club, which welcomed speakers like Leander Perez at the end of 1954, passed a resolution a year later, condemning the "Communist leadership" of SCEF.

21. Who always had a Christian clergyman pray a benediction at their rallies, even the one on November 15, 1960, when Rainach, Perez, and other racists incited the mob action that occurred the next day. See James Lawrence, "The Scandal of New Orleans," *Commonweal*, Vol. 73 (February 3, 1951), pp. 475–476.

22. It was only months later that I discovered the identity of Wagner's emissary. He was Father Carl Schutten, editor-in-chief of the archdiocesan weekly newspaper.

23. The "Communist charges" against Hulan Jack were patently absurd, but his reputation was considerably lessened in 1961 when he got a suspended 1-year sentence on a charge of bribery and was relieved of his office as borough president. He claimed that it was a "loan" and not a "bribe" when a realty operator paid the cost of 4,400 dollars for remodeling his apartment. In December 1970 he was again in trouble, charged with conspiracy to profit illegally from food distributors doing business with Harlem supermarkets. In April 1972 he was found guilty on one count of conspiracy and nine counts of aiding and abetting in the unlawful payment of funds by employers to employees in the grocery industry. See *New York Times*, April 25, 1972.

24. The propaganda of the White Citizens' Councils became increasingly anti-semitic during the next few years. This point has not been noted in the published commentaries on the New Orleans school crisis of 1960.

25. See Chapter Four.

26. The "excuse" was later made that *all* members of the board of the Urban League were booed, and that the archbishop was not singled out.

27. This letter was given wide newspaper publicity. As far as I know, this investigation of me was not undertaken by the FBI. Earlier, in 1948, an FBI agent made enquiries about me to Father Thomas Shields, then president of Loyola University, after I had appeared on a Sodality program at Jesuit High School with Albert Dent, president of Dillard University.

28. Proposed by State Senator Willie Rainach, president of the White Citizens' Councils Association, who helped to prepare at least forty bills on racial segregation.

29. In the *Times-Picayune* of May 25, 1956, Irwin took note of the fact that CHR had not filed a list of its members. "Thus, like the outlawed NAACP, this committee is without right to function in the State of Louisiana. It exists in violation of the laws of the State of Louisiana, and its officers, according to these laws, are subject to imprisonment."

30. The Fund for the Republic, like similar agencies, made its financial grants only to tax-exempt, nonprofit organizations. Because of involvement in interracial activities on and off the campus, since 1948 Loyola University was subject to complaints from alumni and attacks from racist groups. This was unquestionably the main reason why the president and board of directors declined a further grant from the Fund for the Republic in the autumn of 1956.

31. This was the beginning of his "3-year silence" which was not broken till July 1959, when he announced that the Catholic schools would be integrated as soon as possible, but "definitely not later than when the public schools are integrated."

32. And it was at this time that Father Sheehan was preparing to resign from the Catholic priesthood.

33. This was an unexpected proposal. The former chaplain of the Sodalities had consistently prevented Xavier University from admission to the New Orleans College Sodality Union.

34. With easy hindsight, Crain, *op. cit.*, p. 248, could say that in 1960 the public school board members "found themselves even more stranded when the expected moral example of the Catholic Church never materialized. Everyone had expected the Church to pave the way for community acceptance of desegregation."

35. See Stephen Ryan, "After Jesuit Bend," *America* (February 4, 1956). He cites the case of Erath, Louisiana, where Bishop Jeanmard excommunicated two women for physically interfering with racially integrated catechism classes.

36. Inger, *op. cit.*, p. 76.

37. Crain, *op. cit.*, pp. 237–291.

38. Actually they did succeed in preventing public school integration until September 1961.

39. See my articles, "The Catholic South and Race," *Religious Education* (January-February 1964), pp. 30–33, and "American Religion and the Negro," *Daedalus* (Fall 1965), pp. 1085–1106.

FOUR

POLICE HANDLING
OF ARRESTEES

On a Friday morning in March 1964 three public officials in New Orleans received hand-delivered envelopes marked "personal and important," which contained a mimeographed sixty-page report of a survey entitled *Police Handling of Arrestees in New Orleans*. Two of them, Mayor Victor Schiro and Police Superintendent Joseph Giarrusso, paid no attention to it and were taken by surprise 3 days later when the news media carried the story of the report on Monday evening, March 23. They were immediately defensive and outraged by all the "slurs, innuendos, and errors" contained in the report.

The third public official, District Attorney Jim Garrison, read the report as soon as it reached his office and declared it to be "an excellent study with immense practical value." This judgment, differing sharply from that of the mayor and the police chief, was to be expected in view of the ongoing "feud" between the district attorney's office and the police department. In the previous year Garrison had said that he has more trouble with the command of the police department than with all the racketeers in town (1). Meanwhile, Giarrusso was conducting a police investigation of the district attorney's office. He had said in May 1963 that public confidence in the police is irreparably harmed when the district attorney and the police department "are constantly engaged in one public controversy after another."

My research monograph, which evoked this and much more disagreement, reported on an interview survey of a representative sample of New Orleans residents who had been arrested by the police for law violations during 1962 and 1963. The report confirmed the praiseworthy fact that the great majority of policemen handle arrestees in a routine, professional manner. There was, however, selectivity in the arrest procedures that discriminated by sex, race, and social status, and by some types of violations like homosexuality and drunkenness. In spite of obvious and measurable improvement in the police department since a 1954 investigation by the metropolitan crime commission, there remained a hard core of officers guilty of brutality, thievery, obscenity, and sexual aggression against arrested persons.

No interested citizen who watched the New Orleans police—or any other large city police department—should have been "taken by surprise" by a report of this kind. Competent news reporters ferret out some instances of police misbehavior all over the country, and New Orleans is probably no better—or worse—than other American cities. Yet, there were four main complaints about this particular research report. Mayor Schiro felt that this was a most inopportune time to make such reports because the training and morale of the department were constantly improving (2). Superintendent Giarrusso said that information of this kind should be brought to him in confidence so that he could clean up the department "from within" (3). John Kelly, president of the Fraternal Order of Police, complained that it "cast untrue reflection" on every police officer and his family. George Singelman, secretary of the White Citizens' Council, smelled a subversive conspiracy behind the study and called its author "an advance agent of propaganda to neutralize the police force for Negro rights groups" (4).

HOW THE RESEARCH STARTED. In 1962, after returning from Chile where I had spent the previous year studying attitudes toward social change which resulted in a monograph entitled *Cambio Social en Chile*, my research interests were focused on the military. The Catholic chaplains at Lackland Air Force Base in Texas had gathered more than 7,000 questionnaires from Catholic trainees there and had asked me to do a report on their data (5). This aroused my interest in a possible research study of military chaplains as a specialized occupational category within the Catholic church. This was a forlorn expectation. Interviews and correspondence with chaplains and ex-chaplains and two visits to the chief of chaplains office in Washington convinced me that the "brass" would not permit this type of research. Meanwhile I surveyed students in the ROTC program at Loyola University of the South and at Louisiana State University. At that time the ROTC had not yet become a burning issue on the college campus, nor were there any funds available to support a wider research project.

The fact that I then turned to the subject of police and the civil rights of citizens does not mean that this was a new interest for me. Much earlier, in March 1948, I had invited Captain Blancher of the police department to talk to my sociology class on the topic of "police relations with minority groups." He was denied permission by the assistant superintendent, William C. Maher, who told me that he did not want the department to become involved in such controversial issues.

Much had happened in the decade and a half since 1948, and the public issue of civil rights was coming more and more to the fore. It was a subject that cried out for scientific research in Louisiana and a matter I often discussed informally with Jack Nelson who for a while was a legal assistant in the district attorney's office, and with Albert Dent, president of Negro Dillard University in New Orleans. In the fall of 1962 I asked them if they thought it worthwhile to analyze the records of police arrests over the past decade to search for a progressive trend of improvement in the police department. I proposed that we take an annual random sample of arrestees from the punch card files of the data-processing unit of the police department. This proved overambitious because of the enormous file of records and particularly because data processing of records had been only recently introduced. I decided then to explore the records for only one year, 1962, as a pilot study for further research.

I could only hypothesize that our prospective research findings would tie in with problems of civil rights, a matter I discussed in early January 1963 with a subgroup of the Louisiana Advisory Committee to the U.S. Commission on Civil Rights (6). Dent and Nelson were part of this group and present at the discussion, as were Dr. Harold Lief, psychiatrist at the Tulane University School of Medicine, and Professor Ralph Slovenko of the Tulane University School of Law. The main purpose of this meeting was to plan the contents of the next annual report on Louisiana to be submitted to the U.S. Commission on Civil Rights (7).

During the course of the conversation I expressed dissatisfaction with the scattered and vague generalizations that made up the annual reports from the advisory committees of the various states. I realized that these state reports certainly had a cumulative impact, provided a broad picture of violations of civil rights around the country, but they lacked the scientific rigor that tests hypotheses, draws conclusions from reliable data, and leads to realistic programs of social reform. I was not suggesting that the next annual report of the Louisiana Advisory Committee should be delayed until a statewide scientific study could be made of all facets of civil rights. The time, money, and personnel required for a study of this scope were simply not available to us. On the other hand, I was not enthusiastic about involving myself in gathering and analyzing limited data for a generalized report to the commission.

Nevertheless, our conversation that night ranged over the litany of specific areas in which there was evidence of violation of civil rights. We knew that the sugar cane workers and other farm laborers suffered discrimination (8). There was unequal access to educational opportunities and recreational facilities and to public services such as garbage collection, street cleaning and repair, and police and fire protection. Although the problem of denial of civil rights tended to focus on relations between whites and Negroes, I felt that the study I proposed should not "feature" race relations. This decision seems important in the light of subsequent charges made against me, my study consultants, and research assistants.

Among the public agencies serving the adult population, the New Orleans police department dealt potentially with all citizens of whatever category: age, sex, race, education, and occupational and social class. If we studied the arrests made by the police officers we could find whether there were evidences of discrimination in any of these categories of the whole population spectrum (9). A practical consideration favoring this approach was the fact that I had just been awarded a grant of 1,180 dollars from the National Science Foundation under its institutional grant for unrestricted research made to Loyola University of the South. Furthermore, President Dent assured me that there was a small contingency fund for research at Dillard University and that up to 2,000 dollars of that money could be made available for the project.

POLICE CHIEF'S APPROVAL. Since I proposed to study the record of arrests made by the New Orleans police department I needed access to the records and obviously could not proceed without the permission of Superintendent Giarrusso and the cooperation of his employees. It seems necessary to prove at this point that I had this permission and cooperation, because when the report was made public in 1964 Giarrusso stated publicly that he did not know me, that he was unaware the research was being done, and that he did not cooperate with my research team.

On January 9, 1963, I wrote to Superintendent Giarrusso to say that "we are contemplating a sociological analysis of a sample of persons arrested by the New Orleans police." I told him further that "this afternoon I visited the police record room and spoke with both Sergeant Lionel Estopinal and Mr. Desmond Boudreaux. They very courteously showed me around the excellent IBM facilities in use there, and also explained what kind of data are punched onto the IBM cards." After briefly explaining our intended procedures, I concluded with the request: "May I have your authorization to collect these materials and to proceed with the study?"

That afternoon I had told Desmond Boudreaux that I wanted a random sample of about 4,000 cards of adult New Orleans residents who had been arrested in 1962. He said that juvenile records were kept separately, but that other punch cards on arrestees were boxed in sequence by date of arrest, and that it would be a "big job" to separate residents from nonresidents, or even traffic violators from persons arrested on other charges. He was cooperative but indicated that all the employees there were then overburdened with work. The police statistical bureau was still in the process of moving to city hall where all official data processing was being combined. Five days later he phoned me for particulars on my request so that he could estimate the cost and the man-hours required to select and reproduce the punch cards I wanted.

Boudreaux had received instructions from Giarrusso, who on January 16 wrote to me in response to my request of a week earlier. He said that he was authorizing Mr. Robert Develle, director of finance for the city of New Orleans, to release the information I was seeking. He was careful to point out that this was not an order or a "directive" to Mr. Develle, who was in charge of the data-processing unit where the information was stored. At any rate, he graciously suggested that I call on him again in the event that he could be of further assistance in my research.

The police chief's "nondirective" was promptly delivered to the statistical unit of the department. That same afternoon (January 16) I had a telephone call from Major Finerty saying that they had authorization from the superintendent to cooperate with us, but there was a genuine problem of manpower shortage just now to fit this request into their busy schedule. In order to save him time and work, and to save us money, I offered to come to City Hall with my assistant, Brian Jordan, so that we could ourselves select the sample and reproduce the punch cards. We agreed on an appropriate date, the next Wednesday, January 23.

The official police statistics for 1962, which had been compiled but not yet published, showed that there had been 67,486 adult arrests made in New Orleans during that year. I decided that the simplest procedure was to take a 6 percent random sample of this total without regard to place of residence or type of alleged violation. At this point an ethical question arose for Desmond Boudreaux and A. J. Labatut, who agreed on the sample but realized that each IBM card carried the name of the person arrested. They were unwilling to take the responsibility of releasing these names to us, and called for a decision from their superior, Robert Develle, who in turn brought the problem to Superintendent Giarrusso. The latter decided that our sample of arrest cards could be reproduced, but that the names of arrestees must be deleted.

This reluctance to release the names of arrestees was understandable because, as Boudreaux commented, there were
some people of "good reputation" who had been arrested.
This was no hindrance to the initial stage of the research,
which intended simply to analyze and compare categories of
arrestees according to demographic characteristics. At any
rate, I wrote a letter of thanks to Boudreaux on January 26
and raised questions about certain coding problems on the
data cards, to which he supplied prompt answers. Three days
later, January 29, I wrote Superintendent Giarrusso to thank
him again for his cooperation and to say that "this is more-
or-less a pilot study of the available data. If our hypotheses
test out and we find anything that seems interesting we shall
inform you of it."

WHO GETS ARRESTED.   Three months later, at the beginning of May, we were ready with our report covering police arrests during 1962. This was a fifty-five-page mimeographed monograph, containing twenty-six tables of comparative data with interpretive comments and was entitled *Who Gets Arrested in New Orleans?* (10). On May 13
Superintendent Giarrusso acknowledged receipt of this report,
commenting that he had "glanced" through it and thought
that many of the statistics were interesting. He promised to
study the report in more detail as soon as possible. Again on
this occasion he invited me to call upon him at any time I
needed information or help.

All of this seemed to vanish from the police superintendent's memory when he later told news reporters that he was
unaware of the sociological study I was conducting. As we
entered the second stage of the study I asked him for further
information, this time for copies of all letters, both of complaints and compliments, received by the police department
during 1962. On May 21, 1963, he responded to this request,

saying that he would be happy to participate in the survey by providing copies of all these letters.

The report I presented to the chief of police and to the Louisiana Advisory Committee of the U.S. Commission on Civil Rights could hardly be called a "shocking revelation" of police behavior. Probably everybody already knew the conclusion from our data, that "individual police officers wield an unusual degree of discretionary power in making arrests." Probably everyone also surmised that "the type of persons who are arrested differs significantly from the general adult population of the city." Implicit in both of these statements is the fact made explicitly by our data, "that the internal differences in the arrested population evoke differential treatment of arrestees by law enforcement officers."

The empirical data we had so far collected confirmed this finding that the discretionary power of the arresting officer was often employed in New Orleans to select the kinds of people who were arrested. Our subcommittee on the administration of justice saw this as a potential violation of civil rights. The fact that relatively the same findings could have been made from the same kind of probe in many other American cities did not decrease the significance of these conclusions. As far as we know, Giarrusso made no practical use of the report. He probably filed it and forgot it. After all, it was a confidential, unpublicized report, compiled and analyzed as a service to the police department at no expense to either the police or the public.

What were the evidences in this first report that pointed to discriminatory arrest patterns in New Orleans? We find them in the comparison between the population statistics of the city in the 1960 census and the data we collected from police records on the age, sex, race, employment, and other characteristics of people arrested in 1962. The disproportions loom large: for example, although Negro males constituted only 15 percent of the adult population, they accounted for

51 percent of the resident arrestees. Twenty-six percent of white males in the population were unskilled or semi-skilled workers, but 53 percent of white males arrested were in these occupational categories.

Up to this point, and with this kind of comparative information, we did not know how the police actually handled arrestees, or why they arrested proportionately more laborers than white-collar workers, more males than females, more Negroes than whites, or why there were significant age differences between arrestees and citizens in general. We note, for example, that only 15 percent of New Orleans white females were under 25 years of age, but 34 percent of white female arrestees were in this age category.

Insofar as arrest records can be employed as a measurement of law violation, they show everywhere in the United States that crime rates are highest where the people are poorest and where economic conditions are worst. It is a widely reported generalization among criminologists that arrest rates are higher among low-income Negroes than among middle- and upper-class whites, and that the proportions of lawbreakers vary with reference to their age and sex (11). Perhaps less widely known are the following kinds of data derived from the New Orleans arrest records: white women are more likely than black women to be charged with prostitution; on the other hand, a black female is twice as likely as a white female to be arrested in New Orleans. Females of both races are more likely than males to have multiple charges placed against them by the arresting officer. The so-called "round-up" or group arrest, is made more often with Negroes than whites, but a greater proportion of the charges against Negroes are dismissed than are those against whites.

This report on arrestees during 1962 was the end of the "first stage" of our larger research project, and it constituted, as President Dent said, the "police side" of the story. We knew that the small institutional grant from the National Science Foundation could not support the whole study and that stages of a research project are not as clearly defined as they appear to be. In early March I had written up a proposal which Dent submitted to the Field Foundation requesting that a grant of 6,000 dollars be made to Dillard University for the purpose of getting the "citizen side" of the story. This request was immediately honored, and we were assured financial support to continue the study.

The research design called for the selection of an exact rep-representative sample of 200 New Orleans residents to be interviewed from among those who had been arrested in 1962. There were 39 arrested on traffic charges and 161 on other charges. On both kinds of charges we had a distribution by age, sex, and race. This meant that we had to interview 85 whites (74 males, 11 females) and 115 blacks (103 males, 12 females). The attempt to locate these people for interviews constituted the largest problem of the whole study.

ASSISTANTS, PROBLEMS, AND PROCEDURES. It was no problem to construct this precisely proportional sample from the punch cards previously obtained from the police bureau of statistics, but it was difficult to reach these people for interviews because their names and addresses had been erased from the cards. All other information, however, remained on the cards: the serial number of the arrest, the police precinct where the person was booked, the date of arrest, the type of charge, the age, the sex, and the race. It was, then, an arduous, time-consuming job to find the names and addresses of the selected sample of arrestees.

The man who did this arduous task was Brian Jordan, who had a master's degree in sociology from Fordham University and was chief research assistant on this study from January through September, when he left to continue graduate study at Louisiana State University. Fortunately, one of his areas of competence and interest was criminology. He clearly identified himself as a criminologist doing a study for the Loyola Department of Sociology and was received with friendly cooperation among the police officers with whom he came in contact. By this time, the precinct record books of 1962 arrests had been gathered at police headquarters. These were by law a public record open to the investigation of qualified persons, and Captain Murry readily granted Jordan access to them.

Jordan later recalled this experience.

> "I spent about a month down at central headquarters on Broad Street matching the serial number of arrest with the corresponding name and address of the arrestee in the precinct book. On each of the original, selected list of arrestees I copied out all available information including the name of the arresting officer, the circumstances of the arrest, and where given the names of lawyers and witnesses. It took me from about mid-March to mid-April to put together this original list of the 200 people we intended to interview."

As a well-dressed, personable, soft-spoken, and well-educated, white man, Jordan was treated with genuine courtesy. One of the unanticipated but valuable by-products of this situation was that he had many informal conversations, often over a cup of coffee, with various key police officers at headquarters. The same was the case when he had to visit the precinct stations to find names of substitute interviewees who were listed as current arrestees of 1963. There too he talked with friendly policemen, several of whom urged him to "join the force." Nevertheless, on March 25, 1964, the police chief told newsmen he doubted that any of my researchers talked to any policemen, as claimed.

Jordan continues his account:

"After almost 2 months of active interviewing it became
clear that many of the 1962 arrestees on our list had
moved away, given false addresses, or just couldn't be
contacted. As I followed up these people I was reaching
only about one out of three on our list. So, I contacted
Captain Joseph H. Murry, acting supervisor of police dis-
tricts and got from him a carte blanche letter of introduction to the local district captains asking them for their
cooperation in our sociological arrest study (12). Except
for the captain of the second district, they all willingly
opened their books to me."

At this point it was obvious that we needed a team of interviewers if we were to locate and talk with 200 arrestees
within a reasonable period of time. Professor Harold Lief
helped in the construction of the interview schedule to be
used and gave some informal training to the interviewers. Besides Jordan, these were Tom Lief, then a graduate student at
Tulane University, and three Negro interviewers from Dillard University, Barbara Guillory, William Washington, and
Roy Winand. Tracking down and interviewing the arrested
persons continued into September 1963. Gaining their confidence so that they would be willing to talk frankly about
their experiences with the police was eased by the fact that
white interviewers dealt with white arrestees, and black with
blacks. Barbara Guillory talked with Negro women arrestees,
but we did not have a white female interviewer.

The inability to locate many of the people arrested in 1962
meant that their substitutes taken from the police blotters of
1963 were often still waiting for the disposal of their cases. It
meant also, however, that we obtained even more up-to-date
information on police behavior from people whose experiences were fresh in their minds. A minority of arrestees, especially repeaters (as well as homosexuals, alcoholics, and drug
addicts) who were "known" to the police, evidenced suspicion of the interviewers and fear of police reprisals. A minority also was strongly hostile to the police, especially some

whites who claimed they were wrongfully arrested, and some blacks who said they were brutalized by the arresting officer.

During the summer of 1963, part of which I spent lecturing at the Universidad Ibero-Americana in Mexico City, Brian Jordan continued as chief investigator on the study. He and Tom Lief conducted all of the interviews with white arrestees, but the problem of searching out the matching sample was a persistent one. Jordan kept going back to the precinct stations to check the arrest records and to carry on informal conversations with friendly policemen. The officers unwittingly provided considerable "inside" information on their attitudes and behavior to arrestees that was most valuable to us. As a skilled interviewer, Jordan was able to "guide" these conversations, during which he took no notes, but immediately after which he transcribed to his notebook. For accuracy, he regretted often that he did not carry a hidden microphone to record these conversations (13).

Some of the arrested persons on our list were easy to find —they were being held in the parish (county) prison. Jordan interviewed the arrestees of both races there. He reports: "I introduced myself to Louis Hyde, sheriff in charge of the prison, and told him I was a criminologist helping with Loyola's sociological study of arrested persons and told him I wanted to talk with several prisoners whose names I had. He said okay and introduced me to the gate guard. On later visits the guard mistook me for an attorney and would call down any prisoner to the 'talk box' for me." As part of our investigation he also visited the "show-up" of prisoners that took place mornings and evenings in the basement of police headquarters. Here, too, he was given courteous cooperation by the police.

In only one instance did the police raise questions about what we were doing on this research project. This was in mid-July when Roy Winand encountered a Negro ex-preacher who had been arrested and who refused to be interviewed. He phoned the Dean of Students at Loyola University and asked "what's going on out there?" and "are you sending out Negro students to harass people?" He was dissatisfied with the explanation of the sociological study and lodged a complaint with Major Theriot of the superintendent's office. The latter dispatched two officers to talk with the dean to find out whether a "race study" was going on. They appeared to be satisfied with the explanation given by the dean, who suggested that they contact me on my return from Mexico (14).

After the final report of the study was released in March 1964, Superintendent Giarrusso complained that we had not come for information to the "top administrators" of the police department. He must have been unaware of the fact that we did have lengthy interviews with three of his department heads, whose names we did not divulge in the report and who were certainly quite willing to remain anonymous after the report was greeted with such vigorous condemnation by their police superintendent.

PROTECTING INFORMANTS.   This "anonymity" of the research report was particularly irksome to John Kelly, president of the New Orleans branch of the Fraternal Order of Police, who visited me in a belligerent mood 2 days after the report was released. He said that I had "whitewashed" Giarrusso and the top people in the department but had defamed the rank-and-file policemen, of whom he said he represented 97 percent. He insisted that no policeman had ever been interviewed by any of our research assistants and demanded to know where he could find "that liar, Jordan." (By this time, Jordan was continuing graduate studies in psychology at Louisiana State University.)

There was then an odd switch in the conversation when Kelly said that "we've got to protect the reputation of people." He said that the police always protect clergymen "who get into trouble" and why should a clergyman like me try to expose the faults of the police. I agreed that people's reputations should not be sullied and that this was the very reason why I could not give him the names of our informants, whether they were policemen, lawyers, judges, witnesses, or arrested people. At that point I gave him a copy of the final report and asked him to withhold judgment until he had read it. He replied, "I don't care what you wrote there. You defamed the police, and all the damage has already been done. We'll get to the bottom of this."

A special meeting was called that same night by Kelly's organization, at which two biracial investigative committees of police members were appointed. One was charged to obtain from me the confidential information on which the report was based, interview the informants who gave it, investigate all the statments and charges made, determine their validity, and issue a report to the public. As far as I know, this committee did not function at all. No member of it ever contacted me, my five research assistants, or any members of the subcommittee on the administration of justice of the civil rights commission.

The other appointed committee of the Fraternal Order of Police was ordered to investigate "the integrity, character, sense of responsibility, impartiality, and associations of the persons responsible for the report and the real reasons for the issuance of the report." I do not know whether, or how, they conducted this investigation. In a sense their work was done for them by the White Citizens' Council of Greater New Orleans who later published a detailed "expose" of the integrationist, left-wing tendencies and Communist associations of myself and my fellow members of the subcommittee on the administration of justice in civil rights. They also uncovered the "leftist" history of the Field Foundation which had made the research grant to Dillard University.

Quite aside from the promised and expected confidentiality of our sources of information, we could obviously not hand over the names of our informants to angry people like Kelly and the White Citizens' Council (15). In the report itself I wrote that we were "following the example of police officials, who refused to divulge the names of arrestees, as well as of officers against whom complaints had been lodged." This should have satisfied even those who did not recognize the ethics of social science research. I continued,

> we have carefully concealed the identity of all our informants: arrestees themselves, their witnesses and friends, lawyers, policemen, and judges. The code numbers within parentheses, which appear throughout this report, are simply a handy reference to the materials in our files. Since we have promised confidentiality to all our interviewees, these materials will be destroyed at a convenient time in order to protect completely our sources of information.

Because I did not provide specific names of people involved in specific cases of police handling of arrestees, I was accused even by Giarrusso and Schiro of making "unsubstantiated" charges against the New Orleans police. In this instance Giarrusso made no direct request to me for my sources of information, but he did insist that "we look into every complaint against the police and try to correct it." The police department has its own bureau of investigation to check on charges of misconduct on the part of officers. On a previous occasion, in early 1949, I visited the superintendent, then Joseph Scheuring, concerning the charge that a Negro prisoner had been beaten. He had his secretary bring in the file on the case and hand it to me. It contained testimony, in almost identical words, by three policemen who stated that the arrestee had fallen and hit his head against a vending machine, and that this had caused his injuries. When I asked him for the rest of the testimony which might determine whether the truth was being told by the policemen or by the prisoner, he seemed amazed at such a request.

Our research notes, 14 years later, contain this remark: "the police reports of arrests frequently cited a cigarette machine at Parish Prison located between the paddy wagon stop and the cell block. 'Falling and hitting the head' on this machine was the cause of many split heads." Nevertheless, I felt that in 1963 the procedure of investigation in such cases had improved under the leadership of Superintendent Giarrusso, from whom I asked permission to study the central file at headquarters that contained both compliments and complaints about the police. On May 21, 1963, he granted this request with a carbon copy of his letter for Captain Lloyd Poissenot and Desk Sergeant (Miss) L. Torpie, who gave us full cooperation during subsequent weeks (16).

What we found among the documents in the central file were unsolicited letters from New Orleans citizens, running four to one in favor of the police. From January to December 1962 the police department placed in this file 1,235 letters of appreciation and only 301 letters of complaint. None of the latter gave the badge number or name of any policeman, although this information was frequently found in the letters of approval. None of the complaint letters made the kind of serious charge against officers that sometimes appeared in the headlines of New Orleans newspapers.

Since I was seeking a balanced appraisal of the relation between police officer and citizen, "both the good and the bad," I was glad to analyze this large volume of letters of approval, and did so in the final report (17). But the compliments were not balanced by the complaints. I phoned Captain Poissenot in early June and asked whether there were other letters of complaint about police misconduct that were not contained in the central file. He replied that there were many of them, that every case was fully investigated, and that the record was securely locked up in the police bureau of investigation. He said further that I could not be allowed access to these records because "it is necessary to protect the reputation of everyone involved in these cases." It appears that Giarusso made a mental reservation when he promised to let me have copies of *all* letters of complaint received by the Department during 1962. When reporters questioned him in 1964 he said he had investigated sixty-two charges of alleged brutality.

This reluctance to expose the negative aspects of police work is understandable, but I have no idea to what extent —if at all—the "missing" data from the central file would have altered the final report. We kept up our search for information from the public records of arrests as maintained currently in the police precincts. The arresting officer was required to fill out a standard form on each occasion, and these forms are open to public scrutiny. We read there the behavior of the arrestee as well as that of the police. Obviously, none of these accounts indicated any irregularity or misconduct on the part of law enforcement officers.

Superintendent Giarrusso protected his sources of information, and I protected mine. Another New Orleans citizen, Aaron Kohn, who was professionally interested in the behavior of the police, suffered several prison sentences for contempt of court when he refused to divulge his sources of information. He was head of the Metropolitan Crime Commission which had been established a decade earlier by a Special Citizens' Investigating Committee of the New Orleans City Council (18). His persistent refusal to reveal the names of informants brought him harassment from public officials and sympathy from local news editors.

DID WE DEFAME THE POLICE?   Aaron Kohn's massive investigation of the New Orleans police department was reported in six volumes of mimeographed pages in April 1954. It unearthed an embarrassing amount of police corruption and brutality, and although Mayor Morrison and Superintendent Scheuring angrily and publicly denounced the report and its author, there was a notable subsequent improvement of police behavior in New Orleans. The Metropolitan Crime Commission had been established precisely to investigate an intolerable situation that "everybody knew about." In other words, there was an evil situation, and the evil doers had to be ferreted out.

The approach we used in studying the police handling of arrested persons deliberately avoided a focus on the negative aspects of police behavior. It is true that the inspiration for the study came out of the concerns of the U.S. Commission on Civil Rights, but it is also true that the observance of civil rights is as open to social science research as is the violation of civil rights. We expected to find both commendable and condemnable examples of the manner in which police deal with the people they arrest—and our expectations were fulfilled.

The design and intent of the research project would have been entirely different if we had decided to make a study of police brutality. We would have searched out—and easily found—large numbers of New Orleans citizens who complained about the way the officers treated them on arrest. As a matter of fact, during the course of our own research project several lawyers offered to give us a list of citizens who had such complaints about the police, but we refused and told them this was not the type of study in which we were engaged.

The interview schedule we used had been carefully pretested with several arrested people who were not in our representative sample. There were no "lead" questions that might prejudice the interviewees or suggest that we were looking only for the "bad actors" on the police force. Here are a few of the questions we asked: "Would you tell us how the police treated you? Were they polite and courteous? Did they treat you fairly or unfairly? Did the police handle you gently or roughly? They say that they handle people the way they deserve to be handled. Was this true in your case?"

All the information and statistics we gathered in this year-long study pointed to the fact that police officers in New Orleans for the most part acted like well-trained professionals when they made arrests. An editorial in the *States-Item* on March 25, 1964, said that "since most policemen were found to handle arrested persons in a routine, professional manner, the picture seems largely favorable." I argued vigorously and publicly that the report of this objective, scientific survey provided the first genuine demonstration of the improvement that Giarrusso had brought to the police department.

On the basis of the findings, however, I had to say in the report that there was still a "hard core" of police discrimination in the arrest process. This term, "hard core" seemed to arouse volatile emotions as well as deep misunderstanding (19). In her *States-Item* column for March 28, Iris Kelso noted that my report

> saying that a hard core of the police department is still guilty of mistreating prisoners made Mayor Schiro and Superintendent Giarrusso fighting mad this week. In fact, they sounded a good bit like former Mayor Chep Morrison and former Superintendent Joseph Scheuring did when the SCIC report on police graft came out in 1954. "Slurs and innuendos," they said, ignoring the fact that the report really gave the police department a pat on the back for overall improvement.

This statement about "overall improvement" should not lead to the conclusion that we had intended to make a study of all aspects of law enforcement in New Orleans. This would have been an unmanageable task beyond our research resources in money and personnel. In focusing on the relationship between the officer and the arrested person we did find some instances of thievery, obscenity, and sexual aggression on the part of police, but public attention seemed drawn mainly to charges of police brutality (20).

The matter of police brutality was occasionally in the news during the period we were doing our interviews in 1963, but everyone seemed to agree that it was nothing like a decade earlier when a chief of detectives told a luncheon club about the practice of giving arrestees "ice cream and cake," meaning torture to extract information and confessions. In May 1963 District Attorney Garrison, also addressing a luncheon club, said that he "had detected a pattern of brutality, not sanctioned by present officials of the police department, but also not stopped by them through any organized effort" (21).

This was another scene in the continuing feud between Garrison and Giarrusso. The district attorney complained that when the department investigated charges of brutality among its own officers the reports were "doctored up" and "orchestrated." He filed charges in five specific cases, involving nine policemen, but Giarrusso refused to suspend these men until sufficient evidence had been produced. An assistant district attorney said that "we are intent upon abolishing the custom of brutality in this city and making sure that fear and terror are not a part of our law enforcement process."

One of the most significant findings of our study was laudatory of Giarrusso and his policemen: the great majority (79 percent) of the arrestees interviewed by us did not complain about rough handling by the police. There is often a certain amount of "pushing and shoving" in the arrest process that can hardly be termed brutality. It seems significant too that the more serious charge—that the officer actually punched or beat the arrestee—was made by a higher proportion of whites (21 percent) than of Negroes (16 percent). Several of the Negroes who had been frequently arrested said that since Jim Garrison became district attorney there was much less beating of prisoners. None of them seemed aware of the fact that Giarrusso and other top police officials were mainly instrumental in decreasing the amount of police brutality.

During the same year there were a number of headlined cases of "graft," rolling of drunks, and public bribery on the part of the police. When he had indications of such conduct Giarrusso arranged a stake-out and apprehended the guilty officer, who was then suspended and booked. These instances were given full publicity by the superintendent who said "I am determined that the few men, out of more than a thousand, who choose to commit acts of wrongdoing will be detected and suffer the consequences." In our interviews we uncovered instances of alleged police thievery, but the general conclusion was that the "graft-ridden" days of the New Orleans police department had long since come to an end. In the great majority (86 percent) of our interviews with arrested people there were no allegations of such financial irregularities.

One of the complaints made by some people was that police officers abuse arrestees verbally, "constantly using foul and obscene language." Yet, the specific data of our study do not support the common allegation that the New Orleans police always and indiscriminately use foul and abusive language with arrested persons. A higher proportion of women (35 percent) than of men (25 percent) complained about the obscenity used by the arresting officer, but this still leaves the largest majority of instances in which such objectionable language was not used. The sociological significance of our findings was the fact that only certain kinds of people were the objects of abusive, tough and obscene language.

There are still a few policemen in New Orleans who do not believe me when I insist that the purpose of the research project was not to attack the police department, and that its result was not a defamation of the character of all local law officers. If the report itself did not convince them of our scientific objectivity, probably nothing else could convince them. It is a little more difficult to clear myself of the complaint that the research project was part of the whole conspiracy of the "race-mixers" and racial integrationists.

WAS IT A "RACE STUDY?"   Ever since its establishment in 1957, the U.S. Commission on Civil Rights meant only one thing to most white Louisianans: it meant the federal (northern) insistence on integration of Negroes in employment, schools, housing, public facilities, and all other previously segregated situations. The fact that the impetus for this study came from people who were in favor of civil rights for all citizens was enough to brand it immediately as a "race study." In a column-long editorial in the *Times-Picayune* for April 3, 1964, the writer took the trouble to point out that "Fr. Fichter's involvement in race matters and his standing as a controversial figure is recognized." It was to be expected that in a deep-south city like New Orleans the issue of race relations would be of overriding concern.

The most furious and sustained attack on the research report—surpassing even the displeasure of the mayor, the superintendent of police and the president of the Fraternal Order of Police—was launched by the members of the White Citizens' Council. One of its officials wrote that "although the Fichter Report pretends to be devoted to examining Police Handling of Arrestees, the bulk of the text is devoted to attempts to prove that the New Orleans police discriminate against Negroes." Furthermore, "one will notice that a studied attempt has been made to portray Negroes as selected victims of prejudice and discrimination" (22).

Even before plans were drawn up for the study of police relations with arrested citizens, I rejected outright two potential approaches, or perspectives, of the research project. The first was the exclusive study of selected cases of police misconduct. The other was a concentration on the manner in which the police handle black arrestees. The random sample of interviewees was deliberately chosen as proportionately representative of all citizens who had been arrested during the year. The proportions fell into categories by race, sex, age, and type of charge made against the apprehended people. We rigorously adhered to this precise representative sample despite time-consuming difficulties in locating the interviewees.

The fact that we uncovered considerable racial discrimination on the part of law enforcement officers was the result of the study, rather than its intent. After the report was publicized, letters to the newspapers and phone calls to various local radio "talk shows" kept repeating that the crime rate was higher among blacks than among whites—a fact which was not denied in the report but which did not explain away discriminatory treatment of black arrestees.

As a matter of fact, my final report on the research project estimated that the criminal nucleus of New Orleans comprised about 3.6 percent of the resident adult population, a little more than 15,000 persons, and that the proportion (6.6 percent) was higher among Negroes than it was (2.1 percent) among whites (23). On the basis of a complicated formula which included the individual's police record, his reputation for "law-abidingness," the arrest record of his relatives and close friends, and other available evidence, I estimated that less than three out of ten (28 percent) of the arrested persons could be judged the "enemies" of society and of the police. These are the people who, then, seemed to constitute the heart of the crime problem in the city of New Orleans. According to the rough formula we devised they could at that time be numbered at 5,859 whites and 9,174 Negroes. These "precise" figures must be taken as a cautious estimate, but they strongly support the generalization that there were more violations of law among Negroes than among whites.

In my preliminary report to Giarrusso on *Who Gets Arrested in New Orleans* I had suggested that there was police discrimination in the "round up" of groups of Negroes, and also in the fact that Negroes are more likely than whites to have their cases dismissed—which indicates a higher proportion of "groundless" arrests among Negroes. Similar data have been gathered in other communities, but they may be interpreted differently (24). Commenting on our findings, Ralph Slovenko said that "one may be equally justified in concluding that crime is more frequent among Negroes and that the police and the courts release them without further incarceration. In other words, the frequency of arrest among Negroes may indicate that crime is more a part of their mores than it is among whites, and that often nothing is done about it beyond arrest."

This combination of more arrests and fewer convictions among blacks depicts contrasting forms of racial discrimination: that against the Negro individual and that against the Negro community. We did not make a complete study of the disposition of the charges against arrestees because many of our interviewees had only recently been arrested, but we do have sufficient evidence to prove that blacks in New Orleans generally got heavier sentences than whites for the same type of law violation. This is unequal racial treatment of offenders. On the other hand, the fact that large numbers of black arrestees have their cases dismissed—particularly when the offense is against a fellow Negro—means that the black community is not getting equal protection from the law enforcement agencies. This latter point has often been editorialized by the *Louisiana Weekly*, which is owned and published by Negroes.

There is no question about the fact that our research study uncovered racial discrimination on the part of New Orleans police and that the report itself provided a "sordid story of unequal treatment and discrimination." The sources of our information were numerous: the complaints by arrestees, the comparative statistics from police records, and the observations made by witnesses, lawyers, judges, and law officers. A selection from just two interviews with policemen suggests the "flavor" of police attitudes and conduct toward Negroes.

One officer explained that "Negroes expect white officers to discriminate, and any discourtesy reinforces this conviction and lessens the possibility of cooperation between Negroes and white policemen." He said further that "in court, Negroes are treated in Amos-and-Andy fashion. This discrimination leads to further moral decadence among Negroes." He feels that the policeman is simply the "channel of the general white hostility against the Negro. Most white police are not deliberately and consciously abusive, or discriminatory, but are always acting out what the majority of whites in New Orleans feel about Negroes." In other words, the police behave toward Negroes the way they think white New Orleanians expect them to behave (25).

Another policeman told us, "I'm not sadistic like some of the other guys I work with, you know, pistol whipping and all that." He also, however, related the following incident about himself: "So I started to take a punch at this jig, and he feints back before I even hit him, and you'd never guess what the black bastard had on him. When this jig goes back a small gun fell out of his belt and clanked on the sidewalk. If we were on the grass we never would have heard it. Well, anyway, that's all I needed. I took the black bastard up behind some trees and beat the hell out of him." As though to justify this brutality, he added: "Now, you know he was up to no good with that gun."

In a city like New Orleans it is to be expected that the racial aspects of police discrimination would attract much attention. The spectacular publicity surrounding our controversial report on police arrests stimulated the New Orleans branch of the National Association for the Advancement of Colored People to call a special press conference on the morning of Friday, March 27, when they said that the report was of "grave concern" to them. Solomon Borikins, of the

Legal Redress Committee, declared that "to justify the abuse and mistreatment of Negroes because more of them are arrested than whites is to create a police state rather than provide good law enforcement." There is no connection between arrest statistics and police discrimination. "If every Negro in New Orleans to a man were a criminal and warranted arrest, would their physical abuse be justified?"

The NAACP cited eight specific cases—by name, date, and circumstances—of alleged police brutality against Negroes which had not been satisfactorily investigated. They were frustrated by the lack of action of the police bureau of investigation and proposed that this bureau be replaced by a biracial citizens' committee made up of people of "high integrity and standing in the community who have no legal axes to grind." They agreed with the arrest report on the fact that Giarrusso had worked hard to improve the police department, but felt that a citizens' committee with subpoena powers could help to get convictions against the "bad eggs" among the police officers.

The local Negro newspaper, *The Louisiana Weekly*, took up this same theme in a long two-column editorial on April 11. The writer praised Giarrusso for his "record as an excellent administrator," but ridiculed the so-called "probe" of jail conditions by newsmen and police on Easter Sunday, who found no evidence of brutality against prisoners (26). "Just how naive and stupid do they think the general public is?" The writer said that both this probe and the comments by Giarrusso were an attempt "to whitewash the problems mentioned in the Fichter Report." This kind of response to serious police problems "must indeed be considered an insult to the public's intelligence."

A LEFT-WING CONSPIRACY. The racial aspects of the year-long study of police arrests were of particular interest to leaders of the White Citizens' Council, the president of which declared that *The Louisiana Weekly* "is a formidable outlet for the incendiary concatenations of race-baiting Negro Leftwing extremists." He and his associates felt that the report on police handling of arrestees deserved a "special" issue of their monthly mimeographed paper, *The Citizens' Report* (27). This special issue was distributed in two sections. Part I headlined that "Father Fichter's Public Record Reveals Leftwing Linkage," and Part II, "Father Fichter's 'Survey' Unit Flavored with Integrationists." Jackson Ricau, editor and president of the White Citizens' Council, who had been excommunicated by the archbishop in 1962 for voicing opposition to the removal of racial segregation within the Catholic church, demonstrated serious homework in attempting to discredit my report as subversive (28).

The revelation of my "left-wing linkage" included the fact that in 1956, in an educational project to prepare for the desegregation of Catholic schools, I had received a grant from the Fund for the Republic which "supports extreme left-wing groups," and was able to conduct the recent study of police arrests with a grant from the Marshall Field Foundation which has been "successfully penetrated or used by Communists." It appears that the receipt of such "dirty" research money from such "subversive" philanthropic organizations branded me a leftist, or at best an unwitting dupe of the Communist conspiracy.

It was pointed out, furthermore, that in 1959 I had been charged by the arch-conservative Catholic weekly, *The Wanderer*, with having written "a very disturbing book," entitled *Parochial School: A Sociological Study*. The test questions we used in part of that school survey were the kind that "undermine parental authority; thus, indirectly, spiritual authority." In 1960 I was co-chairman of a New Orleans citizens' group, Save Our Schools, with Rabbi Julian Feibleman, whose "public record discloses thirteen instances of connections with subversive groups" (29). In 1962, in a lecture given at Loyola University about my experiences in Chile, I was alleged to have said that "the only solution for Chile is to go Communist."

The survey of police handling of arrestees, and the report issuing from it, were further suspect because of other associations of which I was guilty. One of these was Dr. Harold Lief, psychiatrist of the Tulane Medical School, who was a member of the American Civil Liberties Union, which is "closely affiliated with the Communist movement in the United States." He was also a director of Save Our Schools, of which John Nelson was a vice-chairman. The latter was an unsavory companion for me because he agreed to speak at a combined program of two groups with which I was intimately connected: the Regional Interracial Committee of Catholic College Students, and the New Orleans Commission of Human Rights of the Catholic Committee of the South (30).

This "objectionable" program was held on Interracial Sunday in 1956, "honoring Manhattan Borough President Hulan Jack, Negro, noted for his Communist-front affiliations." Nelson was guilty also of acting as legal counsel for a Tulane University student who was an active member of the "pro-Communist NAACP and CORE." Nelson had received an award from the Catholic Interracial Council together with a Negro leader of the San Diego Urban League, and the National Urban League had been partially financed by the "Communist" Garland Fund. The public record of another consultant and fellow member of the subcommittee, President Albert Dent of Dillard University, "lists five citations for subversive activity."

This guilt by association with other "subversives" was only part of the evidence introduced by the White Citizens' Councils people to discredit both me and the arrest report. The personal charge was that I was following and promoting the Communist "party line" as planned by U.S. Communist Gus

Hall who said in 1964: "If we could launch a national and an international campaign against this (southern anti-Negro) brutality we could make a signal contribution to the freeing of the South." The White Citizens' Council editor then added this comment: "to counteract Communist objectives the support of the Police by all good citizens is especially important now that Communist-inspired race riots are getting to be a regular part of the American scene."

The White Citizens' Council in New Orleans had its own expert on the theory and practice of Communism, who in 1961 had distributed a copyright monograph entitled *What Do Communists Believe?* Hubert Badeaux, ex-policeman and part-time student in my sociology course on social problems at Loyola University, took it upon himself to publish his *Commentary on the Fichter Report*, in which he included the complete text of the arrest study. As an elected officer of the White Citizens' Council, he followed the usual ideology of this racist group in ferreting out the "Marxism and subversion" of the arrest study. "The Fichter Report is skillful propaganda, and fits in quite nicely with the determined political effort being made to compel Americans to practice equalitarianism whether they believe in it or not."

There is no doubt in the author's mind that the latter-day civil rights movement had "its origin in the cunning revolutionary propaganda of V. I. Lenin." The Communist Party has "enjoyed magnificent success" through this movement.

> Now, in the midst of a political battle to enact sweeping civil rights legislation, aimed at giving the utmost in legal immunities and privileges to Negroes, the Fichter Report has been issued. It is an extension of the Communist charge of police brutality and discrimination, it is responsive to the Communist directive of May, 1950, and the timing of its release provided welcome propaganda for those leading the fight to abolish classes (31).

THE MECHANICS OF RELEASE. There was neither connivance with Communists nor a carefully planned strategy behind the fact that I chose the end of March 1964 as the time to make public the results of our study. We had completed the interviews and the collection of other data in September of the previous year, and I had set December 1 as the target date on which to complete the writing of the report. As usual with such self-promises, and with the distraction of other tasks of lecturing and research to perform, I did not meet that date; it was the first week in January before I could present copies of the report to my fellow members of the civil rights subcommittee on the administration of justice.

I was willing to take full and eventual responsibility for the contents of the report, but I wanted it scrutinized by these expert consultants. I wanted also to have their advice concerning practical recommendations for the improvement of the New Orleans department of police (32). Discussions about this latter point stretched over several weeks while the members studied the report. I also asked Aaron Kohn of the Metropolitan Crime Commission to study the report and participate in our conference on recommendations—which was then the only section of the report that had joint authorship. These consultations were completed by mid-February.

From the beginning of the research project, in early 1963, I anticipated that the final report would be published by the Government Printing Office in Washington as part of the continuing series of reports distributed by the federal Commission on Civil Rights. At the February meeting of the Louisiana advisory committee, my report of police handling of arrestees was accepted, approved, and transmitted to Washington. Perhaps I was impatient; perhaps Washington officialdom moves slowly; at any rate, I took it upon myself to release the report.

In a later note to President Dent of Dillard University I wrote that the postponement of decision to publish on the part of the U.S. Commission of Civil Rights finally persuaded me that this study would lose its effectiveness if it did not soon get out into the New Orleans community. You remember that I asked Jack Nelson to get us an answer from Washington by Saturday, March 14, and that he then asked me to wait till Tuesday, March 17. With no answer on that date, I decided to ditto the report single space, and get copies to Schiro, Giarrusso and Garrison on Friday and to the media on Monday.

The contents of the report were timely and topical, and might have lost their local relevance if not made public soon. The impact of the release of the study proved to be explosive, at least, to the mayor and the police chief, to whom it was delivered 72 hours earlier but who had not bothered to read it. The public learned about it through the local news media, the most enterprising of which was the staff of WDSU, operating both a radio station and a television channel in New Orleans. Ten minutes after the report reached his desk, Alec Gifford, news reporter for WDSU, invited me to the studio to discuss it with him and news director, John Corporan (33). We taped a half-hour interview for that evening's radio program, "Conversation Carte Blanche," and also videotaped a 3-minute interview that was televised that evening on the news program.

The *States-Item* carried the story in its final edition that same night, and the *Times-Picayune* had it on the front page the following morning. News reporters could get only "no comment" from the offices of the mayor and the police chief. On Tuesday afternoon Major Albert Theriot phoned Charles Brennan of the Loyola University Office of Public Relations, asking for "'a dozen copies," for which he would "send a police car right away." At fixed periods during that day an editorial was broadcast over WDSU television and radio stations, calling the report a "shocker," and closing with the question: "Why have we tolerated such practices in a mod-

ern, civilized society? Or are we as modern and civilized as
we think?"

Giarrusso called a press conference at his office on Wednesday morning at which "he said the survey was a blanket indictment of the department and caused irreparable harm and
damage. He criticized it as being unsupported by facts, and
incomplete in that none of the top police officers were consulted" (34). At a luncheon of the Young Men's Business
Club, Mayor Schiro interrupted his report on civic progress
to say that the survey was an injustice to the community.
"When you do something like this, and you're not man
enough or honest enough to say 'here are the proofs,' it's dangerous business."

John Corporan of WDSU and Bill Reed of WWL wanted
my response to these statements, and reporters from both
daily papers called for interviews. I told them I would wait
until after the meeting that night of the Fraternal Order of
Police and attempt to answer all three statements on Thursday morning. In my brief reply I simply said that I stand on
the facts, conclusions, and recommendations of the study, and
that nothing that had been said either "disproved or improved" my report.

The WDSU editorial on Thursday discussed the reaction
of the mayor and the superintendent, saying that the study
was "a compliment and not an attack on the police" and ending with the remark that "the superintendent has obviously
been doing his job. The Fichter study merely shows that the
job is not yet complete." Radio station WNOE waited till
Wednesday, April 1, to broadcast its editorial which charged
that the report "violated the cardinal principle of science. It
contains no proof, no evidence in fact." Furthermore,
"WNOE questions whether the Fichter Report has helped to
solve a problem, or has created a new one."

The Sociology Department of Loyola University received
a continuing stream of letters and phone calls, some from

people offering further testimony of police misconduct, some disagreeing violently with the report and its author, many others requesting copies of the report. I could respond to those critics who were willing to reveal their names, but not to those who left vulgar and anonymous obscene messages. I had to insist that the research project was now completed and that further investigation and any concerted movement to improve the police department had to be done by others.

Supplying copies of the arrest report involved problems of time and money. I thought it still probable that the U.S. Commission on Civil Rights would publish it as a monograph from the Government Printing Office in Washington, but this would take time. We had dittoed only forty copies of the report, and this supply was now exhausted (35). Numerous friends asked me if they could be of any help, to whom I responded that I needed money to reproduce and distribute the report. A telephone call to David Hunter at the New York office of the Stern Family Fund resulted in a grant of 900 dollars on April 8, which enabled us to distribute 1,000 copies of an offset monograph to police departments, law schools, civil rights groups, and concerned individuals throughout the country.

To give free and wide access to the results of this research project I did not copyright the arrest report. Hubert Badeaux, however, the White Citizens' Council expert on subversion, did copyright his *Commentary*, which ran to 105 pages, of which 83 pages constituted the complete text of the original report. Since my own "edition" of the report was exhausted by the end of June 1964, I was content during several subsequent years to tell enquirers that they could purchase the copyrighted *Commentary* from Badeaux for the price of 2 dollars and 50 cents. I did not trouble to point out that we had spent only 7,980 dollars on what Badeaux was pleased to call "the 50,000-dollar Fichter Report" (36).

AFTERMATH. This account cannot be fittingly finished without the story of my confidential conference with Mayor Schiro and Chief Giarrusso. On the Wednesday after Easter, Dennis Lacey of the mayor's staff called to say that Schiro would like to talk with me privately and "off the record." We set the meeting time for Friday morning, and I immediately prepared a brief, four-page memorandum for discussion. That night I asked Jack Nelson to look over these points and to accompany me to the mayor's office, which he readily agreed to do.

Lacey picked us up at Loyola University, drove us to city hall, and ushered us into the mayor's office by a back entrance. No one else at city hall was to know we were there, no reporters allowed, no word to be given to the media. I was not sure why this secrecy was required, but instead of waiting for Giarrusso and Schiro to tell me why they wanted to see me, I took the initiative. I said that I resented the public insult they paid me during the previous week in charging that my survey report was false and dangerous, a dishonest criticism of the city administration, and a blanket indictment of all police officers. "You know as well as anyone—and perhaps better than I—that the report was factual and that every criminal lawyer in town would support those facts." I said that their public reaction to our findings was a strategic blunder similar to that made by Morrison and Scheuring to the report of the Metropolitan Crime Commission in 1954.

The mayor replied that the blunder was mine in not bringing the survey report privately to him and the superintendent "because we look into every complaint and try to correct it." In reply I handed him a copy of the preliminary report, *Who Gets Arrested in New Orleans?*, told him that I had submitted it confidentially to Giarrusso in May 1963, and asked what police improvement had resulted from that report. The chief was embarrassed by this question since he had at that time thanked me for the report and then apparently forgotten it. The mayor said he never heard of it, but insisted that the publicity given to the recent arrest study report had seriously undermined the new and improving morale of the police department.

Jack Nelson then asked whose morale was hurt by this report—the policemen who are guilty, those who have no morale, those who resist the reforms the chief is trying to initiate? As a lawyer who had considerable experience in the district attorney's office, he could—and did—cite specific examples of police misconduct. The response to these examples was a plea for understanding on the part of Giarrusso who then told us of numerous recent and current cases of problem officers, how difficult it was for him to maintain discipline and to get airtight evidence against a delinquent officer. He embellished on his statement of the previous week that "since 1960 a total of 550 complaints against the police were investigated and more than eight officers were dismissed. Numerous others received disciplinary action."

Victor Schiro is no longer mayor of New Orleans and Joseph Giarrusso no longer the superintendent of police. I left New Orleans that summer to work elsewhere, but not as the result of pressure, nor to one of the "exiles" to which I was reportedly banished by my superior (37). There was indeed pressure. On the Sunday after the conference at the mayor's office, the president of Loyola University was told by an alumnus that the university was suffering financially because it retained "nuts" like Fichter, Clancy, and Twomey (38). "I can get you 6,000 dollars right now, but I won't as long as you keep Fichter there." I suggested that the president "up the ante" to at least 16,000 dollars before dismissing me.

I was costing the Jesuits money. Even as far away as Detroit a graduate of the Jesuit Xavier University of Cincinnati told the alumni director that he would no longer support his alma mater. In retaliation for the report on police handling of arrestees in New Orleans, he said, "I repudiate the balance of my 1963 pledge, will work no more to collect funds for their annual drive, and the same train of thought is to be given to University of Detroit High" (the Jesuit prep school from which he graduated in 1955). He signed his name under the word, "unloyal" and sent a copy of the letter to the president of Xavier University.

Less threatening than this kind of pressure, and certainly more amusing, was the "warning" sent by the local White Citizens' Council to Sir George Williams University in Montreal, where I was visiting professor of sociology in the summer of 1964. Without realizing that Harold Potter, the head of the department, was a black sociologist, the warning described my "subversive" activities in the field of race relations during more than 15 years in New Orleans. When I moved to the University of Chicago for the academic year 1964—1965, similar warnings were sent to Philip Hauser, chairman of the department of sociology, and Peter Rossi, director of the University's National Opinion Research Center, where my task was to analyze the data of the 1964 graduates of predominantly Negro colleges. Both in Montreal and in Chicago, these warnings from the White Citizens' Council acted as strong recommendations for my qualification as a university professor (39).

NOTES

1. Jim Garrison had even more trouble in 1967 when he tried to prove the "conspiracy" behind John Kennedy's assassination. See F. Powledge, "Is Garrison Faking?" *New Republic*, (June 17, 1967), pp. 13–18, and G. Roberts, "Case of Jim Garrison and Lee Oswald," *New York Times Magazine*, May 21, 1967, pp. 32–35. See also James Kirkwood, *American Grotesque: An Account of the Clay Shaw-Jim Garrison Affair in the City of New Orleans* (New York, Simon and Schuster, 1970).

2. Schiro has been praised as an "old fashioned" politician who succeeded in desegregating the schools in 1961, where the "reform" mayor, Chep Morrison had failed in 1960. See Morton Inger, *op. cit.*, p. 69.

3. This is a notion common to leaders of most organizations, including the ecclesiastical. See Chapter Five.

4. The White Citizens' Council had not forgotten my role in the 1956 campaign to desegregate the Catholic schools of New Orleans. They persistently argued that the civil rights movement was basically a Communist plot.

5. The questionnaire had been constructed and the data collected before I was invited to interpret the results. My mimeographed report, *Religious Backgrounds of Catholic Trainees*, was not publicly circulated and I have no idea whether the military chaplains implemented it.

6. The only previous report of this advisory committee was an eighty-three-page pamphlet, *The New Orleans School Crisis*, dealing with the 1960 failure to desegregate public schools.

7. At that time the California State Advisory Committee of the U.S. Commission on Civil Rights was preparing its report on *Police-Minority Group Relations* (1963). More pertinent to the South was the report, 2 years later, *Law Enforcement: A Report on Equal Protection in the South* (1965).

8. In 1963 the National Farm Workers Union sent people into the rural areas of southern Louisiana to interview farm laborers. I was asked to analyze and interpret the collected data, which I did in an unpublished monograph, *Workers in the Sugar Cane* (with the assistance of Jo Ann Prat.)

9. The New Orleans police officer promises "to respect the Constitutional rights of all men to liberty, equality and justice."

10. This first report did not question the distribution of law violations by age, sex, race, and social status. It did raise the question of equal treatment of all persons arrested for violations of the law. For a study of "police discretion," see Wayne LaFave, *Arrest: The Decision to Take a Suspect into Custody* (Boston, Little, Brown, 1964).

11. Among many examples see Marshall Clinard, *Sociology of Deviant Behavior* (New York, Holt, Rinehart, Winston, 1963) Chapter 8, "Types of Delinquent and Criminal Offenders."

12. We have no evidence whether Murry cleared this permission with Superintendent Giarusso, or whether the latter ever discussed with his subordinates my first report on *Who Gets Arrested in New Orleans?*

13. Besides the ethical qualms we had about such procedures we both agreed that it would have been dangerous to get "caught" by the police with a hidden tape recorder.

14. Mayor Theriot was apparently also satisfied that we were not doing a "race study." He let the matter drop and did not contact me about it.

15. The harassment of "integrationists" by members of the White Citizens' Councils was as organized and persistent in 1964 as it had been in 1956. It was also an effective tactic in silencing many supporters of racial desegregation.

16. See p. 125. This was the letter in which he said he would be "more than happy to participate in the survey."

17. *Police Handling of Arrestees* (New Orleans, Loyola University, 1964), pp. 12 f.

18. His investigation revealed widespread graft and corruption among police and city officials. His report, released in April 1954, consisted of six volumes of information but concealed the names of informants.

19. But the term was not always used in anger. That summer a softball team made up of policemen called itself the "Hard Core."

20. Cries of "police brutality" had been made in the handling of mass civil rights demonstrations before 1963, but had not yet reached the crescendo they achieved later among college students and other young people.

21. Editorial in the *Times-Picayune*, May 18, 1963.

22. Written by ex-policeman and occasionally a student at Loyola University, Hubert J. Badeaux, *Commentary on the Fichter Report* (New Orleans, privately printed, 1964), pp. 7 f.

23. *Police Handling of Arrestees*, pp. 7 f.

24. See the discussion by Edwin Sutherland and Donald Cressey, *Criminology* (Philadelphia, Lippincott, 1970), pp. 132–142.

25. It is a commonplace in the literature on the subject that a community gets the kind of police department that "it deserves." The multiple-volume report of the U.S. Commission on Civil

Rights in 1961 had a separate section on "Equal Justice Under Law." Volume 5 was entitled *Justice*.

26. In May 1963 an editorial in the *Times-Picayune* predicted that "practically all prisoners" would answer affirmatively to the question whether they had been "beaten or threatened" when Jim Garrison's questionnaire was being distributed to the inmates of the parish (county) prison.

27. That is, besides the regular issue (Vol. 5, No. 4) of April 1954.

28. See my comments on this excommunication in Chapter Three, pp. 105-108.

29. There were three clergymen as co-chairmen of SOS, the third being Bishop Girrault Jones. This religious and ecumenical leadership is generally ignored in the accounts of the New Orleans "school crisis" of 1960.

30. See Chapter Three, on school desegregation, and footnote 23 on the subsequent woes of Hulan Jack.

31. Badeaux, *op. cit.*, pp. 1–6.

32. This was the only instance among my research studies in which I tried to make research data "applicable" to social reform.

33. Also in the studio that afternoon was Jim Garrison who congratulated me on the arrest study. This was the first time I had personally met the controversial district attorney.

34. The fact that I had Giarrusso's approval and cooperation for the study is demonstrated above, pp. 123–125, *States-Item*, March 25, 1964, *Times-Picayune*, March 26, 1964.

35. This dittoed version of the report had sixty-eight pages, and the later offset version had sixty pages, whereas Badeaux's "copyright" text of the report ran to eighty-three pages.

36. Badeaux, *op. cit.*, p. 105.

37. John Beecher, "Magnolia Ghetto," *Ramparts* (December 1964), pp. 45–50, mentions the "uproar" caused by the arrest study but adds that "Fichter went on leave to teach at the University of Chicago, his fourth exile since coming to Loyola. Previously cooling-off periods had been spent in Germany, Peru, and at the University of Notre Dame" (p. 46).

38. The president of Loyola University was then Father Andrew C. Smith, a liberal and courageous integrationist. Father Thomas Clancy, political scientist and social activist, became provincial

of the southern Jesuits in July 1971. Father Louis Twomey died in October 1969.

39. These "warnings" were sent also to the student body of both universities and included the special issue of *The Citizens' Report*, April 1964, discussed above, p. 145–148.

FIVE

RESEARCHING
THE CATHOLIC CLERGY

Bureaucrats, whether civil or ecclesiastical, seem to have a fear of "exposure" in the publication of findings from sociological research. This fear was a factor in the suppression of *Southern Parish* and was even more evident in the reaction to my research report on the New Orleans police. The bureaucratic mentality insists that the data should be confidential and argues that needed improvement should and can best be made "from the inside" by the official bureaucrats themselves. This general, self-protective attitude also includes a fear that the "enemy" will use the research data to attack the organization—like the Communists intent upon destroying police morale and the anti-Catholic bigots who are out to besmirch the church (1).

This fear of the enemy was the basis of a warning about "studies of religious sociology" sent out from Vatican City on April 7, 1958, over the signature of Cardinal Angelo Dell'Acqua, who recognized the utility of such studies if they were properly handled. "Unfortunately, however," he wrote, "the publication of statistics on the religious situation prevailing in some countries has supplied our enemies with material capable of being exploited in every possible manner to the detriment of the Church." For this reason he then laid down a regulation for Catholic researchers that such studies should be undertaken only by the Episcopate and the data collected from them "should be placed at the disposal of Pastors and not used for publicity purposes" (2).

Two copies of this warning were dutifully delivered to me in the spring of 1958 through official channels. One came from the Vatican to the apostolic delegate in Washington to Archbishop Rummel in New Orleans to me. The other came from the Jesuit general in Rome to the provincial of the southern Jesuits to the president of Loyola University of the South to me. This was not a personal communication from Rome—like others I received—but it was directed personally to me by the New Orleans archbishop and the southern provincial who were fully aware of the two books I had published on the sociology of the parish (3). Meanwhile I had conducted several sociological surveys of sisters, brothers, and seminarians, the findings of which I had no intention of withholding from publication (4).

As I continued my research on the Catholic church I became ever more convinced that the key people, the agents of change in Catholicism, were the fulltime professionals in the service of the church. The year after the warning came from Rome I decided to do a "confidential" research survey of American Jesuit students who were then, in 1959, studying in their 4-year course of theology. The questionnaire was answered at the five American theologates by 545 men (93 percent of the total at these schools). This was a private survey not meant for publication, the findings of which I analyzed and distributed to the superiors of the ten American Jesuit provinces, with the suggestion that they put this report on the agenda of their next joint meeting in May 1960.

Then I discovered another prohibition: some questions are too "sacred" to be included in a survey. The agenda for the annual meeting of provincials had to be sent to Rome for approval by the Jesuit general and his advisors. On January 19, 1960, Father Carroll O'Sullivan, superior of the California province, where the meeting was to be held, sent the proposed agenda to Rome, and very quickly (February 4) the reply came from Father Janssens, the Jesuit general, who was dismayed that my survey had ever been permitted by the provincials. He disapproved specifically of (a) questions that dealt with personal matters that were practically "secrets of conscience," and (b) the fact that any sociologist would take it upon himself to ask questions that only Superiors had the right to ask: on the system of studies and training, on seminarians' opinions about their professors, spiritual advisors, and superiors. "Such things must never again be permitted; and if they are under way they must be stopped" (5).

As a result of this exchange the provincials removed the Fichter questionnaire and survey report from the agenda of their San Francisco meeting, but I trust that they discussed it informally and that each provincial—and especially the rectors of the five Jesuit theologates—privately studied the findings of the survey. It is an interesting fact that Father Gordon George, a trained sociologist and provincial of the Canadian Jesuits, asked me to conduct the same survey among his theological students. He expressed gratitude for the findings, paid for the survey, and said that it "aroused much interest up here" (6).

THE FIRST PRIEST SURVEY. In early January 1960, after completing the private and confidential survey of Jesuit theological students, I began another survey which was not to be private and confidential. This was a research study of active diocesan parish priests (excluding monsignors). For this I had taken a strict interval sample—every seventh name —from the 1959 edition of Kenedy's *Official Catholic Directory*. Once again I ran into trouble. Within 2 weeks after the questionnaires were mailed out for this survey I had an anonymous letter from a priest in Philadelphia, enclosing a prohibition against answering the survey. This notice from the chancery office was sent to all priests in the Philadelphia archdiocese, forbidding them to answer my questionnaire because the survey had not been "authorized" by John Cardinal O'Hara, archbishop of Philadelphia (7).

The cardinal immediately lodged a protest against me with Father Janssens, the Jesuit general in Rome, who did not bother to contact me about the matter but quickly sent a "stop order" to Father Andrew Smith, who was then my provincial superior in New Orleans. The latter received this order on February 9, 1960, and informed me of it with the wry remark that "two Cardinals—no less—have seen fit to protest about this to Rome." The second protesting cardinal was obviously Francis Spellman of New York, who had been alerted by Cardinal O'Hara on February 11 (8). Spellman, addressing his clergy conference on March 8, announced that O'Hara had complained about me to the Jesuit general and had received assurance that it would "not happen again." The New York prelate did not forbid his priests to answer the questionnaire, but ridiculed the survey, especially items concerning the promotion of priests to the rank of monsignor.

The Jesuit general was quite explicit in his instructions to the southern provincial. I was to be forbidden immediately from continuing this survey and from using its findings in any kind of publication. The general regretted that this work had caused me so much effort, which certainly indicated my zeal but not my "prudence or wisdom." This was from the man who had encouraged me personally in December 1954 to pursue sociological studies of the church, and who in 1959 advised me to do research on social problems (9).

Over the years I have made two generalizations about such prohibitory ukases from ecclesiastical authorities. One is that they are not to be taken seriously because they are part of an elaborate protocol which demands that if a prelate complains to Rome he should get some kind of proof that something was done about his complaint. The easiest response is to send him a carbon copy of the letter of prohibition. The second is that the "guilty" party is given his "sentence" without a hearing. I am convinced that in all of my surveys I could have demonstrated to an impartial jury of experts that I was not entirely lacking in prudence and wisdom.

Cardinal O'Hara's interference with the clergy survey in his archdiocese did not seriously hamper the sample. One of his priests contacted a sociologist in Philadelphia, who in turn suggested to me that they would work together to gather a sufficient number of answered questionnaires from the local diocesan clergy. I decided that this was not necessary since I was making regional (rather than diocesan) comparisons of the data, and since the other Pennsylvania dioceses had "oversubscribed" their responses. It is a coincidence that the American Philosophical Society in Philadelphia made a grant of 2,000 dollars for this research project. The Social Science Research Council also made a grant of 2,000 dollars, and Loyola University of the South absorbed the rest of the cost of the study.

I sent out the questionnaires to the diocesan clergy between January 9 and 19 and included a postpaid reply envelope. I promised to send an "overview" of the findings to any who requested it, an offer which 1,357 priests accepted. While analyzing the data from this project I devised still another research survey, a parallel study of active lay Catholic adults who were the "friends" of the priests to whom I sent the research report in early May. With this report I enclosed

three questionnaires (also with postpaid reply envelopes) asking that they be distributed to the lay people they judged to
be active, practicing Catholics (10).

These two surveys were my first step beyond the simple
IBM equipment, key punch, and sorter-counter I had earlier
installed in the sociology department of Loyola University.
Even such simple machines were nowhere else in use on the
campus, much less any sophisticated computer equipment
(11). I turned to a good friend, Dr. James Sweeney, head of
the computer center at Tulane University, who with his assistants William Nettleton and Daniel Kileen then "compu-
terized" my research findings and dubbed the clergy survey
the "Black Knights Study." With their help I was able to
probe large numbers of variables and test out almost innumerable hypotheses.

Aside from the mimeographed reports I sent to the priest
respondents in May 1960 I deliberately delayed writing up
the results of these two studies for publication until I returned from my year as visiting professor at the Catholic
University of Santiago, Chile, in 1961. Part of my hesitation
lay in my frustration over the apparently intransigent attitudes of leading Catholic hierarchs to sociological research in
the church. I discussed this at length with two men who were
knowledgeable in ecclesiastical politics, Monsignors John
Egan of Chicago and George Higgins of Washington. They
agreed with me that someone had to explain to the bishops
that social scientists were not really attacking the church,
that research was not only useful but necessary for the operation of the church, that if they were unwilling to support research they could at least stay out of the way of researchers.

During 1960, whenever I had occasion to travel from New
Orleans to other cities for lectures, conferences, and conven-
tions, I tried to get an appointment with the bishop of the
place I visited. Three cardinals, Cushing of Boston, Spellman
of New York, and Ritter of St. Louis, were too busy to see

me, but I did confer with their chancery officials and other priests. I was graciously received by Cardinal Meyer of Chicago, Archbishop Alter of Cincinnati, and Bishop Wright of Pittsburgh, all of whom listened patiently and—it seemed to me—with a sense of relief when they realized that I was not asking them for some form of financial support.

As a matter of fact, during that year in carrying out my "research apostolate" I visited twenty-two cities. In three of them, Buffalo, Newark, and Seattle, I talked only with groups of parishioners. In most of them (Atlanta, Dallas, Denver, Detroit, Los Angeles, Milwaukee, Oklahoma City, Portland, St. Paul, San Francisco, Scranton, and South Bend), I met mainly with groups of diocesan priests. Besides promoting among them the importance of sociological research in the church, I had an opportunity to share and discuss the findings of the two research surveys. These meetings gave me important insights into the views and experiences of American Catholics, both clerical and lay, and helped my analyses of the data.

Another reason for delaying concrete plans for publishing the findings of these two surveys was my indecision whether to write two separate books, one on the priests and one on the laity, or to combine the data from both surveys and produce a single book. In the large volume of information I had gathered there was also much pertinent material for articles and lectures, as well as for books. After my return from Chile I was still mulling over this decision when Philip Scharper of Sheed and Ward came to New Orleans for a visit in the spring of 1962.

Scharper asked the usual question put by editors and publishers to authors: "What are you working on now?" I told him about my parallel surveys of Catholic clergy and laity, some of the interesting findings I had, and the problem of how to ready these materials for publication. Both surveys were "originals." Before 1960 there had never been a nationwide study asking priests what they thought about their work, nor one asking lay people what they thought about their priests. Scharper was attracted to the latter, but I made it clear that I did not have a representative sample of Catholic lay adults (12). What I had obtained were the responses of the "better" Catholics as recognized and chosen by the diocesan priests in whose parishes these lay people lived. We decided then to do the book about these lay parishioners and to call it "The Friends of Priests."

I had to write this book while busy with other tasks of research and lecturing. I was soon immersed in a new study —on the New Orleans police—and also spent the summer of 1963 teaching at the Ibero-Americana University in Mexico City. Nevertheless, I had the typescript of "The Friends of Priests" completed by the end of 1963. Some small revisions were suggested by the readers and editors of Sheed and Ward, and the production schedule of the book seemed to go along fairly smoothly. I read and revised the galley proofs in December 1964 while I was at the University of Chicago.

There would be no point in recounting the routine of book publishing except for an almost incredible occurrence in this particular instance. After returning the corrected galleys to Scharper, I waited for the page proofs so that from them I could construct the index for the book. The publisher seemed to be taking an unduly long time for this stage of the process. The delay was explained when a copy of the completed book arrived in the mails, without an index and with a new and inappropriate title, *Priest and People*. This blunder on the part of Sheed and Ward was never satisfactorily explained. It lead to the obvious criticism by reviewers that the title did not fit the content of the book, and it resulted in further confusion with a book of the same title by Conor Ward (13).

Although my 1960 survey of diocesan parish priests was the first of its kind in the United States, I did not publish a separate volume dealing with its findings. I did utilize considerable data from it in the misnamed book, *Priest and People*, and even more, for comparative purposes, in the final report of my second clergy survey taken in 1966.

THE SECOND PRIEST SURVEY. When I went to work for Peter Rossi at the National Opinion Research Center (NORC) of the University of Chicago in September 1964, I had no thought of doing a follow-up replication of the earlier (1960) survey of diocesan clergy. I was busy enough with my specific assignment in Chicago, the analysis and interpretation of data from the NORC survey of graduates of Negro colleges. This study, together with its larger companion survey of the graduates of "non-Negro" colleges, had its own share of difficulties, some of which resembled the process of censorship (14). Why the findings of the larger study of white college graduates have never been published had best be told by someone else.

Before leaving Chicago in September 1965, I completed the typescript report on the Negro college graduates and submitted it, through NORC's Peter Rossi, to Herbert Rosenberg, the government supervisor of the grant out of which the study was made. He and his readers called for considerable revision of the text. As a result I had to spend many additional hours on this work even though I then had taken a full-time appointment as Stillman Professor at Harvard University (15). I had barely finished the revision of the report on Negro college graduates when I received an inquiry from Robert Hoyt, editor of the *National Catholic Reporter*, asking if I was interested in doing another survey of diocesan priests.

There was an air of caution and anonymity about Hoyt's inquiry. A "certain priest" had contacted him with the suggestion that *NCR* might want to underwrite and handle a survey that would get at the attitudes of diocesan priests concerning the Catholic church's law on celibacy for the clergy. This unnamed priest, together with a small group of fellow clergy, had prepared a rough questionnaire of twelve items on which they wanted priests to check a yes-or-no answer. They felt a need for caution because the American bishops frowned on any suggestion that the law of clerical celibacy be questioned.

Hoyt's circuitous inquiry came in May 1966, almost a half year after the close of the final session of the Second Vatican Council, which had by-passed the question of a married priesthood in the Latin rite. My earlier research indicated that the law of celibacy had become a problem in the recruitment of seminarians and in the retention of priests after ordination, but I saw this as only one of a series of problems with which the Catholic priesthood was faced (16). I told Hoyt that I was unwilling to do a survey on priestly celibacy, but would gladly design a broader survey in which the issue of celibacy was included.

The spokesman of the anonymous group of priests later revealed himself as Father Frank Matthews, a 44-year-old pastor in the St. Louis archdiocese and director of the Catholic Radio and Television Apostolate. In mid-July he visited me at the Cambridge Center for Social Studies with which I was then associated while teaching at Harvard. By that time I had roughed out the first version of a questionnaire, a timetable for the research project, and a cost estimate of 8,240 dollars to do the work. He agreed that the celibacy question should be only one segment of the survey items, assured me that he could raise the necessary funds, and took copies of the tentative questionnaire to be "tried out" among his St. Louis confreres.

It was not until August 19, 1966, that I had in hand the fifth and final version of the questionnaire. I had pretested the questions with groups of diocesan priests in Boston and New York, while Frank and his associates sent them to similar groups in Detroit, Milwaukee, and New Orleans. In early August I had held a long conference with seven priests in Chicago, and 6 days later with nine priests in Los Angeles, where I had gone to discuss with Jesuit educators the results of my first survey of Jesuit high school students. After a thorough pretesting of every item and its wording I felt that I had a questionnaire schedule that adequately covered the main areas of concern to diocesan priests who were neither pastors nor monsignors.

In my 1960 survey, in which I had already discerned many of the problems faced by diocesan priests, I had also omitted monsignors but included pastors. The decision to exclude pastors from the 1966 survey came out of the repeated observation that the exercise of authority by pastors was one of the central obstacles for the "forgotten men," the parish curates. It was Bishop Stephen Leven of San Antionio who had made an intervention at the last session of Vatican II in which he called the parish assistants the "forgotten men of the church" (17).

The priests who helped assemble the contents of the questionnaire were generally in agreement that the church was not changing fast enough, even though they were optimistic that much good would come out of the recently concluded Vatican Council. There was widespread dissatisfaction with diocesan administration, with the blame placed sometimes directly with the bishop and other times with chancery officials. Some problems loomed larger in some dioceses than in others. Seminary training was criticized, as well as the system of appointments and promotions. Some priests did not like their immediate working conditions; others emphasized the need to discontinue stole fees and Mass stipends; still others deplored the lack of continuing education for the diocesan clergy.

The questionnaire item that gave me the greatest trouble had to do with decisions of conscience, especially when there was disagreement between the individual priest and his bishop or a difference of interpretation of church regulation and doctrine. This pretesting occurred in 1966, well before the public controversy in 1968 over Pope Paul's encyclical on birth control, but these priests were already bothered "in conscience" about continuing the traditional teaching on artificial contraception (18). Some of them were involved in protest demonstrations of various kinds and felt that they had to continue "in conscience" even against the bishop's orders. Eventually I incorporated a question on the priest's "right in conscience" to act on controversial issues and a question on whether the respondent would support a fellow priest who so acted against the bishop's wishes.

Although I was unwilling to make a survey on clerical marriage—and I still think that it is erroneous to call the actual survey a "celibacy study"—I recognize this as a central problem for some of the priests I interviewed. They were convinced that the old rules demanding a celibate clergy were outmoded and that the Catholic church of the Latin rite had to change those rules. They were sure that the survey would show many diocesan priests with the same conviction. But what about those who conscientiously believed they had the right to marry—and hoped to do so—whether or not the rules were changed? This, again, was a conscience problem for which they wanted a solution.

The timetable I worked out for this research project called for completion of the questionnaire by the first of September 1966, when it would be sent out to a one-third sample of diocesan priests (non-pastors and non-monsignors) as selected automatically by the facilities of the Kenedy *Official Catholic Directory*. The questionnaires were precoded for quick punching onto IBM cards at the Cambridge Center for Social Studies, and then sent to the computer center at Loyola University of the South for electronic data processing. The cutoff date was set for 90 days after mailing so that the preliminary report on response percentages was due in the middle of December. The agreement with Matthews called for a final report of at least one hundred pages in March 1967.

While the questionnaire was being completed I contacted the publishers of the *Official Catholic Directory* to inquire about their special listing of "Secular Clergymen other than Pastors." Although they publish the large directory only once a year in May, they maintain a current census of all Catholic priests in America, constantly updating changes of address. They are able to boast that their special listings contain only a 2 percent error. For this reason I was confident that I had the most up-to-date mailing list obtainable at the beginning of September. Kenedy then addressed envelopes for every third diocesan priest who was a non-pastor, and from them we manually removed those addressed to monsignors. The total mailing went to 5,938 priests in 138 dioceses.

For lack of finances, and also as a guarantee of anonymity to respondents, I decided on a "one-shot" survey, that is, only one mailing with no follow-up of nonrespondents. Another reason was that I already had an extraordinarily high (33 percent) sample of the men I wanted to reach. At the cut-off date I had 3,048 completed questionnaires which represented 17 percent of all diocesan priests who were not pastors or monsignors. For comparative purposes I ought to say that in 1969 NORC did a clergy survey for the Catholic bishops, mailing questionnaires to every tenth Catholic priest, and with two or three follow-ups, and based its final report on the returns from only 7 percent of all American Catholic priests (19).

WHO GETS THE FINDINGS? Because of the earlier experiences I had had with church officials in my research work, I was more cautious and less trustful in 1966 than I had been previously. Before mailing out the questionnaires on

September 7, 1966, I warned everyone with whom I consulted that they keep this project confidential. I saw no reason, as I later told the apostolic delegate, why I should obtain the approval, or "authorization," of a bishop before sending an inquiry to the priests of his diocese. I wanted no preliminary prohibition that might interfere with the project. Since Rome ordinarily moves slowly, I guessed that it would be about 3 months before the inevitable letter of ecclesiastical remonstrance would arrive. It actually arrived 3 months and 2 days later.

What to do with the findings? To whom should they be given? Who could use them most effectively in implementing the renewal of the priesthood indicated in some of the documents of Vatican II? Should the report be public or private? This was not a personal problem for me because I agreed from the start that the ownership of the data was to be with Frank Matthews and his colleagues who had initiated the study and gathered the funds for it. I had no plans for publication, but they made an agreement with Bob Hoyt and Don Thorman that in exchange for a partial subsidy of 2,000 dollars to the study, the *National Catholic Reporter* would have first rights on releasing the findings.

From the very beginning the St. Louis priests were eager that "the bishops find out what the priests are thinking," especially on the matter of clerical celibacy. They wanted the results channeled to the American bishops and through them to the Vatican and the pope himself. They felt that certain progressive bishops—Stephen Leven of San Antonio, Ernest Primeau of Manchester, and James Shannon of St. Paul —would be willing to "make a case" with the American hierarchy and perhaps to act as an intermediary committee in presenting the research findings to church officials in Rome (20).

The prelate most responsive to this idea was Bishop James Shannon whom I telephoned in early September, asking his advice about the most effective means of communicating the research data to people who could "do something about them." He felt that "special pleading" on the part of some American bishops would probably have some influence in Rome, but also that the findings should not be limited to a secret and confidential report meant only for episcopal eyes. He approved the agreement Matthews had made to give "first rights" for news release to the *National Catholic Reporter*. In effect, however, the news release by this paper and my simultaneous mailing of an overview of the findings to the bishops of all American dioceses canceled out the plan to utilize any specially chosen episcopal intermediaries to bring the message to Rome.

Since I had constructed a national sample of priest respondents, the questionnaire reached into every part of the country, and there was neither need nor effort to keep the study confidential any longer. Some priests said that they discussed the questionnaire and their responses with their colleagues. Others, who had not received a questionnaire, wrote to request that they be included in the survey. Only one protested that he would not answer because the questionnaire "does not say that the survey has the approval of the bishop." Inevitably, word of the research project spread among the American hierarchy, several of whom complained to the cardinal secretary of state at the Vatican, so that the matter was brought "to the attention of the Holy See."

I later learned that on November 30 the papal secretary of state relayed these episcopal protests to the apostolic delegate in Washington. I was not aware of these complaints before the "cutoff" date in early December, at which time I sent the overview of findings to the diocesan bishops. Only six of these bishops took the trouble to acknowledge receipt of this preliminary report and its covering letter. Two of them, Bishops George Ahr of Trenton and Maurice Schexnayder of Lafayette, Louisiana, sent a brief note of thanks with no further comment. Constructive criticisms and interested comments were offered by Bishops Romeo Blanchette of Joliet and Bernard Topel of Spokane. One negative response came from Bishop John Russell of Richmond, who wrote briefly to ask what possible good I could hope to accomplish by this widespread publication, either for the church or for the vocation program.

The most positive episcopal reaction I received was from Bishop Victor Reed of the Oklahoma City–Tulsa diocese, who invited me to address his clergy institute on the practical implications of the survey. His chancellor, Father William Garthoeffner, asked me for twenty copies of the overview of findings, as well as of the questionnaire, so that the priests there could make a further study. The vocations director of the Kansas City diocese, Father Earl Eilts, commented on several "valuable insights" of the study. He opined further that "probably many in authority will not utilize other aspects of your study to improve the priesthood and seminary because they reject a change in celibacy."

The fact that the overwhelming majority of the bishops failed to acknowledge receipt of my December communication does not mean that they were antagonistic to the report, or even that they failed to read it. After all, one of the findings of both the 1960 survey and the 1966 survey was that bishops do not communicate well with the lower-echelon clergy (21). Six months later, at the end of June, I had the rare opportunity to deliver two lectures to a select group of American bishops at Fordham University. In the lectures, and the question sessions, the final chapter of my book was discussed (22).

The spectacular publicity attending this research project, especially through the news media in December 1966, made it inevitable that a book be published about it. Eric Lankjaer, who was in charge of religious books at Harper and Row, had already visited me in October at the Harvard Divinity

School when we discussed a possible manuscript. His editorial colleague, Fred Wieck, whom I had known briefly at the University of Chicago Press before my *Southern Parish* study came under fire, took up the contact that resulted in a publishing agreement at the end of January and a manuscript at the end of June.

The original understanding with Frank Matthews and his associates who guaranteed the funding of the research was that they would have a completed manuscript of about 100 pages by the first of March. When it became apparent that a wider audience could be reached through a large book publisher they agreed that I should omit the March report and go ahead with the writing of a book. Meanwhile several other publishers made inquiries about the book potential of the survey. I started writing before Christmas and had the first rough draft completed by the middle of March. It was a fairly smooth and orderly procedure, with my research assistant, Jean Blanning, supplying and checking references and with statistical tables flowing in regularly from John Keller and Norma Batt, of the computer center at Loyola University of the South.

I have never been attracted by so-called "pure research," or the collection and analysis of data simply as an intellectual experience. From the point of view of practical utility for institutional renewal, research data become valuable to the extent that they are analyzed, interpreted, and generalized. The "deadly dull" statistics of the preliminary overview in December, out of which Bob Hoyt made an exciting news story, required objective and patient reflection. As I completed each chapter of the book I sent it to a list of eighteen concerned and competent persons, asking their comments, suggestions, and corrections. This was a task which half of them, though willing, were unable to accomplish. In most cases they were too occupied with other commitments to do a careful reading of the manuscript.

The nine readers who—in the best sense of the term—acted as "censors" of the book provided valuable insights and saved me from some misinterpretations. Three of them were social scientists: Raymond Baumhart, Thomas Garrett, and Edgar Mills. Three were scholars of religion and ecclesiastical studies: James Blanning, Edward Stanton, and Ernest Wallwork. Three were socially concerned and religiously active lay women: Fortunata Caliri, Mary Schniedwind, and Dorothy Willmann. The final version of each chapter of the book was immeasurably improved by the voluntary assistance of these readers.

Even when I had completed the book I still did not have an appropriate title for it. Fred Wieck suggested "The New Priests," but Herder had just come out with that title (23). Since the book dealt with lower-echelon diocesan clergy, I though that "Priests at the Bottom Rung," would be fairly descriptive. Bishop Leven had called the ordinary parish assistant the "forgotten man" of the church, and we thought that the title could be "Forgotten Voices in the Church." For a-while we toyed with the idea of "Priests Anonymous" but remembered that anonymity belonged to alcoholics and others who were trying to rehabilitate themselves. It was only at our last conference when I delivered the manuscript that Eric Lankjaer suggested the title: *America's Forgotten Priests: What They Are Saying.*

SECRECY AND SENSATIONALISM.   By and large I did not believe that the findings of the priest survey, or the manner in which I described them, were sensational. Nor did I believe that they should be shrouded in secrecy. This was the fourth social science project in which I had to face this question of confidentiality versus publicity. I had been scolded by various establishment people on three previous occasions for "rocking the boat." According to them, the facts about urban parish life, about the behavior of city police, about race relations in the school system were the kind of facts that should not be publicly revealed because their disclosure caused "more harm than good." Now for the fourth time I was about to be called publicly to task.

My own attitude toward censorship had changed drastically since the suppression of three volumes of my *Southern Parish* research project. Although I continued always to ask competent persons, especially social scientists, to read and comment on my research monographs before publication, I continued also to oppose the notion that the truth should be hidden from the public. Meanwhile, the Second Vatican Council had itself affirmed: "There exists within human society a right to information about affairs which affect men individually or collectively, and according to the circumstances of each. The proper exercise of this right demands that the matter communicated always be true, and as complete as charity and justice allow" (24).

Pope John XXIII was widely acclaimed for his intention to "open up" the church to an honestly refreshing self-scrutiny. In a sense, the council he convoked was itself an enormous research project, utilizing the talents of many experts and publishing its findings for all to read. But traditional patterns die hard, and many of the bishops who participated in the council were unwilling to relinquish their habit of censorship and control in their own dioceses. Above all, they seemed fearful of sociological investigations published without their permission. A year after the close of Vatican II, the apostolic delegate told me, "I have been asked to recommend to you that in your prudence you not publish the data of this investigation without first bringing the matter to the attention of the National Conference of Catholic Bishops and the appropriate Congregation of the Holy See."

I must assume that this prelate, Archbishop Egidio Vagnozzi, read carefully the preliminary overview of statistical findings which I sent him on December 10, 1966. He certainly saw the news release prepared by the *National Catholic Reporter*, as well as the article and editorial appearing in that weekly on December 14. With all this information at his disposal, the apostolic delegate was undoubtedly prepared for the questions asked of him a week later, December 21, at a press conference arranged by Washington women reporters.

When a woman reporter asked the apostolic delegate to comment on the "Fichter Survey" the prelate did not challenge the facts revealed in the study. Instead he belittled the priests who had supplied those facts in answering the questionnaire. Pastors and monsignors had not been included in the survey, and this meant to the archbishop that "the group was composed of older priests who had not been promoted —possibly for good reason—and of young, rather immature clerics." In effect, he was saying that I had asked the wrong people to comment about life in the priesthood, and was probably implying that I could have gotten the true story had I sampled the mature clerics who had been promoted by their bishops.

One would hardly expect a trained diplomat, the Pope's "ambassador" to American Catholics, to make such a pejorative appraisal of the lower-echelon clergy. I am assuming, of course, that he was accurately reported in the newspapers. The "rather immature" priests to whom he refers are the large number of respondents under 35 years of age. These men are the products of the church's seminary system and are working under the direction of episcopal administration. If they are still immature a decade after their ordination to the priesthood, one may well ask serious questions about the seminary system under which they were trained and about the bishop's leadership of the diocese in which they work.

The "older priests" who had not been promoted to a pastorate or honored with the monsignor's title—"possibly for good reasons," as this papal diplomat said—were almost ex-

clusively from the large American dioceses where priests do
not become pastors until they have been ordained 20 or more
years. Many of them were also in specialized diocesan
activities—chancery office, seminary, Catholic charities,
chaplaincies of various kinds. In most American dioceses,
priests selected for such work are specially trained and trust-
worthy (25).

Two days after this press conference the apostolic delegate
sent me a note acknowledging my letter of December 10, in
which I had explained that secrecy was no longer possible
since I had already mailed out the preliminary overview of
findings. He said that he would bring my response "to the attention of the Holy See." This procedure was apparently to
satisfy the query of the cardinal secretary of state who would
then have some functionary at the Vatican write back to the
several American bishops who disliked unauthorized questionnaires sent to their clergy. Perhaps also there was an expectation that the Holy See would take official notice of the
survey in the form of a condemnation. There was indeed a
flurry of excitement in February 1967 when an American
wire service mistakenly identified an article in *L'Osservatore
della Domenica* as an expression of Vatican censure. It reported a "special feeling of disquiet" resulting from my survey of the clergy (26).

It was too late for secrecy because the overview of findings
had already been sent to all those respondents who requested
it. Editor Robert Hoyt was writing an article to appear in
the December 14 issue of the *National Catholic Reporter*.
Donald Thorman, publisher of *NCR*, prepared a news release
which he sent to seventeen bishops and archbishops. When I
learned that only this limited number of prelates were to receive no more than a news release on the survey, I sent a
copy of both the questionnaire and the overview, together
with a covering letter, to the bishops of all 138 dioceses in the
United States. I felt that they needed this information if they

were to respond intelligently to questions from news reporters.

I have no way of knowing how carefully the prelates studied the preliminary report I sent to them. There is no doubt,
however, that the findings of the survey, as presented in the
article in the *National Catholic Reporter* and its accompany-
ing news release, disturbed some of the American bishops. A
very prompt reaction came from the two Kansas City prelates, Archbishop Edward Hunkeler of Kansas City, Kansas,
and Bishop Charles Helmsing of Kansas City, Missouri. They
challenged the finding that bishop-clergy communication was
bad and that bishops took little personal interest in these
priests. They said the data did not apply to their dioceses—
which may well have been true since I said nothing specific
about the two Kansas City dioceses.

What seemed more to irritate these hierarchs, and to arouse
national attention in the survey report, was the "sensationalism" of optional clerical celibacy. The story in the *National
Catholic Reporter* headlined the fact that 62 percent of the
priest respondents favored freedom of choice for the diocesan
clergy to marry or to remain celibate. This "fearful" topic,
which had been banned from the floor of debate at the Second Vatican Council, was now out in the open. Indeed, it had
not been a closed question among the priests themselves—
more than eight out of ten said they had discussed it with
fellow diocesan priests during the previous year.

I had deliberately refused to focus my research project exclusively on the question of a married priesthood, and I devoted only a small segment of the questionnaire to this topic.
Yet it immediately became the heart of the matter, and the
study was everywhere called "that celibacy survey." Reporters and journalists singled this out as the most newsworthy
item in the survey. The widespread publicity given to the
celibacy question brought charges of "sensationalism" against
both me and the *National Catholic Reporter*. Archbishop

Hunkeler denounced me to a newsman for the *Kansas City Star* as a sociologist who is not thorough in research and "always aims at sensationalism and publicity." I wrote courteously to him requesting that he expand and demonstrate the basis of his comment, but have never received a reply.

Bishop Helmsing in whose diocese the *National Catholic Reporter* is published and who originally sponsored it but who 2 years later (October 1968) strongly and publicly condemned this weekly for its "poisonous character," was worried about what he called my "so-called sociological study." Even before he had read the preliminary report of findings he exclaimed, "God save us from surveys along the lines of the Kinsey Report!" Whether my report can be called scandalous, or whether God can be credited with "saving us" because it was not scandalous, the fact is that the subsequent book, *America's Forgotten Priests*, contained only one chapter (21 out of 254 pages) dealing with the topic of "Married Clergy."

A USELESS SURVEY? A sociological researcher has to be ready to answer complaints about his sample and techniques and charges that the findings are false, or that their public release is harmful. Another kind of criticism is more frustrating: that the survey is useless because it simply "discovers what everybody already knew." A Philadelphia priest, who shall be nameless here, refused to answer the questionnaire because he wanted no part of a study that would "put the church and the hierarchy in a bad light and confirm the malcontents in their rebellion." He said further that "every curate in the country can tell you of the problems of his diocese and of the church in general." It seemed to him that sociologists "like to tell us that what we already know really does exist."

I offered to bet this unbelieving cleric that he really did not know how the Philadelphia priests would answer the questionnaire. To make it easier for him to win the bet I suggested that he select any ten of the opinion questions in the study and that he would be the winner if he could come within 7 percentage points (i.e., 3 percent below or above) of the actual responses of his fellow priests. The winner of the bet would pay for a special report of all research data on the Philadelphia priests. He was apparently not a betting man and did not respond. He had saved postage by sending his criticisms in the postpaid envelope meant for the returned questionnaire.

Obviously I had anticipated some of the main findings of the survey, partly on the basis of my previous surveys and interviews with priests and seminarians and partly on materials I had gathered from the literature on the priesthood. Some of the "problems" publicized as a consequence of my 1966 project were already in evidence to careful observers in the 1950s. The need for church renewal and change was apparent well before the Second Vatican Council. Perhaps no one knew how widespread these problems were among the clergy, nor the intensity with which they existed in different regions of the country, nor the direction in which they were developing.

One of these areas in which I could roughly anticipate the responses to the survey was that of human relations and communication within the ecclesiastical system. Some bishops may have had hurt feelings to learn that their priests think of them as aloof and unfriendly, others may agree with the diocesan paper, *Brooklyn Tablet*, that keeping your subordinates at a distance prevents "paternalism" in the church (27). Frank and open dialogue has long been notoriously absent with bishops and chancery officials and in the seminary system and all diocesan institutions. I was not at all surprised that the survey revealed nine out of ten priests clamoring for due process, personnel boards, grievance committees, clergy senates,

and other institutional changes that would improve communication.

A second anticipation of survey results, which I also based
on wide previous knowledge of conditions, was the dissatisfaction of parish.clergy with their life and work. It was no
secret, even before Vatican II, that many priests were ques-
tioning the meaning and value of their vocational role in
modern society. Many thought that their talents were being
wasted, that the seminary had not prepared them to deal with
contemporary problems, that "working conditions" in the
local rectory and parish left much to be desired. More than
half (54 percent) of the fulltime curates said that the tasks
they performed in the parish were not utilizing their talents
and training. They were bored with the minimal work expectations of their vocation.

A third area in which results could have been roughly predicted, but which seems to have taken many by surprise, was
the clergy attitude on celibacy and marriage. Nevertheless,
there were probably many, like the editor of *Ave Maria*, who
had not believed that the question of celibacy was "an issue of
serious concern to large numbers of American priests" (28). It
was felt that priests generally did not think about this matter,
much less talk about it—and this may have been true in the
1950s. Yet, only 14 percent of the respondents said that they
had seldom or never discussed the question with their fellow
diocesan priests in 1966. Less than four out of ten (38 percent) said that the freedom of choice to marry should not be
open to diocesan priests.

Some commentators who knew that I had proposed the ordination of married lay men in a speech to the national convention of Vocation Directors at Milwaukee in September
1966 thought that I had "rigged" the questionnaire in order
to get the desired answer on optional clerical marriage. In
that same speech I had suggested that seminaries be open to
female candidates for the priesthood and that the church seek

candidates for the priesthood from black Catholics, students in public high schools, and persons in the lower economic classes of Catholics (29). The fact that I held—and still hold—strong preferences on many of the items in the research questionnaire did not mean at all that I was unable to ask and test these questions with scientific objectivity.

I must confess that I was surprised by one of the findings, one which was hardly noticed by the critics and commentators of this research report. I did not anticipate that such a large proportion (64 percent) of the respondents would agree with the statement, "As in other professions and occupations, it should be possible to have voluntary resignation, or an 'honorable discharge,' from the priesthood." The notion that the priesthood is a permanent commitment to Christ and the church had seemed to me much stronger than the notion that priests in the Latin rite were to be permanently nonmarriageable. I probably should have asked how many of them would take advantage of an "honorable discharge" if it were available to them. I did ask whether they would choose to be priests if they could do it over again, and found that better than one out of seven would "hesitate" now to enter the seminary.

In retrospect to 1966 I see that approval of voluntary resignation from the priesthood looked to the future, whereas the fact of relatively few previous resignations looked to the past. Up until this study in 1966 there had been no reliable research information available on the numbers, proportions, or rates of Catholic clergy resignations. I asked the priests how many men were in their ordination class, how many of these had left the priesthood, and how many of these had married. Their responses showed that about 0.5 percent left the priesthood within 3 years of ordination, and that this statistic rose to less than 4 percent for ordination classes of 25 years or more ago.

This was the first factual and reliable information about the much-discussed, and much-rumored, question of the number of men who were leaving the diocesan priesthood. It was a low rate of resignation compared with the known occupational shifts of Protestant ministers and the even higher rate of career changes in some other professions. It also belied the rumors of "wholesale defections" from the American priesthood that were current in 1966 before this research project was launched. I ought to enter the reminder here that these statistics are a reference to the past, to the period up to the autumn of 1966 (30).

It is a peculiar historical fact that I conducted this research project just at the time when the volume of priestly resignations began to increase spectacularly. The Second Vatican Council adjourned in December 1965. One year later, just before Christmas 1966, came the widely publicized news that Charles Davis, prominent British theologian and *peritus* of the council, had abandoned both the priesthood and the Catholic church to marry Florence Henderson, a former American member of the Grail (31). During 1967, and in subsequent years, an increasing number of men left the priestly ministry, most of them taking a wife in the process. There were many among them, however, who wanted to marry but at the same time continue in the active ministry of the church.

PASTORAL RENEWAL. The priests with whom Frank Matthews was associated in St. Louis, and who originated the clergy survey by guaranteeing its financial support, were in favor of a married priesthood. They were also in contact with "priests from all parts of the country who are interested in testing the principle of collegiality." In the spring of 1966 some of them met quietly in St. Louis to discuss the potential utility of the research project, how the results might be implemented, and whether an organized effort could be made to share their concerns with the hierarchy (32). They felt that the concept of collegiality, as expounded by the council, should be applicable at all levels of the church.

Further discussion and correspondence led to the formal establishment in January 1967 of the National Association for Pastoral Renewal (NAPR). Lay people were invited to join, but for the most part its members were Catholic clergymen, some on the verge of marriage, some with no intention to marry, but all with the conviction that the pastoral renewal of the church had to include a married priesthood. One of the avowed purposes of NAPR was to stem the exodus of priests from the church who wanted to get married. Another purpose was to provide a voice for the "forgotten priests" whose opinions were seldom heard by the hierarchy and who might supply information useful for the reform of the priestly role and status of the institutional church. No one suggested that optional marriage was the total solution—or the key to the solution—of all problems of the American priesthood. There were those, however, who felt that it was a "necessary option."

Aside from writing its constitution and by-laws, electing officers, and absorbing large numbers of members, NAPR quickly set three projects in motion. The first of these was a proposal that a "vicariate" be canonically established in which married Catholic priests could carry on the active ministry under the jurisdiction of their own bishop (33). This novel eccelsiastical structure, called also a prelature or ordinariate, had its model in the military vicariate, in which a member of the hierarchy (at that time, Cardinal Spellman) had pastoral responsibility for all Catholic personnel in the military services of the United States. This proposal was submitted to Archbishop John Dearden, president of the National Conference of Catholic Bishops, in January 1967, but it appears to have had little subsequent publicity.

The second project was planned as a nationwide survey of priest opinion and action centering on optional celibacy for the Catholic clergy. Carl Hemmer, a graduate student at Columbia University who later left the Jesuit Order, conducted the survey throughout 1967. Lack of time, money, and experience hampered this survey, but with the voluntary assistance of NAPR members in various parts of the country he was able to sample both diocesan and religious priests in about half the American dioceses. In breaking down the data he found that almost two-thirds of the parish assistants, or curates, favored optional celibacy, a statistic very close to the 62 percent in my clergy survey.

Another aspect of the NAPR survey, developed toward the end of the year, was an attempt to discover the number of men who actually left the priesthood during 1966 and 1967. As a member of the advisory board of NAPR, I strongly encouraged the collection of this information which had been feared and hampered by the hierarchy, particularly the apostolic delegation in Washington, for many years. No one really knew the national figures on ex-priests, whether over 2 years or 20 years. The result of this fear and ignorance was that popular estimates placed the number of ex-priests in America anywhere between 2,000 and 10,000. Even the NORC survey, financed by the bishops in 1969, restricted this question to men who resigned during the 4-year period, 1966 to 1969, but it did find a yearly increase in the rate of resignees, without discovering the total number of American former priests (34).

The third project was a symposium on clerical celibacy, scheduled to be held at the University of Notre Dame September 6–8, 1967. The NAPR executive secretary, Robert Francoeur, started planning for it in March, and George Frein, the symposium chairman, contacted the prospective program participants in April. At this program I presented a paper that had emerged from further analysis of the survey research data in which I made comparisons between priests favoring and opposing clerical celibacy (35). Herder contracted to publish a book, which had to be ready by the middle of August, from these papers.

Bob Francoeur married in May, an action which at that time seemed to me to jeopardize both NAPR and its scheduled symposium. I requested a telephone conference with other members of the advisory board and the core leaders of NAPR and urged that no married priests be directly involved with the program at Notre Dame. My argument— which does not seem so convincing now as it did then— was that we had to try to win over the bishops, rather than flaunt and antagonize them, which I was sure would happen if married priests were to participate in the program. The planners agreed with me, but as a matter of fact some married priests did attend with their wives, and it probably made no difference.

It appears that many of the hierarchy were already antagonistic and unhappy about the "celibacy data" from the research project, and further disturbed by the organization of NAPR. The bishops refused to place the celibacy question on the agenda of their April 1967 meeting, but some of them thought it would be included in the deliberations of the Episcopal Synod at Rome in the autumn. This expectation was shattered in June 1967, when Paul VI issued his papal encyclical calling for continued adherence to celibacy, the "brilliant jewel" of the Roman church. The American hierarchy— whatever any individual bishop thought of it—rallied in public support of the Pope's position (36).

In effect, then, the papal encyclical and the American hierarchy's support of it killed any chance that episcopal representatives would accept NAPR's invitation to attend the September symposium. There were rumors that episcopal pressure was put on the president of the University of Notre Dame to cancel the use of the campus for the symposium. After the event, Bishop Leo Pursley, the local Ordinary of the Fort Wayne–South Bend diocese, complained that the "usual courtesies" had not been observed. He said that he had been informed of the symposium only after it had been scheduled and that one of its chief promoters, Father John O'Brien of the University of Notre Dame, had failed to hold "prior consultation" with the bishop.

The symposium attracted an attendance of approximately 200 persons, but had excellent radio and television coverage and achieved nationwide publicity through the newspapers and magazines. The chairman of the meeting, George Frein, edited the program papers which were later published by Herder under the title *Celibacy: The Necessary Option*. Subsequently he, too, resigned from the priesthood and married. Another man was quietly present at this symposium, the priest who started it all in the previous year when he proposed the research study of the clergy and found the money to support it. On the day after the conclusion of the symposium Frank Matthews announced to his parishioners in St. Louis that he was resigning the pastorate and the priesthood. Subsequently he, too, took the option to marry.

BEYOND CELIBACY.   Before, during, and after my 1966 research survey of diocesan lower-echelon priests I kept insisting that the question of optional celibacy was only one of many facing the American Catholic priesthood, perhaps not the most important one. I tried to point this out, and to put clerical marriage in the perspective of other clerical problems, in an article in *America* discussing the survey (37). In the book itself, *America's Forgotten Priests*, which was published in February 1968, I included a chapter on "Implications and Interpretations" in which I recapitulated eight major findings, of which only one was about "celibate and married priests." There I wrote that "the custom of a celibate diocesan clergy cannot be treated in isolation from the total institutional structure in which it exists" (38).

As a member of the advisory board of NAPR, my interpretation of "pastoral renewal" seemed much broader than that of the leaders and the general membership. Many of them had a personal stake in optional celibacy because they wanted to marry and still remain in the active ministry. I argued that even if the church rules were changed to allow a married priesthood, all the other problems would still have to be solved. I tested this concept at a meeting in Washington with a group of ex-priests and their wives by asking, "Would you come back to the active ministry if you could do so as married priests?" (39).

The wives of these priests raised immediate objections, and the reasons they gave were very similar to the complaints of Protestant ministers' wives: attitudes and expectations of parishioners, the confinement of rectory life, the question of sufficient income, the professional demands on the time and energy of their priest-husbands. The men themselves were more reflective of the entire institutionalized life of the diocese. Before returning to the active priesthood they wanted changes in the appointment and promotion system, due process in grievances, opportunities for sabbaticals and continuing education, better communication with diocesan authorities, and some responsibility in decision-making.

It seemed to me, further, that the lot of the married priest would be even more difficult that that of the celibate priest if he worked in a diocese where the bishop was unmarried. If the celibate bishop had difficulty in understanding the celibate priest, how much greater would his difficulty be in trying to understand his married clergy. Later I did an article for *Commonweal* in which I suggested that marriage should be mandatory for bishops, but optional for priests (40). This was imaginative and sociological speculation, but it also raised some serious questions about the structure of a church in which nothing was to be changed except the rule of imposed clerical celibacy.

Sometimes I have difficulty in judging whether the essential renewal of the American Catholic church has been helped or hindered by the widespread, and almost prurient, preoccupation with the matter of a married priesthood. Most of the bishops were frightened by the very thought of it and generally took their stance on Pope Paul's adamant opposition to any change in the rules. On the other hand, they were finally frightened also by the increasing number of priests who left the ministry and married, and by the decreasing number of seminarians and candidates for the priesthood. In 1966 they looked with scorn on a research project that asked about optional marriage for priests; in 1972 they were studying the findings of a survey they had themselves financed in which they had allowed the "fearful" question to be asked.

Journalists, commentators, and interviewers seemed determined to make celibacy the central issue of church renewal. In Boston during 1967 I participated in several "talk shows" on radio and television and had difficulty—in fact, was unable—to divert the "talk master's" mind off the question of married priests. After the book was published I was guest on an afternoon television show in Cleveland—one of those programs on which the viewers are asked to telephone in their votes on a particular question. The question, of which I was not even aware until the program had started, was, "Should Catholic Priests be Allowed to Marry?". Seventy percent of the 1,143 voters—probably mainly housewives of various religious affiliation—called in affirmatively.

There were a few exceptions to this wide preoccupation with the marriage of Catholic priests. In early March 1968 I appeared on the NBC *Today Show* in New York to talk with Hugh Downs and Joe Garagiola, both of whom had done their homework on my book. They were willing to talk about unrest and dissatisfaction among the diocesan clergy and to discuss the wider implications for church renewal as indicated in *America's Forgotten Priests*. A similar professional approach was exhibited by Irving Kupcinet in Chicago when I appeared as guest on his Saturday night television program, *Kup's Show*. Obviously, these appearances were part of the advertising program arranged by Harper and Row to sell the book.

Meanwhile, NAPR, besides conducting its own surveys, attempting to get the ear of the hierarchy, and mailing out propaganda statements, was planning another symposium to be held at St. Louis University in September 1968. Archbishop Carberry was unhappy with university officials for allowing the program on the campus and also let it be known that he did not want his seminarians and priests to attend it. NAPR continued to be an annoyance to the bishops because it continued to center its efforts on getting the rules changed to allow a married clergy.

The St. Louis meeting of NAPR was notable for the fact that it gave birth to a new organization, the Society of Priests for a Free Ministry. I was present at the informal evening discussion during which this started, and I felt that it was narrowing still further the concept of pastoral renewal throughout the ecclesiastical structure. The proponents of the new group were men who refused to accept their status as "ex-priests" on the grounds that marriage, or laicization, or even formal excommunication, could not take away the sacramental character bestowed on them by Holy Orders. They were willing to support themselves by gainful "secular" employment, but they wanted to provide also a priestly ministry to people who needed their spiritual services.

Another and more representative organization of diocesan priests was established in these years. The National Federation of Priests' Councils had a broad perspective on all problems concerning the Catholic church in America but also in 1969 decided to finance a survey of diocesan priests' opinions on clerical celibacy. I was little more than occasional consultant to John Koval and Richard Bell who carried out this survey and reported its findings in December 1970 at the Chicago meeting of the Society for the Scientific Study of Religion. This report confirmed some of the findings of my own two previous surveys and also anticipated by several months some of the results of the bishops' own survey conducted by the National Opinion Research Center. There could no longer be any doubt that the majority of diocesan priests favored optional celibacy.

As a postscript to this chapter, and as an index of changed attitudes toward sociological research within the Catholic church, I mention that at the end of 1969 I did a "10-years-after" survey of the American Jesuits I had surveyed as theological students in 1959. I enlisted the willing cooperation of all ten Jesuit provincials in finding the names and addresses of these men. As I did in the earlier study, I sent a report of the research findings to these Jesuit superiors. There was no letter of admonition from Rome, nor any command that "this must not be permitted," nor apparently was there any complaint sent to the Jesuit general at Rome about this survey. My impression was that Jesuit superiors, like diocesan bishops, were now quite willing to receive any information that might help them face the continuing problems of church renewal.

NOTES

1. As a matter of fact, *The Converted Catholic Magazine*, edited by former Roman Catholic priests, did precisely this in the issue of November 1952. Data taken from my *Southern Parish* study inspired the remark that "the evidence is, conclusively then, to the effect that the Roman Catholic Church has more *heretics* inside than outside!" (p. 280). In April 1958 the name of this periodical was changed to *Christian Heritage*.

2. This document predated the Second Vatican Council which on December 4, 1963, in its Decree on Communications said that

"there exists within human society a right to information about affairs which affect men individually or collectively, and according to the circumstances of each." (article 5) Then on October 28, 1965, the Decree on Bishops said that "religious and social surveys, made through offices of pastoral sociology, contribute greatly to the effective and fruitful attainment of that goal [adaptation of the apostolate] and they are cordially recommended." (article 17)

3. See Chapter Two for the trouble I had with *Southern Parish*. One of its negative reviewers, Paul Furfey, treated the second book, *Social Relations in the Urban Parish*, with more respect, saying that it was "a brilliant and very significant book which will set the pace in an important, developing field of research." *American Sociological Review*, Vol. 20, No. 3, June 1955, p. 354.

4. I used these and other subsequent and available research studies in my book, *Religion as an Occupation* (Notre Dame, University of Notre Dame Press, 1961).

5. This "never-again" prohibition was not permanent. With a new Jesuit general, Pedro Arrupe, and the post-Vatican II social climate, I participated in the 1966 Survey of American Jesuits, the questionnaire for which replicated many items from my previous Jesuit survey of 1959.

6. Among others interested in the survey was a Jesuit from Brazil, who asked permission to translate the questionnaire into Portuguese for distribution to Jesuit theological students there.

7. This was not the first time the archbishop of Philadelphia criticized me. While I was visiting professor at the University of Notre Dame he found fault with the predictions in my article on "The Teacher Shortage," *Commonweal*, January 25, 1957. See reference to this in Thomas McAvoy, *Father O'Hara of Notre Dame* (Notre Dame, University of Notre Dame Press, 1967), pp. 429 ff.

8. McAvoy, *op. cit.*, p. 481.

9. See Chapter Two for my previous contacts with Father Janssens, superior general of the Society of Jesus.

10. The procedures of these parallel clergy-lay surveys are explained, pp. vi–xiv, in *Priest and People* (New York, Sheed and Ward, 1965).

11. Father John Keller established the computer center at Loyola

University of the South in late 1963. From then on, he and his assistant, Norma Batt, processed the data from my research projects.

12. In other words, the 2,183 priest respondents were a scientifically selected interval sample and reliably representative. The 2,216 lay people were their "best" parishioners and not a cross-section of American adult Catholics.

13. His book was then already on the market: Conor K. Ward, *Priests and People* (Liverpool, Liverpool University Press, 1961).

14. In government circles this is called "clearance," rather than censorship. My book was published as *Graduates of Predominantly Negro Colleges* (Washington, D.C., Government Printing Office, 1967). The grant for both surveys came from the National Institutes of Health, with joint sponsorship by the U.S. Department of Labor and the National Science Foundation.

15. Another research project that I started in Chicago and completed at Harvard was the 1965 survey of Jesuit high school students, discussed in the next chapter.

16. In this connection it may be useful to review the materials in "Executive Functions of Superiors," pp. 255–279, in *Religion as an Occupation* (Notre Dame, University of Notre Dame Press, 1961).

17. The excellent index in Walter Abbott, Ed., *The Documents of Vatican II* (New York, Angelus Books, 1966) has only two references to assistant pastors, but 119 to bishops.

18. Pope Paul's encyclical, *Humanae Vitae*, was issued on July 25, 1968, and it was loyally supported by the American hierarchy on November 15, 1968, with a collective pastoral letter, "Human Life in Our Day." For the beginnings of the controversy see Robert Hoyt, Ed., *The Birth Control Debate* (Kansas City, *National Catholic Reporter*, 1968).

19. The final report of the NORC survey, delivered to the bishops for their meeting in Detroit, April 27–29, 1971, was in part a confirmation of my research findings of 5 years earlier. For a lively discussion of the NORC's findings, see Andrew M. Greeley, *Priests in the United States: Reflections on a Survey* (Garden City, Doubleday, 1972).

20. Bishop Leven was promoted to ordinary of the San Angelo diocese in 1969. In the same year Bishop Shannon married and was formally excluded from the church.

21. I do not know which bishops complained to the Holy See at Rome about this survey. They did not send their protests to me nor, as far as I know, to my Jesuit superiors.

22. This was an off-the-record institute, by invitation only, at which a number of lecturers discussed the changing American Catholic church. By this time I had completed the book manuscript and delivered it the next day to the New York office of Harper and Row.

23. M. de Saint Pierre, *New Priests* (New York, Herder, 1966) translated by Sr. M. Renelle.

24. Walter Abbott, *op. cit.*, p. 322, calls this "the most important statement of the document." Decree on the Instruments of Social Communication, article 5.

25. This rebuttal of the apostolic delegate's remarks was already made in my article, "That Celibacy Survey," *America*, January 21, 1967, pp. 92–94.

26. This Italian newspaper was probably confused with *L'Osservatore Romano*, which often reflects Vatican opinion. Robert Graham, special correspondent for Religious News Service, explained the mistake in February 1967.

27. Patrick Scanlon, managing editor of the *Tablet*, tried to "explain away" my survey in the issues of December 22 and 29, 1966.

28. Nevertheless, John L. Reedy, in his "Editor's Column," accepted the findings of the survey and said he was ready to "eat crow."

29. There is a reference to this speech in the article, "Holy Father Church," *Commonweal*, May 15, 1970, pp. 216–218.

30. For subsequent information on this point see my article "Catholic Church Professionals," *The Annals*, Vol. 387, January 1970, pp. 77–85.

31. Charles Davis explains his position and decision in *A Question of Conscience* (New York, Harper and Row, 1967). See the tightly reasoned response to Davis by Gregory Baum, *The Credibility of the Church Today* (New York, Herder and Herder, 1968).

32. See the introductory remarks by George Frein, Ed., *Celibacy: The Necessary Option* (New York, Herder and Herder, 1968), pp. 8–10.

33. This proposal grew out of an article by Robert Francoeur, "The Priest of the Future," *Jubilee*, October 1966.

34. The NORC survey report, published in 1972 by the United States Catholic Conference under the title, *The Catholic Priest in the United States: Sociological Investigations,* estimated that 5 percent of American Catholic priests had resigned during the 4-year period (p. 313). Perhaps the most significant segment of this study was the supplementary survey of 873 resigned priests. See Chapter 15, "A Look at the Resignees," pp. 275–309.

35. "Sociology and Clerical Celibacy," in Frein, *op. cit.,* pp. 102–122, was specially prepared for the symposium, and not a chapter reprinted from the survey report, *America's Forgotten Priests.*

36. It should be noted that Pope Paul issued his encyclical, *Sacerdotalis Caelibatus,* on June 23, 1967, as though unwilling to wait until the bishops could discuss this subject at the September Synod in Rome.

37. "That Celibacy Survey," *America,* January 21, 1967, pp. 92–94. The only other "defense" I made of the survey was a brief article in the *National Catholic Reporter,* January 4, 1967, p. 6.

38. *Op. cit.,* p. 210. I also provided an appendix, pp. 238–241, "Prescript to Further Research," drawn from suggestions made by the priest respondents to the survey.

39. See my article, "The Re-entry Process," *The Critic,* August–September 1968, pp. 60 f.

40. "Bishops Ought to Marry," *Commonweal,* May 24, 1968, pp. 289–291. The idea for this article came out of the data on priests' career promotion, *America's Forgotten Priests,* pp. 150 f., and was furthered in conversations with Anthony E. C. W. Spencer, British social scientist.

SIX

JESUIT HIGH SCHOOL STUDENTS

The research study I did on the American Jesuit high schools was so "trouble-free," compared with the four other projects described in this book, that any account of this experience may seem out of place. If there is no other reason for telling this story, it may serve as a demonstration that every once in a while a research project can proceed smoothly. Perhaps this is the positive sociological approach applied to research procedures—rather than the negative crisis approach— explaining how "something works," rather than describing "what went wrong."

As may be expected of the typical American Jesuit, I have been involved in education all my professional life. Beyond the role of lecturer on the university campus, I spent a full year at NORC analyzing research data on the college life and aspirations of students in Negro schools of higher learning. Another year of research, at the University of Notre Dame, went into the study of children, teachers, and parents at an elementary parochial school. The missing segment of my research experience in the sociology of education was at the secondary level, and for a while I thought that this gap might be closed by participation in the so-called "Notre Dame Study" of Catholic schools.

This did not occur because there are some professional educators who see little value in the sociological approach to the study of school systems. In early 1962, when preparations were under way for the nationwide survey of American Catholic schools under a grant from the Carnegie Foundation, I met in Washington, D.C. with Frederick Hochwalt and his assistant, O'Neil D'Amour, and later in South Bend with George Schuster. Father D'Amour, a consultant on the survey, was most explicit in declaring that this was a job for educators, not social scientists. The survey apparently proceeded under this assumption. With the exception of Donald Barrett and Andrew Greeley, whose participation in the study was at best peripheral, no sociologists were involved in either the collection or analysis of the research data (1).

American Jesuit educators, operating a large secondary school system for boys, thought that a sociological survey could be helpful. While I was working on the Negro college study at NORC in Chicago, I was asked to discuss a prospective survey of Jesuit high school students. Bernard Dooley, director of a proposed workshop who had suggested the research project, was at first quite vague about it, making two generalizations: (a) "We want to know how we are doing," and (b) "We think we can do better." In other words, he wanted research that could point the way to improved moral and religious training of the students.

When Bernard Dooley invited me to conduct this survey of the boys in the American Jesuit secondary schools in October 1964, I could say that I knew practically nothing about Jesuit high schools. By that time almost 30 years had passed since I had taught the third-year students at Jesuit High School in New Orleans (1935–1936). I was sure—at least

I hoped—that significant changes had occurred in these schools since I had performed in one of them as a young scholastic teacher. That was during the Depression, before World War II, and nothing has been the same since then.

There is always—as there was in this instance—somebody who objects that you cannot study a social situation if you "don't know anything about it," that is, if you are not personally involved in it as participant. This was an objection made by a few diocesan parish priests who said that I could never really understand the operation of a parish or the lifestyle of the diocesan clergy, since I had had no experience in the parochial pastorate. In 1958, when I was invited to give a series of lectures on "religious authority" at the University of Notre Dame, the southern Jesuit provincial, Father Laurence O'Neill, suggested that I was not competent to do so since I had never exercised religious authority, not as a provincial, not even as rector of a Jesuit community (2).

Does one have to be black in order to do research on Negro Americans? This was the hint, made in a gentle and polite way, when I did the research report on Negro college students at NORC and in later years when I gave academic courses on race relations. More recently, and more vociferously, I was informed by a few women liberationists that I was "audacious" in conducting seminars on the subject of "women and religion" and in writing about the role of women in the church. Still more recently, there was the opposite complaint that a sociological review of a book on the woman's movement should not be assigned to a woman as though there were a woman's "point of view" (3).

INVOLVING THE PERSONNEL. The practitioners, especially the older people who have spent all their adult lives in the groups studied by the sociological researcher, are sometimes resentful of the "outsider." They tend to challenge the social scientist: "Do you think you can do it any better?" Or they want all research findings transmitted to them in complete confidence because only they have acquired the wisdom of experience necessary to make reliable and objective judgments about their group. Happily, neither of these attitudes was expressed by Jesuit secondary educators.

Unlike the NORC study of the Catholic priesthood, which seems to have been occasioned by the panic of the prelates who finally realized that there was a crisis among the clergy, the survey of Jesuit high schools was not a sudden decision to meet a crisis. Self-appraisal on both an individual and group level has long been a characteristic of these educators (4). From the beginning there was ample proof of the academic excellence of the Jesuit system—mainly in the large proportions of graduates who attended and finished college. Even in the matter of Christian "formation" the question in 1965 was, "we want to know how successful we have been in forming these young men in accordance with Christian ideals of education."

This was a collective question formulated by a planning committee in the summer of 1964 and carried over into 2 years of intensive self-study among the teachers and administrators at each of the schools and of wide-ranging discussions in each of the American Jesuit provinces. That, at least, was the way that the prospective program of self-analysis was explained to me in November 1964 when I agreed to survey the attitudes of the high school students. Obviously, if there was to be any improvement in these schools it would eventually be introduced by the teachers and administrators themselves. To have them interested and involved throughout the study was, I hoped, a guarantee that development would follow research.

I assumed, therefore, that the people operating these schools knew most about them—certainly more than I— and would be willing to cooperate with me from the very beginning. To test this willingness and, more importantly, to obtain the basic content of the survey questionnaire, I asked that each principal in the forty-four schools send a list of the five largest "problems" of the student body. I stipulated that any principal who did not comply with this request would automatically exclude his school from the survey. I said that I wanted to "discover the extent of interest on the part of principals in this investigation—how many of them answer, with what depth and intelligence, how seriously they are taking this prospective research. There is no use wasting time and money if we are not going to get pretty thorough cooperation at all steps of the survey."

The request to principals went out on January 5, 1965, from Bernard Dooley, director of the study, but 6 weeks later (February 18) there were still thirteen school principals who had not responded. I announced my assumption that these schools did not wish to participate in the survey and my decision that questionnaires would not be sent to them. "I feel that each principal should be left free to participate or not participate in the survey. I do not think that authority or pressure should be brought to bear on the reluctant, but they ought to know ahead of time that they are being left out, or be informed that there is still time for them to respond."

By the end of February, this "threat" of exclusion brought responses from all but two of the school principals. Despite the clarity of the request that the list of problems should focus only on the students themselves, five of the principals misinterpreted it, thinking that the survey was to be made of their alumni. What this demonstrated was that interest and cooperation were manifested unevenly among the Jesuit principals, some of whom cooperated fully and eagerly whereas others had almost to be dragooned into the research survey. I would have been a foolish idealist to expect more from them.

Fortunately one of the most interested principals was right there in Chicago where I was then living while employed at

NORC. Donald Nastold, of St. Ignatius High School, made arrangements for me to pretest two versions of the questionnaire among students in the junior year. The first pretest I conducted on February 26 enabled me to clarify some of the questions for the second pretest on March 11. After each of these I asked the juniors whether they would ask different questions, or ask these questions differently. Their outspoken, even blunt remarks made me realize that this generation of students was quite different from those I had taught three decades earlier in New Orleans.

The next step in the program was the responsibility of Bernard Dooley, who had the questionnaires printed at his headquarters in Baltimore. His staff packaged and sent them to each of the schools on April 5, 1965, with sets of instructions prepared by me for the principals and for the teachers who were to administer the schedules. As far as I could find out, the schools adhered to these instructions: that the questionnaires be answered by both freshmen and seniors at the same hour, that it was not to be called a "test," that no item was to be explained by the teacher, and that no one at the school examine the answered questionnaire (5).

I had not expected perfection in the collection of data, and there were indeed some missteps. The sample called for all freshmen and seniors at the smaller schools, but 100 of each at the larger schools. The balance of planned distribution of the sample was thrown off in one school that produced 135 freshmen but only 56 seniors and in another that produced 128 seniors but only 74 freshmen. In some instances there were freshmen classes that contained sophomores and senior classes that contained juniors. There was also an administrative error that undersampled the seniors at Seattle Preparatory School. With this exception, all errors of distribution could be corrected by a visual inspection of each individual questionnaire so that we ended with an adequate proportional sample from all schools.

It was my original plan that all schools administer the questionnaire during Easter week, but this was not feasible because the principals were then going to be at the annual convention of the Jesuit Educational Association in New York. Most of the schools, therefore, did so in the last week of April and sent the packets of answered questionnaires to me in Chicago. On May 18, however, there were still five schools unreported. Special delivery letters from Bernard Dooley brought in the laggards, but the last packet was not delivered till June 3.

Processing the research data did not require cooperation from the Jesuits in the high schools. I had precoded the questionnaires so that transferring them to punch cards, although an exacting job, was not a complicated procedure. Three coeds at Loyola Univeristy of the South, who had been trained there on previous sociological surveys, completed this work by the end of July. The coded data were then transferred to electronic tapes by Norma Batt at the Loyola Computer Center and processed for tables and percentages under the supervision of the center's director, John Keller.

THE WORKSHOP.   One of the assurances I had at the beginning of the high school study was that the report of findings would not be filed away and forgotten. I was told that "in August, 1966, the Jesuit Educational Association will sponsor a Workshop on the Christian Formation of High School Students. . . . We are interested in presenting to the Workshop a survey of the attitudes of the young men who will graduate from Jesuit high schools in 1965, or at least of a few typical groups of these graduates" (6). It was most satisfying to know that the survey report was to be discussed by the high school personnel who would be ultimately responsible for its implementation.

For more than a year, till November 1965, I worked under

the impression that the prospective workshop was to focus exclusively on the survey I was conducting. At that time, Joseph Devlin, a seminarian at the Weston College of Theology, told me that a group of Jesuit seminarians was meeting regularly to discuss the forthcoming workshop. On further inquiry I learned that the faculties of all the Jesuit high schools were holding conferences and preparing local reports to be presented at the workshop. In December Bernard Dooley verified this fact and said, "This is one stipulation I insisted upon when we planned the affair, that a full year be devoted to preliminary work and discussion on the local level by the delegates from each school."

What was happening during that academic year 1965–1966 was the personal involvement of high school teachers and administrators who in the long run would be responsible for introducing changes and improvements at the local level. Some schools included the lay faculty in these preparatory discussions, and some schools held as many as fifteen meetings during the year. There was involvement also of the Jesuit seminarians at the five American schools of theology, the largest proportion of whom had had 2 or 3 years' experience teaching as scholastics in the Jesuit high schools (7).

Adhering to a formula provided by the planning committee, each of these groups wrote its own conclusions and generalizations which were then assembled and distributed as the *Report from the Schools*. At the end of January 1966 I had finished the writing of my own report of the survey which I called *Send Us A Boy—Get Back A Man*, and I began to get requests from some of the province prefects of study for subsidiary tabular reports of data for the individual schools. Many of the local groups continued their discussions during the spring, and some of them used my survey data to amplify their own observations of the high school situation (8).

The planning committee for the workshop also invited specially qualified Jesuits to submit "working papers" on fourteen carefully selected topics dealing with the general subject of Christian formation of high school boys. One of these working papers was entitled "The Real Profile of the Jesuit High School Student," and what made it "real" was the set of concrete data I gathered in the survey. The workshop was held on the campus of Loyola University of Los Angeles, August 4–16, 1966, and I was invited to speak about the research findings, the report of which was by that time in the hands of the delegates.

Since the survey had been officially requested by the sponsors of the workshop and since it had been approved and authorized by the top superiors of the Jesuit Order, I felt that I need not spend much time in "defending" the study and its methods. This was not a completely correct assumption, as shown by some of the remarks and questions of the delegates. There was a kind of minority hesitancy expressed at the workshop by the suggestions that I was reporting on the "pooled ignorance" of the students; that these boys should consider themselves the beneficiaries, not the critics, of an educational system distilled from the wisdom and experience of the Jesuits; that the information they provided about family background was inaccurate; that they never take anonymous and nontest questionnaires seriously; that April was the worst time in the whole school year to make a survey of students; that the inherent quality of the Jesuit schools could not be captured and measured in quantitative and statistical tables.

These are the "stock" objections regularly offered to survey research by people who are inexperienced in research methodology, in this case by a few older Jesuits whose philosophical and humanist training made them suspicious of the whole sociological enterprise, and by a few younger Jesuits whose pragmatic approach to problems led them to expect more than the limitations of survey methods allow (9). The great majority of the delegates to the Los Angeles workshop did not question my research techniques, and even those who did make objections did not challenge any of the research findings.

This general willingness to accept the results of the survey may at first seem remarkable, because the findings were basically negative—indicating that the high schools were not entirely successful in "forming these young men in accordance with Christian ideals of education." Perhaps the delegates were not surprised or disappointed with my report for two reasons: first they knew the factual situation because of their day-by-day experience in the schools themselves, and second, because they had just spent a year in the honest group appraisal and self-evaluation of the objectives and attainments in each Jesuit high school (10).

For purposes of internal comparison I surveyed only freshmen and seniors in these forty-four schools on the general hypothesis that as a result of Jesuit educational tutelage the seniors would be "better" than the freshmen. As part of my talk to the delegates I selected five significant items on which to test this "trend" hypothesis. (a) The longer the student remained in a Jesuit high school the greater would be his appreciation of the school and its faculty. (b) Seniors would be better Catholics than freshmen, as shown by their beliefs and practices in their church. (c) Seniors would adhere to higher ethical standards of conduct and demonstrate greater moral integrity than freshmen. (d) Seniors would show an increased appreciation of the intellectual, mental, and artistic influence that the school has on them. (e) Seniors would demonstrate more progressive social attitudes and a keener awareness of modern social problems.

The only one among these hypotheses that "tested out" was a relatively indirect finding of the survey: that students at Jesuit high schools get a good academic training and that the seniors recognize and appreciate this experience more than the freshmen do. It is a well-known fact that Jesuit secondary education competently prepares boys for academic success in college (11). There was no need to gather evidence for this fact. The purpose of the survey lay in another direction: to measure the moral improvement and character formation of the students from freshman to senior year in the school. In this regard the freshmen were "better" than the seniors.

Besides comparing seniors with freshmen, I pointed out at the workshop and in the report that the seniors were by no means a "standardized product" of Jesuit education. The schools succeeded with some and failed with others. There were "loyalists" and "rebels" among the seniors, and the school benefited the former much more than the latter. There were also spiritually "devout" and spiritually "tepid" seniors, differentiated by their adherence to religious beliefs and practices. The important finding here was that the religiously devout seniors were more socially aware and progressive, and less prejudiced, than the others (12).

RESEARCH REPLICATION.   The 2-week workshop in Los Angeles was partially supported by a grant from the Lilly Endowment, and the application for that grant said: "It is expected that this workshop will have a profound effect on Jesuit education in the United States and throughout the world" (13). This may have been an overenthusiastic expectation, but the delegates to the workshop had every serious intention of achieving a "profound effect" on their schools as a result of this conference. The specific task force which commented on my research report said that "the real value of the study will necessarily lie in the studies and analyses of findings at the local level, preferably by entire faculties of each school, and then in the changes introduced at the local level in accord with local findings."

Recommendations and resolutions focusing on the prag-

matic improvement of moral and religious training of high
school students were formulated at the Los Angeles workshop. These were distributed in a pamphlet entitled *The
Christian School—A New View*, which was to act as a
guidebook for faculty and administrators. From the contents
of this pamphlet a checklist was constructed by Paul Siegfried
of the Washington office of the Jesuit Educational Association and sent to all the high schools. There were seventy
items on this "checklist," which required merely a yes-or-no
answer, to be returned at the end of each semester. The returns at the end of the first semester of the 1966–1967
school year indicated that little was being done. At the end of
the second semester they were even less encouraging.

At the workshop itself I had urged another kind of fol-
lowup of the 1965 survey. I suggested that the same questionnaire be administered to the high school students in 1968.
This would allow a comparison of the seniors at that time,
who had been freshmen in 1965, with the previous seniors
and the new freshmen. I argued also in favor of a new survey
to be taken in the spring of 1970, covering those students
who graduated from Jesuit high schools in 1965. Hardly any
research data existed on the alumni of Jesuit high schools, and
I suggested that a continuing research program be instituted
for the future, with surveys to be taken every 5 years (14).

In early May 1967 Paul Siegfried reminded me of these
suggestions, said that he was taking them up with the Jesuit
Secondary School Commission, and asked whether I would
conduct the survey. I was then fully immersed in writing the
analysis of research data from the survey of diocesan clergy,
but was willing to cooperate with any social researcher the
JEA might invite to do the study (15). I had asked that someone with recent high school experience be invited to do secondary analysis, or even a reinterpretation, of the data from
the 1965 survey, but no one could be found to do so.

It was during that period also, starting in 1965, that the

whole Jesuit Order seemed to be afire with enthusiasm for a worldwide self-survey. I was invited to come to Rome for a preliminary conference on this enterprise, but my own research, and especially my regular faculty duties at the Harvard Divinity School, prevented me from doing so. A quick survey was launched in early 1967 to reach all American Jesuit priests and seminarians in preparation for the Conference on the Total Development of the Jesuit Priest (16). Questionnaires began to mushroom in practically all American provinces while I protested in vain that surveys be coordinated at least to the extent of using a standardized questionnaire that would allow comparable research data.

Out of these disparate surveys, dealing with various aspects of Jesuit life and work, there came a flood of disparate statistical tables. The multiplication of surveys surfeited the Jesuit respondents, and the mass of statistical tables apparently overwhelmed the men who sent out the questionnaires. The crucial task of interpretive analysis was performed amateurishly —when it was done at all. There was simply a lack of experienced and trained talent that could extract the meaning from the increasing flow of research data.

Perhaps other Jesuit sociologists were too busy with their own work to replicate the 1965 high school study which was approved by the Secondary School Commission at the end of June 1967. Paul Siegfried and three members of the commission came to discuss it at Cambridge on August 21, 1967, when I encouraged the study but declined to conduct it. At most I was willing to act as consultant on the new survey and, if any revisions were necesessary, to reconstruct the questionnaire for the study. At this meeting Joseph Duffy suggested that the Catholic Educational Research Center (CERC), located on the campus of Boston College, might be employed to do the new survey, and perhaps even provide funds to finance it.

The next morning he, together with Paul Siegfried and Joseph Shea, met with Paul McHugh at Boston College who was eager to have CERC take over the sesearch project. He enthusiastically proposed to enlarge the study by including a representative sample of students from non-Jesuit Catholic schools and from other private high schools. He felt that he could get cooperation from the members of the National Association of Independent Schools. CERC had no funds of its own to put into research, but for a project of this magnitude he envisioned a grant of 500,000 dollars from the Ford Foundation or The Carnegie Corporation.

Since I had agreed to prepare the questionnaire for the second survey, I asked Paul Siegfried to canvass the presidents and principals of the high schools, as well as the province directors of education. Not being in immediate contact with the high schools I wanted to know whether any crucial problems had arisen since the previous survey and whether any essential new item should be included in the questionnaire. The number of high schools had increased to forty-seven and the number of provinces decreased to ten. Responses came from only twenty-four of the schools and from only four of the provinces.

In October I prepared a seven-page memorandum on the basis of these replies after a conference in my office with George Madaus and Paul McHugh of the staff of CERC. The director of CERC, John Walsh, conferred with Paul Siegfried in Washington and with Joseph Shea in Boston, and then submitted a "tentative estimate" of 19,000 dollars to do the second survey. I told the members of the Secondary School Commission of JEA that I considered this a very reasonable estimate, especially since it included the cost of printing 500 copies of the research report and copies of the marginal tables for each school.

I was happy to be relieved of the work and responsibility of the second high school survey, although Paul Siegfried kept insisting that I should have "overall charge" of the study as though I were simply using the services of CERC. On January 8, 1968, I finally met John Walsh, who came with his associates, Madaus and McHugh, to discuss the research program for the survey with Paul Siegfried and myself. This was a crucial meeting, the consequences of which were not clear until 2 months later, March 11, when negotiations were broken off with CERC and I agreed to supervise the collection of data (but not to do the analysis and interpretation for the final report).

These negotiations with CERC clarified for me the difference between educational testing and sociological research. I looked upon every answered questionnaire as a sociological document that had to be separately scrutinized for completeness, consistency, and conformity even before its precoded information could be punched onto IBM cards. Educational testing service simply used Digitek "answer sheets" on which respondents made checks at the appropriate places. Furthermore, CERC revised the original questionnaire, introducing so many changes and new items as well as rewording of old items, that there would not be the maximum comparability that I considered essential between the 1965 survey and the new survey.

THE 1968 SURVEY.   One of the puzzling Jesuit educational phenomena of the 1960s—at least it was puzzling to me—was the continued expansion of the American Jesuit secondary system. In 1939 there were thirty-three Jesuit high schools in the United States. In 1965 there were forty-seven, of which three were so new that they did not yet have senior classes. These three were in Concord, Indianapolis, and Sacramento, and I included them in the 1968 survey. By that time four new schools had been established, in Fall River, St.

Louis, Toledo, and Cuyahoga Falls, bringing the total to fifty-one, but I did not survey these four schools because they did not yet have senior classes.

I am curious, rather than critical, of this multiplication of Jesuit high schools at a time when Jesuit personnel was not proportionately increasing and when serious questions were being raised by younger Jesuits about the concentration of manpower in the high school apostolate. My general impression from the findings of the 1965 survey was that these schools—at least some of them—were in need of renewal and reform, rather than of expansion. I do not know what kind of research is done in preparation for the opening of a new Jesuit high school, or whether the report of the 1965 survey was consulted before such a decision was reached. Since 1968 the Jesuits have withdrawn from several of these schools, and the era of continual expansion seems to have ended. I also do not know whether these decisions were made, at least partly, on the basis of the research surveys (17).

Of course, as I said on a previous occasion, "there is nothing automatic, spontaneous, or magical about a research report" (18). Nevertheless, I was hopeful of the pragmatic utility of the high school research as I took up the task of collecting the data of the second survey. The questionnaires were sent to all forty-seven schools on March 29, 1968, from the Washington office of the JEA, with instructions that they should be administrated to freshmen and seniors during the second week after Easter, April 22–26.

As in the previous survey, it was too much to expect that all schools would adhere to this schedule or meet this deadline. Four of them had the questionnaires answered before Easter. More than half had sent the packets of answered questionnaires to me by May 9, when Paul Siegfried telephoned the principals of all remaining schools to prod them into action. He was worried about "time running short" and was very anxious that every school respond to the study. The last school to administer the questionnaire did so on May 21. In two instances the packets split open enroute, and some of the questionnaires were lost.

At any rate, by the end of June I had edited all the survey schedules, appended identification codes to them, and sent them for processing to John Keller at the Computer Center of Loyola University of the South. In this instance I had agreed to provide marginal tables for each school, as well as composite tables for each of the ten provinces. I also requested computer printouts of data on the numerous contrasting categories of students, similar to those I analyzed in the 1965 survey (19). All of this data processing continued smoothly throughout the summer with the expectation that in the fall some sociological reporter, other than myself, could write up the findings.

The search for a reporter had been going on since March, when negotiations with CERC were broken off. Among the members of a seminar I was conducting at Harvard on religion and education there was a Jesuit scholastic from California whom I tried to persuade to take over the reporter's task on the survey. When he declined I asked Bernard Dooley to do it. As director of the 1966 Workshop on the Christian Formation of Students he had been fully immersed in the previous high school survey. He, too, declined with the modest statement that he had "none of the qualifications" needed for such research analysis and interpretation. At the end of the summer, a recommendation was made for Thomas Gannon, a Chicago Jesuit with plans to do graduate work in sociology, but he was not yet available. In the fall term, my research assistant, Robert Cole, a graduate student at Harvard, tried his hand at reporting but soon gave up.

My inability to find a sociological reporter to take on this task was a frustrating experience. Some of the Jesuit commentators on the 1965 survey report felt that the analysis and interpretation of data should be done by some Jesuit who was either in high school work or had "more recent experience" in high schools than I had. I was more than willing to cooperate with this suggestion, even if it meant training a young Jesuit graduate student in sociology to do the reporting. I regretted that the Cambridge Center for Social Studies had not developed into a research organization where such training would be provided for young scholars (20). There were—and still are—relatively few experienced "older" Jesuit sociologists who could do survey analysis, and they are usually already overworked with their own projects.

Even while I still hoped to find a social scientist competent to write the final report of the survey I worked with the statistical tables regularly produced by Norma Batt in New Orleans. Instead of saving all this information for the final report, as I had done with the 1965 survey, I decided to share some of it with Paul Siegfried and through him with the individual schools. Therefore, even before Christmas of 1968, each of the schools had at hand its own marginal tables of responses to the questionnaire. It was my hope that they would compare and discuss the differences between the two surveys as they pertained to their own student body.

A second comparative scheme I proposed to Paul Siegfried was abandoned at his suggestion. The "checklist" of seventy items taken from the 1966 workshop recommendations had been distributed to the high schools on two occasions since the workshop. This was to indicate the extent to which each school had followed those recommendations. It seemed to me that a rating system could be worked out for the schools from their responses to this checklist. The data from the second survey would allow me to work out a rating system to discover whether the "improved" schools matched those which rated high on the self-report made through the checklist. Paul Siegfried lacked confidence in the school responses to the checklist, and he discouraged me from making the proposed comparisons.

Another device for capturing, or retaining, the interest of the local high schools was a series of interim reports on specific items of the survey. On the first of these I ranked all forty-seven schools according to the amount of "experimentation with drugs" that the students themselves reported. I assigned a comparative "score" to each school and suggested that the whole listing be sent to all the schools. Paul Siegfried was much more aware than I of what he called the "sensitivity" of the Jesuit secondary educators. He sent a "confidential" report to the principal of each school, giving only the score and the rank number of the particular school. Obviously, the principal was expected to discuss these findings with the faculty, and it was probably through these discussions that several "leaks" of information occurred with subsequent unhappy comparisons among some of the schools.

Other reports on the ranking of schools were apparently not quite so sensitive as that on student experimentation with drugs. As I gradually worked over the comparative data on the schools I used the responses of seniors to rank them on the amount of cheating among students, their opinion of religion classes and teachers, their estimate of the moral influence of the school, and their social attitudes. All of these were distributed from the central office of JEA as confidential memoranda to every school principal and to every province director of secondary education. There was relatively little feedback from the schools to Paul Siegfried, and none to me, but I held the hope that these reports maintained interest in the survey and stimulated programs of betterment.

When it became apparent in December 1968 that no one else could be found to do the interpretive analysis of the research data, I reluctantly decided to do it myself. I had finished the report of the 1965 survey in January 1966, and now I was barely starting on the report of the 1968 survey in January, 1969. This time I looked for collaboration among the Jesuits who were actually engaged in secondary education. I asked Paul Siegfried to review each chapter as I finished it and to relay copies of it for review by other Jesuits. He found three men who provided excellent critical commentaries: Joseph Duffy of Boston College high school, Leo Lackamp of St. John's, Toledo, and Robert McGuire of Regis in New York City.

One further contact with the Jesuit secondary educators was at the meetings of the JEA at Easter time, held that year at the University of Detroit. On Saturday, April 5, 1969, I presented a progress report of the survey to the group of ten high school presidents and eleven principals who constituted the Jesuit Commission on Secondary Schools. The theme of the report was this: have the schools shown any improvement since 1965 in the program of Christian formation and training as seen through the eyes of the students? Perhaps the commission members—on the basis of the interim statistics I had provided—were braced for the "bad news." Whatever their expectations were, they now learned that the report was mainly negative.

One of the interesting aspects of this meeting was not only the willingness of these Jesuits to accept the gloomy facts of the survey, but also their desire to explore the reasons why these situations exist (21). They were ready to generalize out of experience, making comments about the "new" attitudes of Jesuit teachers, about the way the students' family life has changed, the manner in which adolescent boys look at religion, and the influence of increasing proportions of lay teachers in the Jesuit high schools. They knew that the problems raised by the survey really existed in the schools; they speculated on explanations for their existence; but they had the ongoing and vexing question what to do about them.

At this same meeting I repeated my recommendation— given first at the 1966 Los Angeles workshop—that the high schools support a research survey of their alumni. The suggestion here was that seniors who had answered the questionnaire in 1965 and had graduated that year be surveyed again 5 years later, in 1970. I no longer had any hope that the Cambridge Center for Social Studies could assume this project, and I had no intention of doing it myself. Actually, the search for a sociologist to conduct this alumni survey had begun in March 1968, after Paul Siegfried and I concluded that CERC at Boston College was not the appropriate agent for sociological research projects.

The best prospective researcher for this job seemed to be Robert McNamara, then head of the department of sociology at Fordham University. He had done his graduate work at Cornell University under the guidance of Robin Williams and had a year's experience in survey research with Peter Rossi at the National Opinion Research Center of the University of Chicago. In 1966 he had declined an invitation to become an associate of the Jesuit Cambridge Center in order to join the faculty at Fordham, where he had adequate research facilities for the survey of high school alumni. This project got under way in the early months of 1970 (22).

Ten days after the Detroit meeting with the Jesuit secondary educators, my calm and orderly work schedule at Harvard University was disrupted by the much-publicized student strike. The ordinary faculty routine of research, lecturing, and writing, was slowed down by frequent meetings and consultations among all segments of the campus. For the next two months scholarly activity at Harvard—if not at a standstill—was more or less sporadic. Nevertheless, I was able intermittently to work on the manuscript of the 1968 survey report. I completed it shortly after commencement exercises in June 1969. This means that it took me 6 months longer than the first survey report, which I had finished in January 1966.

THE GLOOMY REPORT. The dismal finding I had to report on the first survey in *Send Us A Boy—Get Back A Man* was that the moral and religious character of the Jesuit high school student deteriorates between freshman and senior years. In other words, insofar as I could measure the Jesuit system of Christian character formation by means of crude survey techniques that tapped the response of students themselves, the system was far from successful in its apostolic objectives. The second survey, which I reported in *Jesuit High Schools Revisited*, again found a similar decline of ethical and religious effects between the freshman and senior years. The trend had not been reversed, nor had there been even a measurable "closing of the gap" that might indicate the beginnings of improvement.

This continued difference between freshmen and seniors was only one part of the comparative findings of the two surveys. The crucial new variable that had intervened between the two surveys was the 1966 Workshop on the Christian Formation of Jesuit High School Students—with its enormous preparatory studies and its serious concluding resolutions (23). After that event my rough formulation of the research question was: are the 1968 freshmen better than the 1965 freshmen; and are the 1968 seniors better than the 1965 seniors? The answer, out of the mouths of students themselves, was negative.

This negative generalization refers to the comparative data for the whole secondary educational system operated by the American Jesuits. The responses of the students did not provide evidence that the promised changes had taken place. By and large, the basic process of Christian formation and character training—which was the focus of my research effort —continued at about the same pace and in about the same way. This does not mean that no effort at all was expended for reform in the individual schools. I did not, however, attempt a school-by-school comparison of the data from the two surveys to discover which had improved and which had not. I still assumed that this had been done by each school at the local level.

One of the dismal demonstrations of the 1968 survey was the ineffectiveness of the teaching of religion in Jesuit high schools. The religion course became less palatable the longer the student stayed in the school, and there was no demonstrable improvement during the 3-year period between surveys. For the great majority of students everything they listened to in the classroom was more interesting than religion. Some of the teachers of religion got comparatively high rating from their students, but the subject was dull.

The startling fact was, however, that it did not make much difference whether the teaching of religion was good or bad. In terms of Christian formation, ethical behavior, and moral attitudes, the five schools that had the best religion courses achieved no better results than the five schools with the worst religion courses (24). This is a puzzle I was not able to unlock with the research data. I surmise that the desired religious effect of the Jesuit high school comes from the general influence of all faculty members rather than from the specific teaching of courses in religion.

A second and surprisingly negative finding of the survey was the inference from the students' responses that there is a difference between "Christian formation" and "character training." I came to the conclusion that the Jesuit secondary system was more successful in strengthening the character of students than in making Christians out of them. What showed up clearly in the survey was that a student cannot be a good Christian without having love of God, but that a student could have a strong character without being a good Christian. It appeared, then, that these high schools were succeeding admirably in promoting a secular version of character formation. As the students saw it, strong character is a personal development quite separable from the religious and spiritual foundation on which the Jesuit theory of education rests.

This must be troublesome to religious educators because it

supports the "secularist" assumption that an authentic character formation of young people need not be undergirded by religious motives and convictions. It undermines a basic Jesuit educational principle: that true strength of character cannot be developed without supernatural religion, in this case, the religion of the Judaeo-Christian tradition as expressed by the Catholic church. I felt compelled to say in the survey report that "perhaps the time has come to demythologize the religious ideology of Jesuit education and to re-assess the whole concept of the impact of religion on character training" (25).

A third generalization of the survey will be judged negative only if one looks askance at the "bourgeois mentality" exhibited by the students and reinforced by the Jesuit high school. The hypothesis I was testing with the survey data is a very serious one: whether the social philosophy of the Jesuit high school reflects the social philosophy that the middle-class Catholic students bring with them from their family and cultural environment. The majority of the students came from well-advantaged families, decidedly above the American average in social class, and representing what might be called the Catholic bourgeoisie. What I clearly demonstrated with the research data was that attendance at a Jesuit high school promotes and reinforces the social attitudes of this class of people.

These attitudes are relatively unfavorable to the public programs aimed at the alleviation of poverty and to the general concept of social welfare payments. What happened in these schools was that these attitudes became more unfavorable the longer the student remained in the school, as evidenced by the difference between freshman and senior responses. This should not have been the case in the second survey, especially since the 1966 workshop had recommended that "the teacher's aim should be to develop a social awareness and sensitivity to the human needs of all levels of society, especially the poor and the deprived" (26).

I ought to mention one more worrisome finding from the survey because it promises to grow in importance as the proportion of lay faculty increases and that of Jesuit faculty decreases. The research data strongly suggested that the lay teacher's influence on the students was different from that of the Jesuit scholastic and priest. Students who were attracted to lay teachers were more "secular" than the others in the sense that they demonstrated less appreciation for the spiritual and religious ideals fostered by the Jesuit school. Furthermore, the lay teachers, although not as popular as the scholastics, were gaining in popularity over the priest teachers. Since the teacher image is extremely important in the lives of adolescents, it appears that the Jesuit schools are becoming increasingly "laicized" (27).

I pointed out in the report that the Jesuit secondary system had been caught in a dilemma of expansion while the source of Jesuit teaching manpower was contracting. If the opening of new schools, as well as the size of existing schools, had been tailored to the supply of Jesuit teachers, this dilemma would not have occurred. On the other hand, the educational status of American Catholics—particularly of the middle class who send their boys to these schools—may have reached a point in time when the Jesuits could begin to withdraw from the high schools and turn them over to lay administrators and teachers. The research data persuaded me that the typical image of the Jesuit high school had already been altered—whether this critical decision to withdraw is ever made.

PRIVATE CIRCULATION. In spite of those who say that sociologists simply discover and describe "what we already know" I felt that none of the Jesuit secondary educators expected that the findings would be as bad as they were. I had no intention of publicizing the results of the survey beyond the Jesuit family, and I agreed from the beginning with both Bernard Dooley and Paul Siegfried that they, as sponsors of the studies, should decide what to do with them. Both research reports were marked "for private circulation," but copies were also selectively released on request to "legitimately interested parties," that is, educators and researchers.

Ten copies of both reports were sent to each of the Jesuit high schools, but there were also so many requests from "legitimately interested parties" that the limited editions were soon exhausted. No news reporters were invited to the 1966 Los Angeles workshop where we discussed in detail and at length the findings of the 1965 survey. A carefully prepared "press release" was given to the news media at the end of the workshop, and the only journalist permitted to attend the workshop was Jesuit Raymond Schroth who described the proceedings of the meeting in an article for *America*. Out of the press release a writer for the *Los Angeles Times* constructed a story with the interesting title, "Jesuit Schools Accept Teen-Age Revolution" (28).

One of the guidelines laid down for me in both surveys was that I must protect the confidentiality and reputation of individual high schools. I was willing to accept this principle, although I realize now that I was unaware how deeply sensitive the people at each high school were about their reputation *vis-à-vis* other Jesuit high schools. At the workshop I spent considerable time talking about this "delicate and invidious" question of comparative findings among schools and among provinces. I selected twenty-four items from the questionnaire and demonstrated the wide range of responses from highest to lowest—without mentioning names— among the eleven provinces and among the high schools of one province.

No province or school was "best" on all twenty-four items, and none was "worst," but the purpose I had in mind in showing these internal comparisons was to stimulate these

Jesuit educators to analyze their own school reports and to recognize their own weaknesses and strengths. They had access to the national statistics, the marginal tables on all freshmen and all seniors, in the appendix of the survey report (29). Each province director of secondary education had in his possession the marginal tables for the whole province as well as for each school in his province. I urged the delegates to study these comparative findings as they apply to their own schools and argued that serious renewal of the Jesuit secondary system depended on the extent to which they implemented the research data at the local level.

I preserved the utmost confidentiality, and I was protective of the reputation of individual provinces and schools both at the 1966 workshop and in the published report of the first survey, *Send Us A Boy—Get Back A Man*. There were no "leaks" either from my office or from the Washington office of the JEA. I was confident that the high schools were making heroic efforts at self-renewal, and I had the fond hope that the results of these efforts would show up in the 1968 survey. During the summer of 1968, when I studied the comparative tables of the two surveys, my confidence was shaken and my hope shattered. The expected "renewal" had not taken place, at least not in a way measurable by the marginal tables of responses.

In this discouraged frame of mind I wrote on August 2 to Paul Siegfried: "Despite my effort to make the statistics meaningful in my 1965 report, most of the schools really did not make the effort to interpret their own situation against the national findings—and to do something about it. Somehow we have to give them a jolt with the 1968 report." I said further that I had changed my mind about the wisdom of protecting the reputation of specific schools. "I think we ought to come right out and name names. No school is at the top of the listing on everything, and none is at the bottom on everything."

At that time I was still looking for someone to analyze and interpret the data of the 1968 survey and to write the final report. Nevertheless, I worked out the rank order of the forty-seven high schools on certain items like drug experimentation, cheating, and the teaching of religion, I devised a system of "scores" for each school, and I sent the listing to Paul Siegfried with the recommendation that they be circulated to all the schools. He was appalled at this lack of discretion on my part and assured me that such a revelation would alienate the high school principals and teachers. His position, of course, was different from mine. As the executive secretary for the secondary schools he had to try to "please everybody" while dunning them for their share of the expenses of the research project.

Although I agreed that it might be harmful, and perhaps uncharitable, to single out schools that were doing poorly or were at the bottom of the list, I thought it might be helpful to name the schools at the top of the list. In the 1968 report, *Jesuit High Schools Revisited*, I made several comparisons on selected criteria between the five schools with highest scores and the five schools with lowest scores, naming the former but leaving the latter unnamed. Thus the reader is able to find out which five schools had the friendliest faculty, were best in the teaching of religion, produced the best Christians, were judged most popular by the students. In one comparison, however, based on the economic status of the students, I named both the five poor boys' schools and the five rich boys' schools (30).

It was one thing to forestall internal rivalry and jealousy among the Jesuit high schools themselves, but it was another thing to worry about the "undue publicity" that might weaken the image of Jesuit education among "outsiders" (31). Even while the questionnaires of the 1968 survey were still being collected the Jesuit Secondary School Commission was meeting in San Francisco and expressing reluctance to have the survey findings made public. One year later, at the Detroit meeting of the commission when I presented my preliminary report of the research findings, there was even greater concern about negative publicity. The commissioners had no doubt that the facts would "get out" to the broader public, but in order to "thwart possible negative criticism of our schools" they urged that some writer be found who would present a "favorable review of the survey and its findings."

I discounted the suggestion that I write a "favorable" review, or summary digest of the findings, of my own report. I did suggest, however, that the final chapter on "Generalizations and Speculations" be reprinted in pamphlet form for wider distribution among Jesuits, or that it appear as an article in the *Jesuit Educational Quarterly*. These alternatives, which were not done, would not have "softened" my interpretations of the hard facts of the survey. On July 23, 1969, Paul Siegfried sent copies of the final report to all the high schools with a covering letter that said in part: "Father Fichter is honest, straightforward, even blunt in his assessment of findings and his evaluation of our efforts in the realm of Christian formation." The most heartening thing he could say in the foreword to the report was a word of praise for the schools' courage in seeking honest answers, their spirit of openness, and their eagerness to improve.

As far as I know, there was no "undue publicity" in any journal article or news media during the months immediately after the distribution of *Jesuit High Schools Revisited*. Raymond Schroth agreed to do an article for *America* in the autumn of 1969, but it appears to have been unacceptable to the editors of that Jesuit weekly. He worked closely with some of the members of the Jesuit Secondary Commission, revised the article, and had it published in the special "education issue" of *Commonweal* at the end of January 1970 (32).

Thus the survey report came to the attention of the public even while it continued to circulate privately among the Jesuits.

HARSH EVALUATION.   The analytical interpretation of research data appears to be a skill that cannot be taught in a classroom or laboratory. The collection of data through observation, interviews, and questionnaire is a time-consuming, methodical process at which many students of sociology become quite proficient. The next step in the research project is the crucial one. What does one do with the assembled information? How does one "make sense" out of it? Research reports may range from one extreme of statistical sophistication which takes on mathematical rather than sociological significance to the other extreme of descriptive generalizations that could have been made without the laboriously collected data.

I have always felt a heavy responsibility in steering a course between these two extremes. I strive for scientific detachment and objectivity in handling the research data even while I am intensely concerned about the problems that the data reveal. I want to write research reports in such a way that the meaning I have found in the study is clearly intelligible to the people who read the report. Obviously, the interpretation that I place on the findings is ultimately *my* interpretation, even after I have asked readers and critics to review preliminary drafts of the manuscript. The question always remains: would another social scientist have written a different report? (33).

The four other research projects I describe in this book elicited an affirmative answer to that question. Each of them would have been interpreted and written differently: by the pastor of southern parish, the white racists of New Orleans, the police chief or Mayor, the apostolic delegate. None of these is a social scientist, but each of them saw different meanings in the data I collected, different from the meanings I drew out of them. The two surveys of the Jesuit high school students did not eventuate in such explosive attacks and criticisms. I like to think that the reason for this was a combination of the good sense of the Jesuit secondary school personnel on the one hand and of my own honest objectivity of reporting on the other.

In the opinion of Paul Siegfried, my assessment and evaluation of the survey findings were "honest, straightforward, blunt." At the New Orleans meeting of the Jesuit Secondary School Commission in December 1969, each chapter of the report *Jesuit High Schools Revisited* was reviewed by a designated member of the commission. One of the reviewers, John Reinke, raised the question of whether the interpretation would be different if the data were "reworked" by someone else. He suggested that "it would be interesting to read what another sociologist might make of the identical data." This is a suggestion that I completely support. It underscores one of the reasons why I was so eager to find someone else to undertake the second (1968) survey of the Jesuit students. I wanted to know whether the replication of the 1965 survey would demonstrate not only a difference in the schools, as a result of changes, but also a difference in the interpretation of the data, as a result of another sociologist's evaluation.

The suggestion, however, has a dreamlike quality about it. During the last few years the American Jesuits have been on a splurge of data collection. Dozens of questionnaires have been designed, and thousands have been distributed, to investigate practically every phase of Jesuit activity. Collectors of data have proliferated; analysts of data are scarce. The nationwide survey of Jesuit priests and seminarians, conducted early in 1967, provided a mountain of data that lies virtually untouched in the computer center of St. Louis University

(34). Research data are piling up in other Jesuit institutions, but only a trickle of analytical reporting is coming from them. I think there ought to be a moratorium on data collection among the American Jesuits while social analysts are trained to evaluate the data already on hand.

What could I have done to relieve the "harshness" of the high school survey report? Did I set the standards of expected student behavior too high? The fact is, of course, that I did not construct my own behavioral model to which I expected the high school students to conform. In evaluating the findings of the 1965 survey I employed a set of norms taken directly from the educational goals proposed in high school catalogs and promoted by contributors to the *Jesuit Educational Quarterly*. One of the papers prepared for the 1966 Workshop on Christian Formation dealt with the "Ideal Profile" of the high school student. My report at that meeting was meant to provide the "Real Profile."

My evaluation of the data from the 1968 survey was sharpened and specified by the concrete norms and resolutions newly established by the delegates to the 1966 workshop (35). These were not grandiose educational goals dredged up from past centuries of Jesuit academic glory. They were decisions based on recent experience in American Jesuit high schools. They were meant to be up-to-date and, I trustingly assumed, attainable. I am not always sure what it means to take a thing at its "face value," but I think that is what I did when I took the workshop resolutions as a set of norms with which to evaluate the student responses to the second survey.

If the educational goals are set unattainably high, the Jesuit high schools may be considered relatively successful in doing as well as they did. While writing the report on the second survey I wrestled long with this question of goals, and of how to evaluate the findings against the goals. My frustration was lessened considerably when I came across a remark by Jesuit Walter Krolikowski: "Whenever educators or students propose educational aims, these aims turn out to be absolutely unattainable, or unattainable by means available to educators, or cheap and pragmatic. What educational institution in all seriousness can say that it produces the perfect Christian gentleman?" (36)

I was unwilling to conclude that there was a lack of seriousness among the Jesuit educators assembled at the 1966 Los Angeles workshop. What made my research report seem harsh and blunt was the probability that I took their resolutions more seriously and idealistically than they did. While writing the report I began to realize that they were talking about practical steps to *approachable* goals, whereas I was thinking about a thorough overhaul of the secondary system aimed at reaching *attainable* goals. Whatever normative standards I might prefer, I had no choice as a social analyst except to employ the goals established and spelled out by the people who are operating the Jesuit secondary school system.

Although I am deeply interested in the reform of Jesuit education, I still maintain that the function of research is separate from that of development. I have had no direct part in the decision making that has introduced changes in the Jesuit high schools since the beginnings of the renewal program in 1964. My contacts with the secondary school personnel have been limited to the 1966 Los Angeles workshop, the Detroit meeting of the Secondary School Commission in April 1968, and the New Orleans meeting in August 1969 of representatives of the six high schools of the southern province.

Nevertheless, my analytical interpretation of the 1968 survey findings included a final chapter on "Generalizations and Speculations" from which I select the following remarks:

> "It appears that the desired religious effect of the Jesuit high school must come from the general influence of all faculty members. Perhaps catechists have been naive in assuming that religion courses significantly improve the attitudes and behavior of students." (p. 180)

"Perhaps the time has come to demythologize the religious ideology of Jesuit education and to re-assess the whole concept of the impact of religion on character training." (p. 182)

"As long as the system is geared to the aspirations of upper-middle class Catholic families it cannot be expected to focus on the educational needs of lower-class boys." (p. 185)

"It would seem the part of educational logic to scrutinize these better Jesuit schools, to select the factors that account for their success, and to apply this information to the renewal of the less popular schools." (p. 187)

As I reread these generalizations I try to place myself in the position of a Jesuit secondary educator whose confidence in Jesuit education is being shaken by four statements. (a) I am being asked to question the sacred dictum that teaching religion in the classroom has a good effect on moral behavior. (b) I must question also the traditional belief that religion is the basic ingredient of good character. (c) I must ask whether it is a mistake to expend so much educational effort on middle-class youths. (d) I should seek my operational criteria in the successful schools of the system rather than in the traditional philosophical maxims of Jesuit education.

Here I must let the matter of Jesuit high school education stand as a concluding chapter of two decades of sociological research. It represents for me a satisfying polar experience in contrast to the unsatisfactory and quarrelsome research experience of *Southern Parish* in 1948.

NOTES

1. For the report on this study, which could have profited enormously from sociological interpretation and analysis, see Reginald Neuwein, Ed., *Catholic Schools in Action* (Notre Dame, University of Notre Dame Press, 1966).

2. For these lectures on religious authority see my contribution, "Sociological Aspects of the Role of Authority in Religious Groups," pp. 9–74, in Joseph Haley, Ed., *Proceedings* of 1958 Sisters' Institute of Spirituality (Note Dame, University of Notre Dame Press, 1959).

3. See the remarks and references by Cherry C. Kinney, "Reflections on the 1969 Resolutions of the Women's Caucus," *The American Sociologist*, Vol. 6, No. 1, February 1971, pp. 19–22.

4. The *Jesuit Educational Quarterly*, which was inaugurated in 1939 and suspended publication in 1970, carried many articles that demonstrated this continuing concern. This excellent periodical was published for "private circulation" but is probably available to scholars at the libraries of Jesuit colleges and universities.

5. The rationale for the survey is explained in Chapter 1, "The Quest for Facts," pp. 1–19, of *Send Us A Boy—Get Back A Man* (Washington, D.C., Jesuit Educational Association, 1966).

6. The personal quotations in this chapter are largely from my exchange of correspondence with Bernard Dooley on the 1965 survey, and with Paul Siegfried on the 1968 survey.

7. These five Jesuit theologates, previously located in rural areas of California, Indiana, Kansas, Maryland, and Massachusetts, have now moved closer to large universities. Since the Second Vatican Council they have also become involved ecumenically with Protestant divinity schools.

8. Eighteen of the forty-four schools did not order a copy of the statistics drawn from their own school. It may be a coincidence that most of these ranked fairly low on the several comparisons I made in both surveys.

9. There are other reasons why practitioners do not always take research projects seriously. See Hyman Rodman and Ralph Kolodny, "Organizational Strains in the Researcher-Practitioner Relationship," pp. 93–113, in Alvin Gouldner and S. M. Miller, Eds., *Applied Sociology: Opportunities and Problems* (New York, Free Press, 1965).

10. See the account of the Los Angeles workshop by Raymond Schroth, "And Get Back A Man," *America*, October 1, 1966, pp. 382–384, and also his article, "Hard Work and Good Company," *Jesuit Educational Quarterly*, Vol. 29, January 1967, pp. 165–168.

11. Statistics on college attendance by these high school graduates are scattered throughout the issues of the *Jesuit Educational Quarterly*. Over the past 30 years approximately 85 percent of them went to college.

12. The relationship between religion and prejudice has been variously researched. Examples are in Gordon Allport, *Personality and Social Encounter* (Boston, Beacon, 1960), pp. 257–267; also Russell Allen and Bernard Spilka, "Committed and Consensual Religion: A Specification of Religion-Prejudice Relationships," *Journal for the Scientific Study of Religion*, Vol. 6, 1967, pp. 191–206.

13. A news release by Paul Reinert, president of the Jesuit Educational Association, in early May 1966 said that the Lilly Foundation made a grant of 10,000 dollars "to secure a broader group of experts and resource persons to participate in the August workshop on the Christian formation of high school students."

14. The paucity of research on alumni was pointed out in Appendix A, "Some Old Grads," pp. 211–223, in *Send Us A Boy*. In 1967, however, Paul Besanceney surveyed the alumni of the two Jesuit high schools in the Detroit province. Probably other similar surveys have since been made.

15. See Chapter Five.

16. This conference was held August 6–19, 1967, at the University of Santa Clara. The first volume of the *Proceedings* consisted of 212 statistical tables, without analysis or interpretation.

17. From personal conversations with the administrators of these schools my impression is that the deciding factors are lack of finances and of Jesuit manpower.

18. *Send Us A Boy*, p. 15.

19. *Ibid.*, Chapters 7, 8, 9.

20. This center, which opened in 1965 and closed in 1971 was in the main a residence where Jesuit social scientists had excellent facilities for writing monographs.

21. Their explanations tended to go beyond those demonstrated statistically in the research report and were thus somewhat speculative. Recommendations for change, however, were their task and not that of the researcher.

22. By this time McNamara had shifted to the post of academic dean at Loyola University of Chicago, a change that slowed

down the alumni research project. In the early summer of 1972 the questionnaires were shipped to William Mehok, who did the data processing at the Center for Applied Research in the Apostolate (CARA) in Washington.

23. This was not "just another" meeting of secondary school personnel. As Bernard Dooley remarked in *The Christian School —A New View* (Washington, D.C., Jesuit Educational Association, 1966), "It is expected that this Workshop will have a profound effect on Jesuit education in the United States and throughout the world," p. vi.

24. This is discussed in detail in *Jesuit High Schools Revisited* (Washington, D.C., Jesuit Educational Association, 1969), Chapter 4, "Teaching of Religion," and also in my article of the same title in *Religious Education* (May–June 1972), pp. 178–187.

25. *Ibid.*, p. 182. See also Chapter 5, "Making Better Christians."

26. *Ibid.*, p. 153, footnote 17. See the whole of Chapter 7, "Social Class and the Bourgeois Mentality." In criticizing this chapter a conservative Jesuit commented that in all my activities I tend to take my stand on the "extreme left." See also my article "High School Influence on Social-Class Attitudes," *Sociological Analysis* (Winter 1972), pp. 246–252.

27. *Ibid.*, pp. 185 f. See also Chapter 3, "Student Preference for Teachers."

28. Under the byline of Paul Houston, Tuesday, August 16, 1966.

29. *Send Us A Boy*, Appendix C, pp. 226–239.

30. On these several criteria the schools are named on the following pages: 42, 86, 107, 128, 151 f., of *Jesuit High Schools Revisited*.

31. After reading this manuscript Paul Siegfried commented that Jesuit schools want to be known as "the best in town," and are not concerned about comparisons with other Jesuit schools.

32. Raymond Schroth, "Jesuit High School," *Commonweal*, Vol. *91*, January 30, 1970, pp. 472–475.

33. Obviously, the "findings" in the form of research data would be the same. The difference, if there were any, would lie in the interpretative explanations of the data. This again is not the same as secondary analysis, which means testing old data with new hypotheses.

34. Except for the secondary analysis I made of these data and published in three articles in the *Jesuit Educational Quarterly:*

"Hardworking Jesuits" (October 1968), "Preparation of the Jesuit Professional" (January 1969), "Pastors and Professors" (March 1969).

35. See *Jesuit High Schools Revisited*, p. 177.

36. Walter P. Krolikowski, "Jesuits and the University," *Jesuit Educational Quarterly*, Vol. *31*, January 1969, pp. 131–142.

SEVEN

REFLECTIONS AND
SPECULATIONS

At the end of the spring academic term in June 1970, I completed my 5-year, nontenured appointment as Stillman Professor at the Harvard University Divinity School. After conducting a summer seminar at the Iliff School of Theology in Denver, I felt the need for a period of quiet reflection during which I could reassess my experiences in small-time research over more than 20 years. This "writing sabbatical" was made possible by invitations from Samuel Blizzard to spend half the academic year on the Princeton campus and from Morton King for the second half on the campus of Southern Methodist University.

Reflection need not stop at the end of one's sabbatical year. I write these lines now back at Loyola University in New Orleans where my earlier research projects antagonized sensitive clerics, bigoted racists, and self-righteous policemen. That it is not the same city as of old may be suggested by the fact that the American Sociological Association, for the first time in its history, held its annual convention here in 1972, and there were no complaints about the housing of black sociologists. That all is not yet perfect, however, is attested by the protests of some women sociologists who were barred from taking luncheon at the Men's Grill of the Hotel Monteleone.

RESEARCH IN A MINOR KEY. The university to which I returned remains relatively small—with about 4,000 students—but has undergone a kind of minor academic and intellectual revolution in my absence. The trend toward secularization, which for a while seemed to affect most American church-related colleges, has been slowed down—if not turned around—at this Jesuit university. The earlier involvement—almost dedication to—empiricism, positivism and technology, has been deemphasized and turned toward human and transcendental values. This may be a reflection of the general counterculture in the larger society, especially among students and intellectuals. At any rate, the attempt here and now is to fulfill the latent promise of the private, independent college as a distinctive contribution to higher education.

In this setting, the kind of low-key, one-man research in which I have been engaged appears to be more viable than ever. Limited areas of sociological investigation are still numerous, and the financial means to study them are also still limited. Schools like Loyola continue to make small research grants available to graduate students and faculty, but the sources of "big" research money seem to be retrenching, if not drying up. Perhaps the difficulty of getting access to big social science grants and of participating in large-scale research projects—which have always been a problem in small colleges—will turn the young sociologist to modest studies. It is interesting to note that research papers presented at regional meetings of sociologists deal in most cases with microstudies by people from small colleges.

Opportunities for modest but significant research lie at hand in the vast store of data that have never been fully analyzed. This seems particularly true in the sociology of religion and education in which large surveys have been taken but of which secondary analysis of data is at a minimum. This is an inexpensive procedure which promises to yield results far beyond the time and effort involved in it. It had been my own hope to involve students in such analysis and interpretation of the data from my own studies that had accumulated on this campus over the years. To my dismay I discovered that my file cabinet containing more than 30,000 data cards —as well as the computer tapes on several studies—had been discarded in my absence. The computer center was moved into the new science complex, new people were put in charge, the IBM 1620 was replaced with a CDC operation —and no one is willing to admit having made the decision to throw away my research data.

Being once-removed from actual data collection and contact with human beings this manipulation of statistical data is attractive as a methodological exercise. Yet it is the kind of experience every young sociologist should have because one of the most difficult tasks for social scientists is to extract the *meaning* of research information. This task is often not successfully achieved even by the most sophisticated statistician —except perhaps in the rarified level of the statistically sophisticated community of scholars. For most young sociologists today the preference seems to be the study of observable behavior among people with the expectation that the findings can be usefully returned to the people in explanatory terms that are useful and intelligible to them.

PEOPLE AS SUBJECTS.   We have all done our share of data handling, which is an essential stage in the research process stretching from the people studied to the people who read the study. It is a constant effort to remind ourselves that the statistics we manipulate are actually representative of live human beings in the social world around us. I have the impression that many graduate students who do the mathematical "hack" work for their research professors are repelled by the aridity of the materials with which they are dealing. They want some experience of getting at the source of the data, the people who are being studied and who are giving information about themselves and their social behavior and attitudes.

This desire to deal with people at the level of personal contact, whether by interviewing or by participant observation, is most often met by using fellow students as objects of research. No category of people in America has been more thoroughly and frequently "sociologized" than college students. Perhaps it is time for a moratorium on the study of students and for a deliberate switch to other subjects of study. One of my colleagues, Jerrol Seaman, has a very small financial grant, but enough to enable him to interview a sample of adolescent dropouts who have been in trouble with the police and a matching sample of youths who have a "clean" record. His interviewers are getting first-hand contact with human beings.

It appears to be no accident or fad that young sociologists with limited financial support are moving in this direction. I see it as partial evidence of the humanistic concern that is now spreading among professional sociologists. Becoming an expert social scientist and learning the skills and using the tools of research are still important, but not as ends in themselves nor mainly for personal and occupational advancement. The younger sociologists on the various campuses in New Orleans, and their students, have developed a broader perspective, asking themselves Lynd's famous question: "knowledge for what?" Most of them are unabashedly for social reform and want their findings to be of utility for the improvement of the local community where their research is conducted.

RACE IN NEW ORLEANS. One of these humanistic concerns continues to focus on the phenomenon of race relations in New Orleans, an area in which both black and white sociologists have been working over the years. There is no question that changes have occurred during my absence from the city. Many factors have helped to alter the patterns of racial discrimination, but the most dramatic impact seems to have been made by professional sports. There is no doubt that teachers, religious leaders, lawyers and judges, and the various civil rights groups had prepared the way for the breakthrough by professional football players who refused to come to New Orleans unless the black players could obtain equal accommodations at the same hotel. There was big money in professional football, even before the New Orleans Saints got the national conference franchise and started regular season play in 1967. The economic advantage to the city finally outweighed the objections of a dwindling number of raucous racists. It became "good business" to remove remaining racial barriers in public facilities of all kinds.

The current mayor, Maurice "Moon" Landrieu, graduate of Loyola University, is reputed to have brought a pragmatic and humane approach to the city administration. He has the reputation also of "catering" to the Negro community and of being less than friendly to the social elite who have for so long dominated the life of the city. The present superintendent of police, who works closely with the mayor, is Clarence Giarrusso, brother of the man who was in charge of the department when we did the controversial study of arrestees in 1963.

It would be naive, of course, to suggest that the "race problem" has been completely solved in New Orleans —or in any major American city. The disproportions are still weighted heavily against the blacks: in rates of unemployment and levels of occupation, in the amount and quality of housing, in the amount and quality of schooling. In the 1970 census Negroes constituted 45 percent of the population, whereas the adjoining Jefferson Parish (county) to the west had 12 percent, and St. Bernard to the east had only 5 percent. As is the case in many other large cities, whites are moving to the suburbs while blacks continue to crowd the less desirable areas of the inner city. This is a relatively new phenomenon for New Orleans, which used to have a stable and broad residential distribution across racial lines. Low-cost public housing projects set the original pattern for segregated residential concentration.

SCHOOL DESEGREGATION.   One of the major controversies of the late 1950s, the racial desegregation of the schools, has largely subsided. The "tokenism" gingerly introduced at Loyola University, and later at Tulane University, seems to have changed to the normal acceptance of students, regardless of race, who can meet the entrance standards (as well as the tuition requirements) at these two private universities. Stated negatively, it may be said that there have been no protests, much less legal actions, demanding desegregation on the campus. Dormitories and all social functions are open to all students, but there are still some elitist groups, social sororities, and fraternities, that continue their policies of exclusive membership. On the other hand, black students now tend to withdraw into their own campus groups.

The long crusade for black admission to formerly white southern colleges has been replaced by a demand for the "survival" of Negro higher education. The private universities, Dillard and Xavier, continue to have predominantly black student bodies. Despite the fact that the New Orleans campus of Louisiana State University admits large numbers of black students, the state also established a branch of Southern University in the city. This was at first resented as an official attempt to evade court orders to integrate. The resistance is now in the opposite direction as black college presidents, faculties, and students insist on maintaining the long-established Negro campuses.

One hears little now of the White Citizens' Councils, who were so outraged about our program for the desegregation of the Catholic parochial schools. Although there are unquestionably still a few reactionary Catholic pastors who are reluctant to allow black pupils in their parish schools and some white parents who have withdrawn their children to private schools, the pattern of integrated Catholic elementary schools has now been set. In a sense, this has been a one-way movement. Few, if any, white children have entered the elementary schools of black Catholic parishes. In 1956 there were 6,653 pupils in the twelve "colored" parochial elementary schools in the city of New Orleans. By 1972 the number of pupils had shrunk to 4,370 in the same number of schools. Some of them are now in desegregated schools.

This does not mean that all of these "missing" black Catholic pupils are now in the parochial schools that had previously been all white. Proportionately, the white parochial schools have undergone an even more severe decline. In 1956 there had been forty-eight white parishes with elementary schools enrolling 31,196 children. By 1972 this number had shrunken to thirty-five parochial schools with 16,835 pupils. During that period fifteen white schools had closed down and two new ones had opened. Most of the existing white parochial schools have experienced drastic reductions in numbers of pupils, and the decrease seems to have been greatest in those that accepted black children. There were, however, five schools that experienced a phenomenal increase of pupils (going from 2,769 in 1965 to 3,903 in 1972) These are located in the "better" residential areas that are predominantly white and in which new houses have been built during the past decade.

It is certainly time for another survey of Catholic parochial schools in this southern city. To what extent have the dire predictions of the racists come true? In what degree have the several experts who were involved in the school desegregation campaign on 1956 been proven correct? When I reread

the *Handbook on Catholic School Integration*, which resulted from the program of the Commission on Human
Rights in that year, I am almost embarrassed that we were
forced to take seriously the arguments of the racists: that
school desegregation would bring disease and delinquency,
psychological maladjustments, and lower intelligence quo-
tients among the pupils. At that time we even had to argue
that the switch to integrated schooling was a moral and constitutional process, and that the Bible carried no prohibitions
against it!

We argued then that desegregation of Catholic elementary
schools would work out *in practice*. This was not an expectation or a promise that all problems would be solved. It seems
to me that a sociological survey of Catholic parents who now
send their children to the parochial schools could indicate
what success has been achieved and what problems remain,
particularly how the racial attitudes of parents and teachers
differ across racial lines and from one school to another. It
may well be that "black pride" and the relatively new mood
of separatism are factors in the continuation of black parochial schools—as they have been on the secondary and
college levels—and that the quality of education obtainable
is more important than the social equality symbolized by attendance of both races at the same school.

SOUTHERN PARISH.   What about Catholic parish life?
Since my return to New Orleans I have been frequently
asked whether I intend to "revisit" southern parish. The present pastor, Father James Benedict, is an old friend whom I
had known well when he was campus chaplain at Tulane
University. Some of the "old-timers" among his parishioners
tell me that many changes had already been made during the
pastorate of Monsignor Pyzikiewicz, mainly as a result of the

thorough investigation we had made of the parish. This kind of remark is subject to verification, but there are now other parochial phenomena open to research.

One of these is the concept and practice of so-called "floating parishes" located at nonparochial centers, to and from which territorial parishioners "float." They use the term "community" in referring to their membership and are officially recognized by Archbishop Hannon as "experimental parishes." Thus they are not examples of the so-called "underground" church. What is noteworthy here is that these communities do not fit the canonical definition of a parish, which requires a specific church building and territorial boundaries. The problem of parish statistics, that is, the records of baptisms, marriages, and other necessary information, is solved by having them deposited at the nearest regular parish church.

Analogous to these experimental communities are the numerous centers for Charismatic Renewal, where prayer meetings are regularly held and the Eucharist celebrated. These groups are open to anyone, including non-Catholics, without regard to parochial boundaries. The Charismatic Renewal Movement—sometimes called "Catholic Pentecostalism"—is a relatively new and rapidly expanding phenomenon in New Orleans. Its clergy leaders keep in close contact with the chancery office and are careful to schedule meetings on weekdays only so as not to interfere with the regular Sunday mass attendance by people in their home parishes. Among these leaders are several priests on the Loyola University faculty who are now cooperating with me in a sociological study of the movement.

Two other parochial innovations are team ministry and parish councils which I have discussed in some detail with graduate students at the local archdiocesan seminary. New administrators now run the seminary which was closed to me in the old days when Father Balduc was its rector. The sociological study of the parish has become respectable as a field of investigation for seminarians and has led to an examination of team ministry and the parish council. Team ministry means, for the most part, the erasure of the old distinction between pastors and curates so that clergy functions are planned and shared in common. In some instances, religious sisters are part of the team and do most of the work of associate pastors, even though this title is not approved for women by Vatican officials. Although these sisters are not ordained clergy and cannot celebrate mass, they do distribute communion, visit the sick, maintain the census, counsel parishioners, and carry on the work of Christian education and convert instruction.

The introduction of parish councils implies, at least theoretically and ideally, much more participation of the laity in the affairs of the parish. Before the Second Vatican Council most American parishes had two lay trustees, whose usefulness depended largely on the extent to which the pastor consulted them and accepted their advice. The council recommended the establishment of pastoral councils at both the diocesan and parochial level to be made up of clergy, religious sisters and brothers, and laity. Like the team ministry, the parish council has met with indifferent success in New Orleans.

NEW ORLEANS POLICE. It would be too much to say that the police department of this city has become the best among the major cities of the country, but there is no question about its improvement in personnel and performance. A restudy at this time would undoubtedly reveal as much improvement during the past decade as there had been between the time of Aaron Kohn's extensive investigation of 1954 and our own specific study 10 years later. Nevertheless, the black newspaper, *The Louisiana Weekly*, continues to uncover evidence of racial discrimination by the police and the courts.

Representatives of the Southern Christian Leadership Conference tend to be broadly critical of the police department, whereas spokesmen for the National Association for the Advancement of Colored People occasionally compliment Chief Giarusso for his efforts to protect the black community from criminals.

Whatever the case, members of the police department are getting better training than ever before. The City College of Loyola University conducts a popular and successful academic program for young officers, who regularly graduate with a bachelor degree in police science. This program had been started by Raymond Witte even before we did the study of arrestees, and part of that research was a questionnaire answered by rookie police attending those courses. Plans are now underway to expand and develop this training into an academic major in criminal justice. About 10 percent of these rookies are women, and 20 percent are black. Giarusso has announced equal employment opportunities in the police department.

One of the Loyola sociologists, Walter Maestri, is a regular lecturer at the police academy, where all prospective members of the force must take a period of technical training. He and his research assistants are now interviewing a sample of New Orleans residents for a study of the "public perception" of the law enforcement officers. At this point one can only speculate whether the citizens have a higher or lower opinion of the police than they had 10 years ago. At any rate, Superintendent Giarusso has given his permission and approval for this study, with apparent confidence that the findings will be positive.

THE BROADER PERSPECTIVE. As is evident from the story I have told in this book, the areas of sociological enquiry in which I have had the deepest interest are race relations, religion, and education. In all three fields tremendous changes have occurred in America, and significant research and writing have been done by sociologists. It would be impossible in these concluding pages to recount all these happenings and what the social scientists have done and said about them.

Yet, one generalization may be allowed. It seems to me that in all three areas—race, religion, and education—and perhaps before sociologists became aware of it, there was a deemphasis of the "equilibrium theory," with its notions of harmony, integration, and balance, and an emphasis on the "conflict theory," with its notions of cultural pluralism and structural diversity. It was as though the triumphant American society emerging from World War II, with hopes of great unity and progress, gradually became dissatisfied with itself and wanted to make things over.

When President Truman issued his executive order in July 1948 for the removal of discrimination in the military, we were on our way to an integrated society. Thurgood Marshall won case after case in the courts, culminating in the school decision of 1954. The Rev. Martin Luther King, Jr., electrified the country by bringing leaders of both races together in a moral crusade against segregation. It looked as though the Equal Rights Amendment of 1964 could maintain equilibrium, but it was not enough and it was too late.

In spite of all the "gains" listed by white liberals and black conservatives, there was growing discontent in the urban ghettoes, increasing "crime in the streets," and countercalls for "law and order." Black Muslims were suspect, Black Panthers were feared, and the whole movement for black power bespoke conflict rather than harmony. Negroes became blacks while their churchmen issued manifestos for reparations and their college students rioted on the campus and demanded Afro-American study programs. The Kerner report saw our nation "moving toward two societies, one black, one white—separate and unequal." Racial conflict increased among the soldiers in Viet Nam and among the sailors at sea.

In the religious field the immediate postwar period promised brotherhood between Christians and Jews, a movement toward unification among Protestant denominations, and even some ecumenical stirrings between Catholics and Protestants. Pope John XXIII excited the whole world by convoking the Second Vatican Council which was meant to usher in the *aggiornamento*, the renewal of Catholicism internally and externally. People talked of a religious revival, a new understanding of human relations that would offset the secularization of the technological age. But the Council also was apparently too little and too late.

Thomas O'Dea diagnosed the "Catholic Crisis" and Jeffrey Hadden foresaw the "Gathering Storm in the Churches." Catholics disagreed among themselves on the issues of birth control and divorce and began to question the authority of their priests and prelates. The matter of priestly celibacy became front-page news and the large-scale resignation of priests and religious sisters suggested growing dissatisfaction among church professionals. Catholic prelates seemed to be in panic when they finally decided to invest in a series of historical, psychological, sociological, and theological studies of the American priesthood. Meanwhile, the sectlike fundamentalists and conservatives grew in numbers and influence. The Jesus movement was impatient with structures and institutions. Catholic Pentecostalism promised to introduce its own kind of religious revivalism. Even the prestigious efforts of the Consultation on Church Unity (COCU) began to flounder as religious pluralism again became popular.

The sociology of education took on added importance in the late 1940s when the colleges were crowded with military veterans who took schoolwork seriously. Faith in education as a means of personal fulfillment and of social salvation was never so high. The baby boom promised that elementary schooling would flourish, and then secondary schools. The drive then was for constant improvement in a system that was considered basically sound. A new thrust was made when the launching of sputnik turned the attention of students and educators towards technology and "hard" science.

Every educator and social scientist could point to imperfections in the massive American educational system, but no one foresaw student strikes on campus after campus. The generation gap seemed widest among middle-class youth. High schools in the inner city deteriorated while those in the suburbs flourished. Private colleges, even in the Ivy League, began to talk of financial crisis, and parochial elementary schools closed down at an alarming rate. Confrontation replaced cooperation as parietals were relaxed, the drug cult gained publicity, communes became preferable to dormitories, and students dropped out of school in unprecedented numbers. The Coleman Report and the work of sociologists like Jencks and Riesman were among the many attempts to describe and interpret the changing educational scene.

CONCLUSION.   One generalization about equilibrium versus conflict, stability versus change, does not exclude all other generalizations. What is happening in the society at large is reflected now in the ways sociologists are reacting to it and theorizing about it. Advanced scientific technology has not fulfilled its promise of a world of peace and plenty. In spite of unprecedented discoveries and inventions, we are still left with gigantic human problems of institutionalized and personal injustice. The strong get stronger, the weak get weaker; the rich get richer, the poor get poorer.

These discrepancies have not been lost on reflective sociologists who are not satisfied that their professional role is simply to advance the field of sociology, to evolve ever more refined methodologies, or to develop grand systems of theory. The demand for change and reform by the various "movements"—women, blacks, chicanos, radicals—within the sociological profession, is accompanied by a shift toward "humanistic" sociology. Nevertheless, there is still much reluctance to admit that scientific positivism is not the full and final approach to the study of the sociocultural system. "Can Science Save Us?" was a question asked decades ago by George Lundberg, and answered affirmatively by him. Sociologists today are very dubious about that answer.

Sociological generalizations are never absolutes, but it seems to me that the current attention to humanistic change is a healthy and promising trend among sociologists. It is an emphasis on social change that may still encompass a flexible stability, and an emphasis on humanism that may still preserve the canons of science. I like to think that the central concerns of my small-time research in the areas of race, religion, and education have always been guided by these two generalizations. I am reasonably confident that some "good," that is, change and reform, has resulted from these five projects. I do not think I would have conducted any of them without a conviction that human beings are, and should remain, at the center of the sociological enterprise.

INDEX